THOMAS HARDY, MONISM, AND THE CARNIVAL TRADITION:
THE ONE AND THE MANY IN *THE DYNASTS*

G. GLEN WICKENS

Thomas Hardy, Monism, and the Carnival Tradition

The One and the Many in *The Dynasts*

UNIVERSITY OF TORONTO PRESS
Toronto Buffalo London

© University of Toronto Press Incorporated 2002
Toronto Buffalo London
Printed in Canada

ISBN 0-8020-4864-1

Printed on acid-free paper

National Library of Canada Cataloguing in Publication Data

Wickens, G. Glen, 1947–
Thomas Hardy, monism and the carnival tradition :
the one and the many in The Dynasts

Includes bibliographical references and index.
ISBN 0-8020-4864-1

1. Hardy, Thomas, 1840–1928. Dynasts. 2. Bakhtin, M.M.
(Mikhail Mikhailovich), 1895–1975. 3. Carnival in literature.
4. Monism in literature. I. Title.

PR4750.D83W53 2002   822 .8   C2001-904208-6

University of Toronto Press acknowledges the financial assistance to its
publishing program of the Canada Council for the Arts and the
Ontario Arts Council.

This book has been published with the help of a grant from the Humanities
and Social Sciences Federation of Canada, using funds provided by the
Social Sciences and Humanities Research Council of Canada.

University of Toronto Press acknowledges the financial support for its
publishing activities of the Government of Canada through the Book
Publishing Industry Development Program (BPIDP).

For Pam, Brandon, and Marina

Contents

Acknowledgments

My interest in Hardy was nurtured during my graduate student years at the University of Western Ontario; my interest in Bakhtin came later when I began teaching at the University of Alberta. I am indebted to Gary Kelly for introducing me to Bakhtin's theories and to everyone in the Beer and Bakhtin circle at Alberta for many stimulating discussions that first gave me the idea for this book.

I am also grateful to friends at Bishop's University and elsewhere for their interest, help, and encouragement. My thanks to Garry Retzleff, Ken McLean, Joanne Craig, Michael Childs, Janyne Hodder, Gary Mullins, and Doug Kneale. My greatest debt, however, is to three good friends and former colleagues who generously gave me their wise counsel on a number of occasions: Brian Jenkins, Tracy Ware, and David Bentley.

My book has also benefited from much professional and technical expertise. I was fortunate to have two readers during the evaluation process who offered insightful suggestions for revision. At the University of Toronto Press, thanks go to my editor, Kristen Pederson, for her sympathetic advice, and to Jeannie Scarfe, Barbara Porter, and Diane Mew for their care in seeing the book through to its final form. My thanks as well to Cheryl Porter at Bishop's University for persevering so cheerfully in the preparation of the manuscript.

Some of the research for this book was made possible by a grant from the Bishop's Senate Research Committee.

Finally, I thank my wife and children who have endured the writing of this book with the patience, though not indifference, of Egdon Heath. The book is dedicated to them with love and respect.

Introduction: Relocating *The Dynasts*

Over the years, the reputation of *The Dynasts* has risen and fallen as steeply as the grain prices in *The Mayor of Casterbridge*. What Hardy considered to be his best work did not excite most Edwardian reviewers, yet by 1912 *The Dynasts* had emerged as a work of magnitude. When some younger writers sent Hardy a tribute in 1921, they thanked him '"most of all, perhaps, for *The Dynasts*"' (Hardy, *Life* 446). By 1938, ten years after his death, there seemed to be 'almost universal agreement that the *Dynasts* is the greatest of Hardy's writings' (Rutland 269). This consensus, lasting through the 1950s, shrunk to a relatively small critical circle in the 1960s and 1970s. Praise continued to be a matter of superlatives, but critics who questioned *The Dynasts'* elevated status saw at best a 'splendid failure' (Carpenter 201) or, at worst, 'a vast and awkward hybrid' (Howe 157). Once considered Hardy's masterwork, *The Dynasts* remains the one major work that 'the majority of his critics, even the sympathetic ones, continue to ignore' (Seymour-Smith 651).

The last monograph devoted entirely to *The Dynasts* – Susan Dean's *Hardy's Poetic Vision* – appeared in 1977 and, as Charles Lock points out, 'did not provoke the debate that *The Dynasts* sorely requires, nor the upward revaluation that would surely follow' (114). The present study tries, with the help of Mikhail Bakhtin, to renew the conversation about a work that critics have treated almost exclusively on the distant plane of sombre epic themes and tragic tone. In the broadest, generic terms, a Bakhtinian reading redefines *The Dynasts* as a novel and relocates it within the serio-comical genres. All the defining features of the menippea also characterize *The Dynasts*: the combination of fantasy and history, of philosophical dialogue (the Spirits) and slum naturalism (stragglers, deserters, and camp followers), the concern with the ideological issues of the day (monism), the two-planed construction of world and Overworld, the destruction of the hero's epic and tragic wholeness, the many scenes of scandal, eccentric behaviour, and inappropriate speech (in the domestic intrigues of the dynasts), the wide use of inserted genres (everything from ballads and letters to decrees and proclamations), the multi-styled and multi-toned scenes, the mixing of poetry and prose, the appearance of the comic alongside the tragic, the misalliances of all sorts as war brings together people and things normally separated.

If, as Bakhtin argues, a carnival sense of the world permeates all the genres of the serio-comical, determining their basic features, a generic approach to *The Dynasts* raises the question of how carnival influenced Hardy. As a member of the Rabelais Club, founded by Sir Walter Besant, he experienced directly the themes and symbols of carnival in one of its elite and official guises. Hardy recalls that during the Club's inaugural dinner in December 1879 one member 'made himself the clown of our court, privileged to say anything by virtue of his office' and to do things in reverse, so that 'when we rose to drink the health of absent members he stayed firmly sitting' (*Life* 135, 136). Although Hardy had little success in being Rabelaisian with his literary friends, he understood carnival in the far deeper sense of the culture of folk humour.[1] Folkways in Hardy cease to have mainly a serious meaning[2] when viewed within the carnival tradition. The numerous attempts to explain *The Dynasts* in terms of its official 'philosophy,' gloomy and serious like the Spirit of the Years, ignore the comic folk aspect of the world and Will. In the spirit of the menippea, carnivalization 'penetrates to the very philosophical core' (Bakhtin, *Problems* 134) of *The Dynasts*; laughter sounds even in the realm of ultimate questions.

The title of my book reflects the historical importance of one of these questions. Hardy worked on *The Dynasts* at a time when the tendency towards a monistic view of the universe in all the high genres of thought revived the old and central philosophical controversy about the relation between the one and the many.[3] The two worlds of *The Dynasts* bring this relation into focus without effacing the controversy. The Spirits 'see,' with varying degrees of belief, the unity of the Will in the diverse historical and natural scenes. Yet the Will cannot be explained, as Hardy himself never tired of saying, in terms of a 'single scientific theory' any more than the Spirits, whose ideas remain inseparable from personality, can be reduced to a single consciousness in an abstract system of thought. In order 'to express his age in poetry' (*Life* 441, 344), Hardy makes the Spirits participants in an open-ended dialogue that belongs to history as much as do the 'Persons' they watch. Chapter 1 draws on Hardy's reading to reconstruct the context of monism as the dialogizing background of the Overworld. My survey situates such familiar influences as Schopenhauer and Hartmann in a disputed field of voices that includes numerous writers ignored or scarcely mentioned in critical accounts of the Spirits. In Hardy's menippean novel, 'a genre of ultimate questions' (Bakhtin, *Problems* 149), the historical struggle of diverse monisms – neutral, spiritualistic, idealistic, critical, analytic – gets inscribed as a plurality of unmerged voices covering a wide range of accents.

Chapter 2 examines the way the dialogue of the Overworld unfolds as the crowning/decrowning of its dominant voice, the Spirit of the Years. The dynastic plot begins with reference to Napoleon's coronation at Notre Dame and ends with his crushing defeat at Waterloo, the Emperor turned fugitive in the wood of Bossu. Like the Overking of Europe, Father Years, the Will's official Spirit and chief interpreter, starts as the leader of a hierarchy of Intelligences and ends as one voice among many, his authority mocked and subverted by the laughing word. The only prose speakers in the Overworld are also the only Spirits to appreciate the comedy in things. The Spirits Ironic and Sinister continually mock the false or narrow seriousness of the other Spirits and dynasts. Irony even usurps and parodies the Years' exclusive role as 'Showman' in the hilarious scenes at Carlton House that end Part Second.

Bakhtin's concept of reduced laughter proves very useful in illuminating the many gradations of laughter in *The Dynasts*, while Hardy, in turn, helps remove the lingering suspicion that this concept is just a loophole for smuggling serious writers into the carnival tradition. Hardy felt he 'had a born sense of humour, even a too keen sense' for reviewers who, accustomed to 'Dickensian humour,' mistook his 'Swiftian' humour for 'the deepest seriousness.' Hardy's reference to 'verses of a satirical, dry, caustic, or farcical cast' (*Life* 324) aptly describes the range of humour in *The Dynasts*.

The laughter in the Overworld reflects the way monism had become a serio-comical field of thought before Hardy wrote *The Dynasts*. The Years' changing dialogic position mirrors the historical development of monism when the reigning voices of naturalism and agnosticism became subject to a devastating irony and sarcasm. James Ward in particular uses carnivalesque strategies of parody and double-voicing to turn agnostic science inside out. The gaps and loopholes that Ward uncovers in neutral monism also characterize the Years' discourse about the Will. Nothing suggests that Hardy 'took the scientists of the nineteenth century at their own estimation' (Rutland 104). Instead, the pretensions of science sound in the epic and prophetic voice of the Years proclaiming his eternal verities. The Years' truth about the world depends on a fiction of detachment that suits his personality and this personality has all the arrogance and inconsistency of the Apostles of science. His speeches often transgress the agnostic limits of the knowable and point in the spiritual direction Ward predicted when the drift of monistic authority began to change.

The Years' agnostic imagination makes the Will much more than an empty signifier. Each time the One appears in the many, the preternatural transparency resembles the intricate anatomy of the human brain. Conceived in terms of the physiological Unconscious, the cosmic web consists of volitions rather than ideas and reason becomes only a moment in an otherwise blind Will. Yet within the seemingly confident and unified voice of the Years, different languages intersect and collide. The competing claims of agnostic naturalism and speculative idealism turn the theme of the Will into a microdialogue of conflicting truths. By the standards of the metaphysical Unconscious, the Years' somnambulistic Will can also be seen as a transcendental Intelligence. Forced to defend the Will and to explain how Its perfect timeless whole can be composed of imperfect changing parts, the Years makes It a mind as well as a brain, a transformation that reflects the search for a satisfactory monism in the context of post-Kantian thought. Whereas Schopenhauer separated Will and Idea, the course of modern thought reunited them. By greatly expanding the realm of the psychical, monism gave provisional support to the idea that everything belongs to one mind-penetrated unity. Chapter 3 shows how various monists came to speculate that there may be a Universal Mind both above and below the human. Negatively or mechanically defined, It is inferior, processive, and unconscious; positively or spiritually defined, It is superior, purposive, and superconscious.

My detailed interpretation of the context of monism allows us to rethink the relationship between the Spirit of the Years and the Spirit of the Pities. Their exchanges characterize the way science itself seemed pregnant with a new metaphysic and even a new theology. Instead of remaining opposites, Hardy's Spirits become reflected in one another, the Years assuming a religious voice to convince the sceptical Pities to believe in the Will. In the After Scene, the Pities construct their idea of the awakening Will out of the Years' monism, the 'It' of agnosticism displacing the 'Thee' of traditional theism. The last word goes to the Pities but nothing is finished or concluded. *The Dynasts* ends with prediction, not prophecy, and a vision of the future that has more in common with the tentative affirmations of critical monism than the confident assertions of Absolute Idealism. The Years' static Will becomes subject to time and change, the block universe of the Absolute transformed into a novelistic world where God emerges as the most ideal portion of the larger whole. The same spiritual naturalism that makes *The Dynasts* Hardy's novel of the future also underwrites the theology of the future.

While the first three chapters show how Hardy needed a novelistic range of voices in the Overworld to represent the changing thought of his day, chapter 4 examines how the mixing of poetry and prose in the world's dialogue makes *The Dynasts* 'a multi-styled genre, as is the authentic novel' (Bakhtin, *Dialogic* 25). Critics have appreciated the prose as good writing and the laughter that often accompanies it as comic relief, without suspecting that these 'low' forms of speech might constitute an essential truth about the world. The main stylistic project has always been to justify the 'wooden' blank verse by connecting speech to knowledge (or ignorance) in a hierarchy that has poetry at the top and prose at the bottom or on the periphery of vision. This strategy cannot explain the novelistic layers of poetry and prose at all levels of speech from Spirits and dynasts to common people. The relation between the various forms of prose, including the narrator's stage directions, and the blank verse and lyric poetry, with all their high generic associations, can best be understood as a system of intersecting planes. The tendency of the menippea to parody itself (Bakhtin, *Problems* 142) gets accentuated in *The Dynasts*: it is full of parodic doubles and laughing reflections of the serious word in all its limitations. A sudden shift into prose brings out the other or hidden side of official truth; the dialogue begins to sound in a novelistic zone of familiar contact or historical events receive a second, carnivalistic plane.

The so-called dynastic style becomes an object of representation set off by the prose, including the prose of the dynasts themselves. In a series of scenes, the Prince Regent keeps slipping into prose, majesty becomes a joke, and what starts as a crowning occasion or official celebration turns into a scene of scandal and disclosure, the future king revealed as a carnivalesque pretender. As in carnival, 'Life itself is on stage' (Bakhtin, *Rabelais* 258) but the meaning of the drama as a whole cannot be understood without hearing the chorus of the laughing people. The spectacle of kings and emperors has a different look when viewed through the prose consciousness of soldiers, servants, street persons, or country folk. The clowns and fools of folk humour reappear in various low figures who unmask the pretensions of dynastic authority to speak for the good of the whole nation. That the Durnover folk should uncrown the effigy of Napoleon just as they do the effigy of Henchard in *The Mayor of Casterbridge* suggests that *The Dynasts* is no 'strange intruder' (Noyes 98) into Hardy's canon. Napoleon and Henchard belong to the same generic world, a world that in the *Mayor* already mixes history with carnivalized time.

It is not so much that Hardy's novels provide the key to reading *The Dynasts* as the carnival tradition provides the key to reading both, even when the subject is war. Chapter 5 explores the connection between carnival and the Napoleonic wars while taking into account the common criticism that Bakhtin does not sufficiently acknowledge the violent aspects of carnival. The germ of my argument lies in a small but potentially significant point in *Rabelais and His World* where Bakhtin admits that catastrophes can be represented as a carnival with its masquerades and disorderly conduct. The historical calamity of the Napoleonic wars allows Hardy to use carnival's way of seeing the world as one great communal performance to represent the mass actions of armies and crowds. As a clash of peoples, rather than professional armies, the struggle for power in Europe transforms the battlefield into a marketplace that can challenge all authority. The battlefield appears not simply as a place of carnival but as a reversal that threatens its regenerating ambivalence. The negative moment of the grotesque prevails, both the body and language opened up in a threatening or terrifying way. Napoleon's military success depends on his grasping the carnivalesque nature of war. The new dynast remains the great manipulator of carnival forms, always ready to uncrown himself in order to direct the power of the crowd.

The battles may be numerous but Hardy often foregrounds not so much the events as what people say about them. Chapter 6 considers the way the dialogue and narrative report the European conflict as a struggle between different speech zones and genres, with the result that heroism always looks and sounds ambivalent. In trying to restore the 'true proportion' (Preface to *The Dynasts* 4)[4] of England's role in the war, Hardy did not end up writing a patriotic work in which 'a few individuals, mostly English, are singled out for our attention as admirable and heroic' (Orel, 'Hardy' 97). Even the English leaders – Pitt, Nelson, Moore, Wellington – have a side that faces the carnival square. The so-called new (Dean 124) heroes still have old concerns that make them subject to the laughter and debasement of grotesque realism. In Part First, Pitt keeps hearing about Napoleon through the low or everyday speech genres important to the novel, until the rumours, reports, and news of disasters make him as prone and emaciated as the body of Europe. If the dynastic system Pitt so strenuously defends is like one of Bakhtin's already completed genres, Napoleon is like the novel, 'born and nourished in a new era of world history' (Bakhtin, *Dialogic* 4). He never fully embraces an outdated epic heroism, any more than he speaks solely from the distant zone of the proclamatory genres. Authority alone does not make his words persuasive; he also relies on familiar speech, bodily humour, and a cynical frankness. The old order constantly hears him as a rude and sarcastic speaker, a carnivalesque intruder into a closed system whose historical inversion makes the past higher and more authentic than the contradictory present.

Napoleon also differs from the established order through his relationship with the crowd – the subject of chapter 7. Hardy makes him the only leader to see, in Elias Canetti's terms, that the 'eruption' of the 'closed' (22) crowd has changed the nature of war. When he pulls war out of its usual rut, he has a sharp eye to the attributes of Canetti's crowd and how they can work to his advantage. Yet not even Napoleon can control the conditions of mass war that he helps bring into existence. By Part Second, the outbreak of war depends on the eruption of the patriotic crowd rather than official alliances, the people gathering emotionally in the public squares and streets of Europe before fighting desperately on the fields of battle. The crowd scenes in Berlin (1806), Madrid (1808), and Vienna (1809) deepen the carnivalesque picture of war while showing how the nation begins to emerge as something higher than king or emperor. In the Russian campaign of 1812, history becomes a massive spectacle without footlights and for all the people. The crowd scenes make possible the transfer of ultimate questions from the Overworld of abstract thought to the world of concrete historical events. The crowd and the Will turn out to be two versions of the same problem of the one and the many. For Hardy, the authentic meaning of the Napoleonic era lies as much in the crowd events at the beginning of the nineteenth century as in the monistic thought at the end of the century. The images of the crowd, including the impressive aerial perspectives or panoramas, do not serve only a negative, satirical purpose, as if Hardy still felt haunted from his London years by 'a monster whose body had four million heads and eight million eyes' (*Life* 141). Even when the crowds of war appear as insects or reptiles, collective action still has a transformative power. For all its violence and destruction, the 'open' crowd gives the old devouring world of war something of the contradictory unity of grotesque becoming.

The last chapter focuses on the way we see the death-birth of this world through the chronotopes closely related to carnival space and time. In a note about the British Museum, dated 9 March 1888, Hardy tropes both the scene and his own chronotopic imagination as 'Time ... looking into Space.' Like the great circle of the library where bodies appear to dissolve (though not without a smile – 'slightly hampered by renovations') and books sound 'risen from the dead' (*Life* 215), time in *The Dynasts* simultaneously destroys and renews, mixing the old and the new in a deeply ambivalent unity. Napoleon's strange career, so full of stunning reversals, lends itself to a carnivalized conception of the historical process.[5] Hardy chooses his scenes to deal with the great turning points of the era when history seems to take on some of the logic of carnival with its radical shifts and metamorphoses. We keep seeing Napoleon at extreme moments of triumph, ultimate decision, or catastrophe. Everything he says and does remains linked to the chronotope of crisis and break in life, or to the related chronotopes of the street and square. On the battlefield or in the palace, he lives to cross the threshold that determines his whole life. When the Imperial stakes carry the risk of losing all, he talks like the gambler or the condemned prisoner, living the moment equal to years. His thresholds of disaster and moments of crucial decision remain subordinate to carnival and mystery time. In the final war culminating at Waterloo, the atmosphere of crisis joins with the idyll of agricultural labour to emphasize the fullness and unity of time. The chronotopic Napoleon has a folkloric basis that makes his fate inseparable from the life of the people and the transformation of an era. Although the Napoleonic wars allow the old dynastic system to continue, the grotesque world of historic conflict may be a new world still in the making. At least the uncrowning of Napoleon requires a carnival spirit of communal performance that makes history for the first time a mass experience.

My goal in the pages ahead is not to restore the 'great' reputation of *The Dynasts*, but rather to bring it up close enough to be read and appreciated within the carnival tradition. Bakhtin allows us to escape the cul-de-sacs that even the most appreciative critics of *The Dynasts* have reached. He himself may have 'never fully learned ... the value of close reading' (LaCapra, *Rethinking* 309), but his methods of analysis suggest ways of closely reading and carefully relating Hardy's text and its context. Although Bakhtin proves to be an antidote to pessimistic readings of *The Dynasts*, Hardy's spectacle of war challenges some of his cheerful conclusions, bringing out the disturbing implications of both his theory of laughter and carnival.

The two main concerns of my book – monism and the carnival tradition – link Hardy and Bakhtin as writers interested in both popular and elite forms of culture. By the time Hardy wrote *The Dynasts* he was reading widely in the same philosophical tradition that, as Katerina Clark and Michael Holquist have shown, helped shape Bakhtin's early work – neo-Kantianism. The very structure of *The Dynasts*, an Overworld of interpretation never quite coinciding with the events that provoke thought, reflects the split between mind and the world that preoccupied Kant, became the foundation of monism, and made Bakhtin receptive to the idea of an unfinished world with a contradictory form of unity. The belief that, in the words of one monist whom Hardy quotes, 'our world is one of growing perception, and not one of fact' (Worsley 316; Hardy, *Literary* 2:408) underwrites Bakhtin's whole conception of the novel. Indeed, 'when the novel becomes the dominant genre, epistemology becomes the dominant discipline' (*Dialogic* 15). The philosophical problem that *The Dynasts* explores is central to Bakhtin's own work, 'work that stands under the sign of plurality, the mystery of the one and the many' (Clark and Holquist 1).

THOMAS HARDY, MONISM, AND THE CARNIVAL TRADITION

ONE

Hardy's Longest Novel
and the Monistic Theory of
the Universe

Right from the start, reading *The Dynasts* posed the problem of where to locate it in literary tradition. In 1906, after receiving Part Second from Hardy, Arthur Symons wrote back to say that 'I watch it as an unparalleled spectacle, which I cannot wholly accept as coming within any known limits of art' (175). The usual way of overcoming this strangeness, to read *The Dynasts* as an epic or tragedy, has not successfully explained its heterogeneous features, though these include aspects of all the elevated genres. The one possibility not explored will be the subject of this book: *The Dynasts* as a novel or, as Hardy apparently told Virginia Woolf, his longest (Woolf 91) novel.

Clearly length alone does not exhaust the obvious differences between *The Dynasts* and Hardy's earlier fiction. Narration shrinks to the stage directions and Dumb Shows, blank verse and lyric poetry greatly outweigh the prose, both world and Overworld take the shape of a play, and the idea of the Will repeatedly intrudes on the action. To call *The Dynasts* a novel we need a theory that can allow for these differences and yet reveal the deeper continuity between the new work and the novel writing that Hardy claimed to have given up after *Jude the Obscure* (1895).

While not identical concepts, carnival, the novel, and the menippea remain so closely connected in Bakhtin's history and theory of genres that we may speak of *The Dynasts* as a menippean novel in the carnival tradition. Bakhtin mentions the epic and the rhetorical genres as two of the three fundamental roots of the novel (see *Problems* 109) but by far his most important source is carnivalistic folklore. In antiquity, popular laughter gave rise directly to the serio-comical genres and these, in turn, became the authentic literary predecessors of the European novel. The characteristics that distinguish the novel from the epic also define the whole field of the serio-comical, including the menippea, with its carnivalistic base. The first of these constitutive features, the multi-styled nature of the novel and the carnivalized genres, will concern us in later chapters when we examine the mixing of poetry and prose in *The Dynasts* and Hardy's use of inserted genres and different speech zones. The other two features, essentially one, involve time and remind us that no epic distance separates Hardy from his historical subject of the Napoleonic wars. By 'embodying the real, if only temporary, thought of the age' (Hardy, *Life* 344), *The Dynasts* inhabits the zone appropriated by the novel: 'a zone of contact with the present in all its openendedness' (Bakhtin, *Dialogic* 7). Contemporary reality, at least on the level of its most advanced concerns, becomes the starting point for an artistic and ideological thinking about the past. 'In point of literary form,' comments Hardy, 'the scheme of contrasted Choruses ... was shaped with a single view to the modern expression of a modern outlook': the 'Monistic theory of the Universe' (Preface to *The Dynasts* 5). As this chapter will show, the question of what Hardy meant by this form-shaping ideology has a very different answer if we approach *The Dynasts* as a carnivalesque novel in touch with the inconclusive present rather than a lofty epic with no place for indeterminacy and little room for laughter in its representation of thought and events.

Although Hardy repeatedly emphasized his attempt 'to spread over art the latest illumination of the time' (*Life* 344), he felt uncomfortable giving his 'crude thoughts such a high title as a philosophy.' Words with a loophole make his definitions unstable and keep open the possibility for altering, as he often did, the final meaning of his own words about *The Dynasts*. His hesitancy over how to categorize his 'drama, or poem, or whatever it may be called' (*Letters* 3:308, 207) extends to the 'philosophy which gave rise to the form' (*Personal Writings* 145) of world and Overworld. 'My philosophy,' he admits, 'is ... of a very tentative and inconsistent pattern' (*Letters* 5:276).[1]

Hardy did not own this philosophy. Its inconsistencies, like the 'contradictions and futilities' that struck him 'after reading various philosophic systems' (*Life* 333), belong to the 'mind of the age' (*Life* 343) and are accentuated by the dialogic form of the Overworld where the last word never sounds and the play of voices does not serve the author's totalizing judgment. In a letter (22 March 1904) to Edward Clodd, Hardy reveals that 'there are inconsistencies' even in the Phantoms who most obviously represent 'the best human intelligence of their time in a sort of quintessential form. I speak of the "Years"' (3:117). From another position 'outside the drama' (*Letters* 3:204), he says of all the Spirits, 'Their doctrines are but tentative,' before singling out the Spirit of the Pities as 'impressionable and inconsistent in its views' (Preface to *The Dynasts* 4, 5).

If Hardy's 1903 Preface anticipates objections, his later comments answer them, especially the one he detected 'under the cloak of an objection to the form' (*Letters* 3:99). We hear the novelist at work intensifying the words of his detractors to the point of indignation: 'On what ground do you arrogate to yourself a right to express in poetry a philosophy which has never been expressed in poetry before?' (*Life* 343–4). Hardy casts his answer in a Postscript (1904) to Part First of *The Dynasts* in the rhetoric of late nineteenth-century naturalism, just one of the many discourses of the Overworld but one that shaped or misshaped much subsequent criticism.[2] Though carrying the weight of direct authorial speech, the Postscript is every bit as dialogic, and in a strikingly similar way, as the exchanges of the Spirits. It is at once a rejoinder (to a *Times* critic) and a revoicing of words already uttered. Caught up in the controversy about his own work, Hardy went far beyond explaining that 'ideas of some freshness' do not constitute a 'new philosophy' (*Life* 343). The modern outlook of the Preface turns out to be an immanent version of something very old: 'The philosophy of *The Dynasts*, under various titles and phases, is almost as old as civilization. Its fundamental principle, under the name of Predestination, was preached by St. Paul.'[3] Hardy borrows his strategy for mitigating 'the real offence of *The Dynasts*' from 'our men of science ... among whom determinism is a commonplace' (*Personal Writings* 145). In fact, as he well knew, by 1904 many men of science – James Ward, George J. Romanes, C. Loyd Morgan, Sir Oliver Lodge, to name only a few whose work he knew – were unwilling to 'exchange the determinism of God for that of matter and energy' (Turner 251). Such an exchange belonged to a time when the 'fashionable creed of advanced thinkers was scientific agnosticism' ('Bergson and Balfour' 474; Hardy *Literary* 2:218). T.H. Huxley preceded Hardy in pointing out that 'Physical science ... did not invent determinism': 'Whoever asserts the combination of omniscience and omnipotence as attributes of the Deity, does implicitly assert predestination' ('Science' 801, 800).[4] Leslie Stephen also claims, and with the same disregard that the Spirit of the Years shows for the threat posed by the metaphor of the ruler and his laws, an unimpeachable orthodoxy for determinism. 'The theologian,' says Stephen, 'agrees with the man of science in admitting that we are governed by unalterable laws' (*Essays* 351).[5]

When Hardy wrote the Postscript there were 'no outstanding champions of Naturalism like the Huxleys and [John] Tyndalls of thirty years ago' (Armitage 733).[6] His backward-looking attempt to defend the Unconscious Will suggests Hardy was already moving away from the importance he once attached to the 'theory on which "The Dynasts" is based' (*Letters* 5:212). While planning his novelized epic-drama, he felt himself going against the grain of the 1890s aestheticism: 'in the full tide of a fashion which seems to view poetry as the art of saying nothing with mellifluous preciosity, the principle of regarding form as second to content is not likely to be popular' (*Letters* 2:208). Whereas the 1903 Preface maintains a careful balance between outlook and expression, the 1904 Postscript defends his philosophy as 'a plausible theory only,' almost a theory without consequences, given Hardy's conviction 'that, whether we uphold this or any other conjecture on the cause of things, men's lives and actions will be little affected thereby' (*Personal Writings* 146). After the completion of *The Dynasts* in 1908, he could retreat behind the powerful late nineteenth-century assumption that 'an invocation of the literary code directed the reader to ignore the text's implication in matters of ideology and power' (Henricksen 786). After all, 'like "Paradise Lost," "The Dynasts" proves nothing' (*Letters* 3:298). In his unpublished French Preface (1927), Hardy imagines a more favourable reception for 'la theorie *moniste* des Causes et des Effets' from the countrymen of Descartes, whose mechanical theory of the universe formed the corner-stone of naturalism, and even considers that one day it might prove to be 'la vraie théorie de l'univers' (*Personal Writings* 60). The conception of monism here is the one that Ernst Haeckel, the most popular naturalist of the 1890s and the chief propagandist for monism, brought back into prominence by arguing that mechanicalism is synonymous with monism. What finally matters to Hardy, however, is that this theory be appreciated as a 'système dramatique' rather than a 'philosophie' (*Personal Writings* 60).

Hardy's own shift in emphasis from the content that initiated the form to the imaginative expression of the thought anticipated the basic divergence in critical accounts of the plurality of unmerged voices in the Overworld. His list (3 August 1907) of contemporary clichés includes 'That T.H.'s philosophy is all that matters' and 'That T.H.'s writings are good in spite of their bad philosophy' (*Letters* 3:266). The first assumption sent critics, especially the earlier ones, down the monologic path to look for a 'philosophic document' in which 'the human action is an illustration of a thesis' (Bailey 82). They require less a dynamic field of historical utterances than a single or collective voice within it, whether Schopenhauer's pessimism, Eduard von Hartmann's philosophy of the Unconscious, or the assumptions of a science already outdated by the time Hardy began to write *The Dynasts* in 1902.

Generic assumptions about *The Dynasts* do have ideological implications. To look for the single and unified world view of the epic (see Orel, Brennecke, Webster) has usually meant finding Hardy's familiar determinism. The results are ominous: an epic at odds with itself, an epic hero, Napoleon, who is a paradox of power and powerlessness, and a reader expected to interest himself/herself in an historical drama rendered meaningless by the Overworld's commentary. William Rutland tries to salvage something from this wreck by arguing that 'the Spirits are the real characters in the *Dynasts*,' but there is no escaping 'the dilemma in which Hardy's philosophy landed him' (333, 334). 'His dilemma,' R.J. White concurs, 'is inherent in any attempt to make a tragedy out of characters who have been robbed of moral choice' (98). Criticism of *The Dynasts* has many dead ends of this kind. When Hardy's grim outlook appears to block the path of appreciation, it becomes a 'bad philosophy': 'If he had only been able to let his philosophic notions lie at rest, or let them go, or let them go hang' (Howe 159).

The belief that 'Hardy depicts human fate as determined' (Maynard 104) has proved surprisingly tenacious, an almost predetermining idea. The scaffolding of nineteenth-century science no longer matters, but the structure of a coercive Will remains even after the linguistic moment. For J. Hillis Miller, the Immanent Will is 'a universal field of signs' even more tyrannical than physical force: 'Each person is programmed from without by a vast circumambient network of language that invades the self from all sides in incoherent abundance and forces her or him to act, think, and feel in certain ways' (310, 311).

For most critics the relation between speech and speaker, rendered irrelevant in Miller's account of the priority of word over mind, remains important. The very position of the Spirits above the world has encouraged the search for authoritative speech, especially when they are regarded as the supernatural spectators of an epic poem. According to Keith Wilson, the 'commentator is then so often faced with the question of which of two contradictory authorities, Years or Pities, to trust' (125). The question of who speaks most for Hardy has never been settled. 'We cannot say for a certainty,' Harold Orel admits, 'which speeches of the Spirits in *The Dynasts* represent Hardy's personal doctrine; many of them do, but not all' (*Thomas* 24–5).

The tendency persists to treat the dialogue of the Overworld as a logical structure, either as an argument between the Spirit of the Years and the Spirit of the Pities or, more generally, as an abstract debate involving all the Spirits. If the Years always have the best of the argument, we are reading an epic of determinism; if the Pities are granted an equal status, we end up with an antinomial structure, 'thesis ... set against antithesis ... to form an ironic complex, which is left unresolved' (Hynes, *Pattern* 44). To William Buckler, this either-or construct suggests that the Ironic Spirits provide the 'most pointed insight into the overall nature of the total experience of *The Dynasts*' ('Thomas' 219). If, however, the Spirit of the Pities represents Hardy's point of view, a new synthesis emerges from the dialectic between Pities and the other Spirits. Now we are reading a continuation of the patterns of choice and responsibility indicated by the novels. At best, the reaction against determinism helps us reconsider the roles of all the Spirits and the importance of the historical drama. At worst, it redirects the search for closure to the human scene or produces Roy Morrell's contention that 'the real subject appears to be not the Will Itself, but Its remoteness, Its irrelevance.' We may forget about the hackneyed passages in the Fore Scene comforted by the thought that the Will 'is Something that, literally, isn't there' (76) – a remark that either misses the point (a metaphysical Will literally isn't anywhere) or restates the obvious. Morrell's 'Boy Scout moralizing of Hardy' (Goode 24) generates 'the almost complete disjunction ... between world and overworld' (Stewart 207) just as surely as the determinism it contests.

Alternatively, and on the whole more recently, critics have chosen a different path than the one of substituting 'the discourse of Possibility' for 'the discourse of the Inevitable' (Wotton 28). Now we are closer to the position Hardy eventually took that *The Dynasts* contains the 'discrepancies that are to be expected in an imaginative work' (*Life* 343). If 'Hardy was primarily an artist, not a thinker' (Buckler, 'Thomas' 227), then ideas 'are not the central stimuli to his *poetic* vision' (Dean 13) in *The Dynasts:* 'the artistic form preceded and directed the metaphysic' (White 119). On the face of it, the view that the Spirits have primarily an imaginative rather than an ideological function looks like a new direction. What the philosophical critics usually mention in passing now comes to the forefront. The conflicts in the Overworld are left unresolved 'because individually the Spirits express conflicting aspects of Hardy's own attitude towards experience' (Hynes, *Pattern* 168). The poetic or mythic bias then adds that Hardy 'was able to objectify his own personal responses' (Southerington 153) by creating Spirits who also evoke 'the different elements of our conscious nature' (Chakravarty 32).

Hardy provides some support in his Preface to *The Dynasts* for the view that the Spirits are abstractions from humanity but not without conditions attached. There is not just one voice for any of the main Spirits but many and these never completely merge with a single attribute of a universal human nature. One group of Spirits, the Pities, 'approximates to "the Universal Sympathy of human nature"'; another group, the Years, 'approximates to the passionless Insight of the Ages.' The rest of the Intelligences 'are eclectically chosen auxiliaries' (5). Regarded in this way, the Spirits are not philosophic spectators 'except in the most experientialized terms' (Buckler, 'Thomas' 227). The Years and Pity are the poles of Intelligence, representing a contrast between head and heart, experience and innocence, or scepticism and hope.

As we can see, the aesthetic approach to the Overworld converges with the ideological in one important respect. The viewpoints of the Spirits again gravitate towards a single consciousness, whether Hardy's own or that of an abstract humanity or both. Critics have been hesitant to treat the Spirits as fully valid consciousnesses.[7] They might be linked with characters in the historical world, Sinister with Napoleon, for example, to help flesh out their individuality or human identity, but their epic function is still to represent 'human nature, abstracted into a number of simplified essences' (Keith Wilson 132). At one point in his argument, Buckler suggests that 'Hardy has disturbed the balance of the Spirits as simple ideologues by allowing them to approximate ... personalities too.' Unfortunately, he lets the conjunction of idea and personality slip away. The Spirits remain 'archetypes of awareness' within a 'universalizing consciousness' ('Thomas' 217, 212), while ideology amounts to little more than the misleading contrast between the Years' empiricism and the Pities' idealism.

In escaping the narrowness of philosophical arguments or the looseness of background studies (Rutland, Wright) with their emphasis on multiple sources, aesthetic readings impoverish the Spirits by detaching the Overworld from the ideological horizon of its epoch, framed by the mosaic of quotation, summary, and paraphrase in Hardy's *Literary Notebooks*. If the Spirits represent no more than different general forms of perception, 'It is hard to see,' as Susan Dean admits, 'how these spiritual entities are "the modern expression of a modern outlook"' (6). Buckler creates a similar problem by counterpointing monism and the perceptual pluralism of the Overworld. We may agree that the Spirits do not speak for Hardy, but when both author and Spirits are distanced from the monism of the piece we are left wondering how this 'cultural metaphor' ('Thomas' 212) governs the total perceptual process.

Every thought in the Overworld should be heard as the position of a personality, but just as thought is not simply an ideological event so, too, is personality not merely an aesthetic event. Some of the temperamental and axiological differences between Hardy's Spirits were also marked out in the context of monistic thought. Hardy's 'Literary Notes II and III' contain excerpts from *The Problems of Philosophy* (1905) and *The Philosophy of Religion* (1906) by the Danish thinker and critical monist Harald Höffding.[8] In many respects, the Overworld dramatizes what Höffding calls a religious problem, for 'such a problem is always the expression of spiritual discord.' It 'can only arise when other sides of the spiritual life ... begin to emancipate themselves and to claim free independent value' (*Philosophy* 2). This 'differentiation of the intellectual life of man,' which Hardy impersonates in the form of Intelligences called Spirits, means that 'evaluation and explanation of existence no longer simply coincide' (*Philosophy* 214–15).

To explain why events happen as they do, the Spirit of the Years displays some of the 'Will-webs' (Fore Scene 27) without any concern for 'those highest spiritual values, the conservation of which,' according to Höffding, 'is the business of all true religion' (*Philosophy* 4). 'Mercy I view, not urge,' the Years admonishes the Spirit of the Pities, 'nor more than mark / What designate your titles Good and Ill' (Fore Scene 24). In the After Scene the Spirit of the Pities recounts how the Will 'that fed my hope was far from thine,' a 'Thee' instead of an 'It,' 'Good' as well as 'Great,' not lacking in 'tendermercy' (703). As the past tense indicates, food for hope no longer nourishes convincing thought. Clearly the comprehension of existence has passed to other forms of the spiritual life, while traditional religious ideas have lost their value as knowledge. The Pities' attempt to deduce a divine reality from values only intensifies the religious problem.

If 'every great religion has appeared in history with a conception of the world' (Höffding, *Philosophy* 15),[9] any new religion in *The Dynasts* must work out its destiny within the monistic theory of the universe. Monism 'supplies the stage for the great drama ... and the stage determines in many ways the nature and course of the play' (*Philosophy* 120). In this conceptual theatre, where man is both spectator and actor, the relation between the unity and the manifold constantly provokes the thought of the Spirits. Were they spectators only, their mood throughout would remain purely intellectual or aesthetic. Long before Hardy created his Overworld, Huxley imagined how to 'a being endowed with perfect intellectual and aesthetic faculties, but devoid of the capacity for suffering pain, either physical or moral,' the universe 'would seem ... to be a sort of kaleidoscope, in which, at every successive moment of time, a new arrangement of parts of exquisite beauty and symmetry would present itself' ('Scientific' 198).[10] These patterns, like Darwin's 'endless beautiful adaptations' (Francis Darwin 1:279),[11] appeal especially to the Spirit Sinister who claims to enjoy the 'sound artistry of the Immanent Will' (391; Part Second, Act V, Scene viii). In a drama without footlights, however, all the Spirits to some degree possess values at stake in the world of the many, while 'only an oriental "overman" ... could ... sit in his heaven [or Overworld] and find his existence harmonious' (Höffding, *Philosophy* 269). The Spirit of the Years aspires to be, in Henry Maudsley's terms, 'a being of another and higher order of intelligence – remote, separate, superhuman – calmly [surveying] human history' (120)[12] in the aesthetic context of the Will's 'Eternal artistries in Circumstance' (Fore Scene 21). Yet the eldest Spirit recognizes the difference between good and ill (see Chakravarty 52). He rebukes the 'lewdness' (383; 2.5.6) of the Ironic Spirits and dismisses the English aristocracy as a 'glib throng' (270; 2.2.3) and their Parliament as 'insular, empiric, un-ideal' (51; 1.1.3). After Pitt's death, the Spirit Sinister remarks that even the Years 'can show ruth / At man's fag end, when his destruction's sure!' (195; 1.6.8).

All the Spirits are bound together in a gradation of feeling as well as thought. Irony and Sinister care enough about the historical situation to cast their judgments of it in ethical terms that reveal an inability to adjust emotionally to the course of events. Irony is not content with an explanation of existence that turns the Many into mere 'painted shapes' (117; 1.4.5) within the unfeeling One and denies the possibility of evaluation. Value 'presupposes a subject which is capable of feeling pleasure and pain': 'All feeling, i.e. all pleasure and pain, of whatever kind, expresses the value that an event in the inner or outer world has for us' (Höffding, *Philosophy* 106). Thus when suffering evokes Pities' complaint against 'the intolerable antilogy / Of making figments feel' (117; 1.4.5), Irony replies, with a glance at the Years for whom 'Affection ever was illogical' (65; 1.1.6), 'Logic's in that' (117; 1.4.5).

More difficult to see perhaps is that 'the sympathies of the Sinister Spirit are with the Pities on the whole' (Ransom 181). Like the Spirit of the Years, who labels Sinister the 'Dragon of the Incorporeal World' (62; 1.1.6), most critics find either 'a malicious Iago of cosmic proportions' (Weber 244) or 'a grimmer and more cynical Spirit Ironic' (Rutland 340). They assume that Sinister's caustic and extreme words emerge in the exterior dialogue without any inward struggle. Yet accents of conviction often imply an internal resistence on the part of the speaker's other self. In the Spirit Sinister's case, Hardy may have remembered Milton's Satan, 'Vaunting aloud, but rackt with deep despair' (*Paradise Lost* 1:126). The Napoleonic world gives Sinister every opportunity to proclaim openly the defiant theme of one side of Satan's internal speech in Book IV of *Paradise Lost*: 'Evil be thou my Good' (110). If not despair, at least evaluation and regret still inhabit such Sinister inversions as 'Good. It is the selfish and unconscionable characters who are so much regretted' (485; 3.1.11); and 'Excellent Emperor! / He tops all human greatness; in that he / To lesser grounds of greatness adds the prime, / Of being without a conscience' (687; 3.7.8). During an exchange over the impending invasion of England, Pity hears an exaggerated cynicism in the only other Spirit to have 'paean'd the Will' (35; 1.1.1). 'My argument,' says the uncanny Phantom, 'is that War makes rattling good history; but Peace is poor reading. So I back Bonaparte for the reason that he will give pleasure to posterity.' Whereas the Chorus of the Years can reply only with the flat admission, 'We comprehend him not,' Pity tries to bring another Spirit Sinister into the open with the angry charge of 'Gross hypocrite!' (88; 1.2.5). Dean takes much the same approach in renaming Sinister the Spirit Cynical in the sense of the 'voice of disappointed idealism' (30). It is helpful to keep in mind, as Havelock Ellis does in exploring the many manifestations of the Spirit of the nineteenth century, that 'every true Cynic is, above all, a moralist and a preacher' (97).[13] This kind of cynic has already broken through the sabre-rattling of Sinister's tart logic. What Pity does not hear is the condemnation of future readers for whom the best way the world can speak itself as a story is in the shape of a narrative about war. The bluntness and crudity of the argument should not prevent us from recognizing how Sinister expands the problem of war and its appeal into the textual realm of events the historian chooses to record and narrate.

Here and elsewhere in comments on the historical spectacle, Sinister sounds very much like a disillusioned Maudsley for whom 'the best history is no better than a tissue of ingenious fictions' about progress. What the past really teaches is how human nature 'fails not to make its greatest heroes of the men who, in mightily managing it, have unscrupulously trampled on its moral rules' (121, 118). While hoping that the 'evolution of the living sentiment of human solidarity' will bring a better future, Maudsley succumbs to the doubt deeply embedded in naturalistic monism. He takes the long view that 'like everything organic, the human race carries the seeds and causes of inevitable dissolution within itself' (313, 315).

For the Spirit of the Pities, the Napoleonic battles create a strife between value and reality: 'Why should men's many-valued motions take / So barbarous a groove!' (670; 3.7.4). Values must be discovered or produced in the world of experience before they can be assumed or conceived to exist in a higher world. More than any other kind of experience, war offers the challenge that every particular process of realization involves a disproportionate destruction of values at other points. The Spirit of the Pities detects mockery in the Spirit Ironic's remark that the deserters from the retreating British army in Spain constitute the 'Quaint poesy, and real romance of war' (290; 2.3.1). Yet the fact that both Spirits feel a discord is also a proof that existence contains value. The simple courage and loyalty of a Marshal Ney, exemplifying 'war's generous impulses' (669; 3.7.4), may be undone by the destructive context of his actions at Waterloo, but on the margins of war, among its deserters and bystanders, others, like the Pities, 'find / Poesy ever lurk where pit-pats poor mankind!' (290; 2.3.1).

The religious moment does not begin until the Pities compare their estimation of human value to the Years' conception of the One. The questions that Höffding asks, the Pities are almost afraid to raise:

> Is there any interconnexion between values and the laws of the forces of existence? Are these laws and forces themselves ultimately determined by the highest values? or are we precluded from attributing validity to our concept of value beyond the sphere of human life? (*Philosophy* 9)

What legitimizes these questions takes us back to the historical conditions in which 'the great web of things' (*Philosophy* 218) became the dominant metaphor for existence as a whole.[14] During the critical period Höffding identifies with monism, science and religion were drawn into a new dialogue.[15] Most obviously, religion could not 'continue undisturbedly to describe its circle round its centre without troubling itself how science establishes the interconnexion of the points it has discovered.' Yet science in its turn could not continue 'to move in the periphery of being without bethinking itself that there may be perhaps a centre, and that this centre may conceivably be identical with that assumed by religion' (Höffding, *Philosophy* 26).

Within the full circle of existence, a paradoxical boundary without limits, the centre could change and lie at a different point. The new point took the form of an enabling presupposition. The scientific understanding proceeds on the basis of an underlying principle of unity that makes orderly dependence and reciprocal action possible. While Hardy's Spirits do not agree about the meaning and value of events, they do not contest the idea of unity. The monistic principle could bring to mind the concept of God and open up the possibility that the rational and causal web of inter-relations 'may be the framework or the foundation for the unfolding ... of a valuable content' (Höffding, *Philosophy* 245). In Hardy's Overworld the great thought in which science and religion meet comes from an unexpected source. If the interest of religion lies in 'regarding all events ... as expressions of one and the same power' (Höffding, *Philosophy* 24), the Spirit of the Years has already occupied the religious centre by assuming an Immanent Will.

Spokesmen for naturalism, who wanted to become a power in the domain of practical life, needed a substitute for Christianity. In *The Riddle of the Universe* (1900), Haeckel argues that 'scientific faith ... leads to a monistic religion' that will replace 'the irrational superstition ... of a perverted Christianity' (9)[16] made to sound as 'grossly logicless' (465; 3.1.4) as Russian Orthodoxy to Napoleon's secular ears. W.K. Clifford 'saw that the methods which are commonly called scientific, though they might rear up a vast superstructure of knowledge, yet left the foundations of it to take care of themselves' (Mallock 252).[17] It became increasingly clear that in some respects 'science was never more intuitive than in the nineteenth century' and that anyone with a mechanical view of the universe 'has an ideal religion or none at all' (Chamberlain 2:244, 291).[18]

For now the point to be stressed is the one that Höffding opposes to the 'current opinion that personality and scientific research are antagonistic' (*Problems* 2): 'the deepest foundation for the principle of natural causation is the need for continuity which lies in the nature of our consciousness' (*Philosophy* 23). Cosmological unity rests on the unity of the personal life. In this respect, any easy distinction between the Spirit of the Years and the Spirit of the Pities in terms of an opposition between a sceptical science and an idealistic religion becomes problematized. Clearly, for religion the 'soul is situated at the centre of the world' (Ellis 232), for 'it is personality which in the world of our experience invests all other things with value.' But 'scientific thought is itself a spiritual activity which can only be exercised by a person' (Höffding, *Philosophy* 279, 317). It is 'one and the same thing which enables us to find values in existence and which makes this existence comprehensible to us.' Thus in life personality comes first, not over but under the world: 'it is that which supports all – even science, and which impresses its seal on all things,' so that existence itself looks 'like a great individuality' (Höffding, *Philosophy* 115, 317, 262).

As Hardy struggled to distinguish his Spirits or Intelligences, often reassigning speeches in the rough draft and manuscript, he also found that their inconsistencies and overlapping moods reinforced the monistic theme. By the time he wrote *The Dynasts*, the belief that 'in consciousness we have a unity and a truly "monistic" stand-point' (Guenther 389)[19] had superseded the Kantian division of the mind into distinct faculties and categories of thought. The need to incorporate feeling in the constitution of rationality made the frontier between philosophy and art difficult to mark. Philosophy could appear 'more a matter of passionate vision than of logic' (James, *Pluralistic* 176).[20] In one sense to Stephen, philosophies 'are really to be considered as poetry, rather than as logic': 'substantially, they represent the emotions with which men regard their dwelling place' (*Social* 192). 'A great philosophical system,' claims Höffding, 'is a work of art, a drama' (*Problems* 127).

The picture which each of Hardy's main Spirits forms of the whole of the drama is not without practical consequences. The Spirits agree about the genre of existence but as the cloud curtain rises and falls they disagree as to what kind of drama they are watching in the 'theatre of history' (Hartmann 2:304).[21] When the Spirit of the Pities says 'terrestrial tragedy,' the Spirit Ironic replies, 'Nay, comedy' (Fore Scene 25). To the latter, 'Where the humour comes in, ... makes the play worth seeing' (336; 2.4.5), especially if 'the episode is frankly farcical' (214; 2.1.2). The Spirit Sinister also looks for 'good sport' (35; 1.1.1) or 'good antic' (111; 1.4.3) in the 'rare dramas' (Fore Scene 23) that unfold in the human scene. War makes 'excellently high-coloured drama' (232; 2.1.6), while corresponding natural disasters generate pleasing 'comedies' (30; 1.1.1).

The tension between the tragic and the comic perspectives is closely bound up with the problem of the One in the many and the fact that monism could be inflected in very different ways. Of all the philosophers whom Hardy read, Schopenhauer relies most heavily on the metaphor of 'the great drama of the objectification of the will to live' (*World* 3:113–14) on 'the stage of the world' ('Counsels' 53).[22] Although belonging to the first half of the nineteenth century, he was appropriated by later thinkers, especially Eduard von Hartmann, as part of the 'tendency to Monism' (Hartmann 2:239) in all philosophies of the modern epoch. William Caldwell approves of the way Schopenhauer 'never allows himself to speak of [the thing-in-itself] in the plural, as Kant does, and so keeps consistently to a monistic point of view' ('Schopenhauer's' 357–8; Hardy, *Literary* 2:160).

Schopenhauer claims that 'we are possessed of two different, nay, absolutely contradictory, ways of regarding the world' that shape our emotional and evaluative responses. If we regard existence according to the principle of unity, all creatures reveal their identity with ourselves and so we feel pity and love for them. If we regard existence according to the principle of individuation, they appear as strangers to us and consequently we can have only negative feelings for them. This double awareness allows Schopenhauer to explain how 'at one moment I regard all mankind with heartfelt pity, at another with the greatest indifference, on occasion with ... a positive enjoyment of their pain' ('Human' 79, 78–9).[23] More importantly, the way Schopenhauer connects thought with emotion suggests that the compassion of the Pities, the indifference of the Years, and the cruel delight of the Spirit Sinister, who hopes for 'pleasing slaughter' (87; 1.2.5), represent more than temperamental differences.

The monism of *The Dynasts* allows for very different responses to suffering but the feelings which accompany the One or the many in Schopenhauer's analysis switch places in the Overworld. It is the sight of the many, not the Years' revelation of the One, that awakens the inexhaustible sympathy of the Pities. The ethical and intellectual components of what constitutes the superior response to suffering, 'really at one with the spirit of the New Testament' ('Studies' 16) in Schopenhauer, become separate voices in the Overworld. By Schopenhauer's standards, the eldest Phantom has fulfilled the true aim of life. His intellect has risen to the point 'where the vanity of all effort is manifest' ('Studies' 45; Hardy *Literary* 2:29) but the drama does not become tragic (or comic for that matter) as a result. The tragic awareness leads to a resignation that fulfills the highest moral aim of sympathy, not the Years' advice to the Mild One, 'be not too touched with human fate' (414; 2.6.5). Although Schopenhauer anticipated 'something of the scientific spirit of the nineteenth century' (Saunders, Preface to Schopenhauer's 'Religion' v), his pessimism does not mean the 'worthlessness of life' that struck some late nineteenth-century observers as 'an idea that agrees with science' and 'meets the mood of the age' (Ross 742).[24] By assuming a fundamental misfit between value and reality, the pessimist 'is compelled to admit that there is something valuable in the world' (Höffding, *Philosophy* 226).

Whatever critics may mean by the Years' stoicism (Bailey 52; Weber 244), it cannot be Schopenhauer's: 'This is the Stoic temper – never to be unmindful of the sad fate of humanity ... but always to remember that our existence is full of woe and misery' ('Counsels' 108). Instead, the Years' 'unpassioned essence' (42; 1.1.3) strives to look at the world with a 'colourless emotion' (Stephen, *Agnostic's* 18). His prevalent mood derives from a late phase of scientific agnosticism in which 'the moral fervour, the enthusiastic resignation, of a Clifford or a George Eliot' was replaced 'by a tone of pure neutrality, as of men conscientiously analyzing a Cosmos for which they are in no way responsible' (Myers 679).[25] Earlier agnostics such as Maudsley and Huxley could speak of 'the long-drawn human tragedy' (Maudsley 123); the Years refers only to the 'Drama' (414; 2.6.5) or 'Play' (696; 3.7.8), never to 'the great drama of evolution, with its full share of pity and terror' (Huxley, 'Science' 802).

While the tragic awareness depends on a grasp of the One in Schopenhauer, this cosmic viewpoint generates a sense of the comic as well. When we return from contemplating the world as a whole and 'look at life in its small details, as presented, say, in a comedy, how ridiculous it all seems!' ('Studies' 24). A knowledge of the underlying Will becomes 'the source of the comical, the burlesque, the grotesque, the ridiculous side of life' (*World* 3:118), so that our 'terrible activity produces a comic effect' ('Studies' 24). Hartmann explains that the encounter with pain and suffering can turn the indignation of the 'sympathizing soul' into a 'Mephistophelean gallows-humour, that with half-suppressed pity and half-unrestrained mockery looks down

with a like sovereign irony both on those caught in the illusion of hap-
piness and on those dissolved in tearful woe' (3:118–19). Neither the
Ancient Phantom nor the young Shade ever laugh but in one speech
Pity feels tempted to express 'that humour which is the last concen-
trated word of the human organism under the lash of Fate' (Ellis 87).
The plightful scene of King George's madness

> Might drive Compassion past her patiency
> To hold that some mean, monstrous ironist
> Had built this mistimed fabric of the Spheres
> To watch the throbbings of its captive lives.

By comparison, the Years' 'nescient Will' (414; 2.6.5) seems preferable,
for at least 'It accomplishes that which appears so designed and
planned' though 'without reflection and without conception of an end'
(Schopenhauer, World 3:78). But, as Hartmann points out, such a blind
Will can become 'the "Sinister"' (3:158). This sense of the One underwrites the gallows humour and perversity of Hardy's Mephistophelean Spirit. If the cosmic Artist is a kind of 'monstrous ironist,'
tragic terror turns into black comedy: 'It's merry so; / What damage
mortal flesh must undergo!' (685; 3.7.7). A humble servant in the
'under' world agrees that 'there's comedy in all things,' then adds his
own telling qualification to the generic dialogue '– when they don't
concern you' (551; 3.4.3).

Although 'the straits that ... arise often look comical enough' to
Schopenhauer, there is still 'the misery which underlies them' (World
3:118). Tragedy, with the ethical value it places on suffering, goes
deeper than comedy. 'If you look beneath the surface of any farce,'
Hardy comments in one definition, 'you see a tragedy; and, on the contrary, if you blind yourself to the deeper issues of a tragedy you see a
farce' (Life 224).[26] Such deliberate blinding produces the insights of the
Spirit Ironic who views the Will as something that 'plays at flux and
reflux' (my emphasis 227; 2.1.5), though from the standpoint of ethical
values 'It does not ... quite play the game' (117; 1.4.5) since Its 'throws
of good and bad' are 'choiceless' (173; 1.6.3). A 'burlesque of what he
should be' (Schopenhauer, 'Studies' 13; Hardy, Literary 2:29), man is
caught in the 'grotesque shape' of 'Life's queer mechanics' (The
Dynasts 336; 2.4.5). Thus pity can be half-suppressed and laughter half-
unrestrained. To the Spirit Ironic, existence seems woven of such tragi-
comic stuff that the riches of potential values can never be realized.

Schopenhauer and Hartmann illustrate why Hardy found the monistic theory of the universe so amenable to a carnivalized conception of history and the high forms of thought. Schopenhauer continually takes the carnival liberty to turn inside out the lofty aspects of the world and world views. T. Bailey Saunders, the editor and translator Hardy read, assigns Schopenhauer a very carnivalesque role: 'Schopenhauer can be said to have brought down philosophy from heaven to earth' (Preface to 'Religion' v). Hartmann's attempt to reunite the Schopenhauerian Will and the Hegelian Idea does not restore reason to its former throne. Indeed the scientific evidence Hartmann so carefully examines shows that 'passion ... uses reason to reach its ends' (Ribot 440).[27] Existence still strikes Hartmann as a 'frenzied carnival' (3:119), just as civilization appears to be a 'big masquerade' ('Human' 13) to Schopenhauer. For all their gloomy outlook, these two pessimists helped make monism a serio-comical field of thought that Hardy could represent only through a novelistic range of voices in the Overworld.

The bitter mockery and dark humour of a Schopenhauer or Hartmann represent one extreme of laughter in *The Dynasts*, the point where comedy begins to pass over into tragedy. In his book on Rabelais, Bakhtin argues that irony, sarcasm, cynicism and the like mark the decline of true carnival laughter, but his own premise that carnivalized literature unites the serious and the comic allows him in the revised book on Dostoevsky to show that laughter can be reduced and still express a carnival sense of the world. In *The Dynasts*, the negative aspects of laughter seem less an indication of carnival's demise than a sign of laughter's confrontation wih suffering and oppression. Laughter does not stay muffled; it keeps breaking into the open to bring out the ambivalence of the world and the Will. The official air of the Spirit of the Years cannot prevent the playful antics of Irony and Sinister, any more than war can silence the laughing people who preserve the unofficial aspects of language and thought that characterize the novel.

In a monistic universe where the final word can never be uttered about the mysterious One, existence becomes double-voiced and 'why the whole tragi-comedy exists cannot in the least be seen' (Schopenhauer, *World* 3:114). Hardy's chronicle-piece, like World History in Carlyle's *The French Revolution*, is 'ludicro-terrific' or 'comico-tragic': 'Transcendent things of all sorts, as in the general outburst of multitudinous Passion, are huddled together; the ludicrous, nay the ridiculous, with the horrible' (Carlyle, *French Revolution* 200, 377, 222).[28]

Both works create an internal distance within their generic forms that extends well past the tonal shifts between the comic and tragic. Carlyle's first biographer, James Anthony Froude, had as much difficulty in defining *The French Revolution* as Hardy did *The Dynasts*. 'It is a prose poem' and a 'spectral' (1:88, 90; Hardy, *Literary* 1:161) history as well. 'It has been called an *epic*' by Carlyle himself but 'It is rather an Aeschylean drama composed of facts literally true' (1:88; Hardy, *Literary* 1:161). Hardy knew that

> Where the poet is bound by history he can hardly have a real plot with a real dramatic unity ... and the dramatist, instead of one central action to which all else is subordinate, is often obliged to content himself with a panorama of shifting scenes. ('Some' 318; Hardy, *Literary* 2:70)

He followed Carlyle in the belief that 'the drama of history must have a central idea' (Stephen, *Studies* 237).[29] Beyond relying on the reader to connect his historical scenes, Hardy uses the 'monotony with which the Spirits insist upon the influence of the Will ... to bind the drama into one organic whole' (*Letters* 3:352).

As the monistic theme passes through a whole range of accents, every important personality in the Overworld brings the reader in contact with religion. 'It is strange,' comments Havelock Ellis about the New Spirit of the nineteenth century, 'men seek to be, or to seem, atheists, agnostics, cynics, pessimists; at the core of all these things lurks religion' (228), in the sense of a hunger for the Infinite. In 1899 it struck Hardy as an 'amusing fact ... that the conception of a First Cause which the theist calls "God," and the conception of the same that the so-styled atheist calls "no-God," are nowadays almost exactly identical' (*Life* 326).

When Hardy said that the 'old theologies ... will not bear stretching further in epic or dramatic art' (*Life* 344), he did not mean that 'Theological imperatives do not concern [him]' (Maynard 63) and that *The Dynasts* should be read as 'a strange new form of secular epic' (Keith Wilson 132). Hardy paraphrased J.A. Symonds's attempt to redefine God as the 'name of a hitherto unapprehended energy, the symbol of that which is the life and motion of the universe' (*Literary* 1:66). However, simply to call the Immanent Will 'God' would be to ignore the powerful challenge to theism that came from some theories of monism: 'belief in ... [God] is now rudely challenged by the Agnostic and the Monist' (Goldwin Smith 723).[30] Hardy's remark that he used a 'generalized form of what the thinking world had gradually come to adopt, myself included' (*Letters* 3:255), locates him within an interpretive community but, if the Spirits are any indication, without ignoring its diversity. The distinctions between voices in the Overworld constitute 'one of the most important ways in which historical difference gets inscribed within works of fiction' (Thomas 149).

History in *The Dynasts* has almost always meant the period from 1805 to 1815, as if the Overworld, though it may have sources, has no history of its own. Hardy's long interest in the Napoleonic period more than matched Carlyle's in the French Revolution, but not 'as illustrating signally his own conclusions on the Divine government of the World' (Froude 2:325). The conclusions of others sound in the Overworld and to recover their voices we need to reopen the question of what Hardy might have meant by the monistic theory of the universe. There have been few direct answers, but their variety is so striking that we begin to suspect that monism, in spite of its name, did not have one meaning.

Passing from one extreme to the other, we discover that 'Hardy's world-view ... is Idealistic Monism' (Brennecke 66) or 'Shelleyan monism' (Elliott 1188), then 'mechanistic monism' (Laird 201) and 'monistic determinism' (Wright 6), and finally that 'Hardy tried to make a poetry of monistic materialism' (Hynes, *Pattern* 40) and that by monism he meant the 'contemporary belief in scientific materialism' (Dean 5). Most critics hear a scientific sanction in Hardy's 'doctrine' of the Immanent Will and proceed to use the terms mechanism and naturalism, together with determinism, materialism, and agnosticism, as if they were single-voiced and interchangeable. Removed from their tension-filled historical environment, these words reveal nothing of the contradictory development of science and the subsequent transformation of monism from a materialistic into a spiritualistic theory of the universe.

Although the term monism, in contrast to dualism, was invented by the German rationalist and Enlightenment philosopher Christian Wolff (1679–1754), the word dropped out of use until Hegel adopted the term to characterize his system of thought. It was again forgotten when Hegel's influence subsided, only to be reintroduced by Darwinians like Haeckel. It entered English scientific and philosophical discourse in the 1860s just before agnosticism (Huxley coined the term agnostic in 1869) undercut the materialistic grounds of science.

In *A Pluralistic Universe* (1909), William James identifies the 'materi-

alistic generation' with 'that in the fifties and sixties' (148). In retrospect, it appeared that 'up to about 1850 almost everyone believed that
sciences expressed truths that were exact copies of a definite code of
non-human realities' (James, *Meaning* 232–3). As monism came to have
a history, its scientific origins in the nineteenth century could be traced
to materialism or the earlier of two distinct and very different forms
of naturalism, the one that allied itself with materialism. In Germany
naturalism and 'the newly awakened *materialism*, which appeared in
1855' (Haeckel, *Riddle* 93) in the work of Ludwig Büchner and Carl
Vogt, remained synonymous late into the nineteenth century, so that
Hartmann felt himself in the minority compared to 'the prevailing
rationalistic and materialistic tendency of our time' (1:109) typified by
Haeckel. Whereas mid-Victorian naturalism tended to work out into
atheism, Haeckel's monism merges God in matter. Scientific materialism became one source of religion, Theodore Christlieb listing the
belief in 'a universal *Material Substance*' (138) as one of three modern
non-Biblical conceptions of God.[31]

In England, however, there was nothing contemporary to *The
Dynasts* about materialistic monism. The thinking world whom Hardy
addresses felt contempt for the sales of the six-penny translation of
Haeckel's *Riddle of the Universe* and invoked the public mind to explain
either the 'idolatory of material force' ('Mr. Footman' 515)[32] or the 'horror of "Materialism"' (Huxley, *Hume* 286).[33] In the struggle for survival
among ideologies, the old-fashioned materialist had become 'as extinct
now [1905] as the dodo' ('Self and Space' 527).[34]

W.L. Walker reported in 1906 that 'although the Materialism of a
quarter of a century ago has largely passed away, a new and more sub-
tle (if more silent) Agnosticism has taken its place' (10).[35] According to
another monist, A.T. Ormond, this new ally transformed naturalism
into 'a much more powerful conception ... that breathes the very spirit
of the times.' The result was that a neutral or agnostic monism supplanted the older materialistic one. Instead of conceiving nature as a
system of material forces, this second form of naturalism 'identifies
itself with some sort of living principle which it plants at the heart of
nature and represents as the spring of nature's processes and movements' (Ormond 594, 593).[36]

By 1886, in one of the many speculative essays Hardy read, 'The
World as an Eject,' George J. Romanes predicted that 'Monism is destined to become the generally accepted theory of things' (58).[37] Four
years later the first issue of *The Monist* appeared out of Chicago. 'If I

may so express it,' David Ritchie said in 1898, 'all our sciences seem to assume a monistic metaphysics' (22).[38] Hardy also knew from his reading that, in Walker's words, monism 'goes beyond Science, strictly so called' (13). It seemed, for example, most paradoxical to the philosopher Hartmann that although both he and the scientist Haeckel professed a monistic outlook, they should be so far apart in their respective interpretations of the One.[39]

Hardy was right, then, in claiming a wide acceptance for the monistic theory of the universe, 'For whatever else may be affirmed of the thought of the century just past and gone, one thing is certain, – viz, that all schools tended to the doctrine of philosophic unity' ('Spiritual' 9; Hardy, *Literary* 2:107). However, the fundamental principle not in dispute made possible the terms of disagreement, especially during the 1890s when the concept of monism underwent a radical revaluation. James Ward charts a movement in monistic theory that Hardy reflects and refracts at different angles through the viewpoints of his phantom Intelligences. The Chorus of the Pities concludes *The Dynasts* where Ward ends *Naturalism and Agnosticism* (1899), 'on the threshold of Spiritualistic Monism' (1:v).[40] Hardy re-voices the 'struggle of diverse monisms' (Ward 2:202) that arose in the late nineteenth century when the untenable monism of materialism gave way to a neutral monism whose instability led to various panpsychist views of nature, including the cosmic mind of *The Dynasts*.

By the early years of the twentieth century, the struggle between rival monisms entered a new phase pertinent to the play of thought in the Overworld. Surveying the current situation in philosophy in 1909, William James used the evolutionary metaphor popular at the time to describe how monism 'breaks into two subspecies, of which the one is more monistic, the other more pluralistic in form' (*Pluralistic* 31). Hardy studied many of the exponents – F.H. Bradley, David Ritchie, R.B. Haldane – of the first subspecies, 'spoken of sometimes ... as "post-Kantian" or absolute idealism' (*Pluralistic* 24). A.J. Balfour recalled (and Hardy recorded his observation, quoted in a review) that:

> 'In the last twenty years or so of the nineteenth century came (in England) the great idealist revival. For the first time since Locke the general stream of British philosophy rejoined, for good or evil, the main continental river. And I should suppose that now in 1911 the bulk of philosophers belong to the neo-Kantian or neo-Hegelian school.' ('Bergson and Balfour' 474; *Literary* 2:218–19)

'We hear,' Felix Adler also commented, 'much nowadays of the necessity of a return to Kant' (192).[41] It seemed to one commentator in 1901 that 'all the thought of the present time is still centring round the lines drawn by Immanuel Kant' ('Spiritual' 10). For Ormond, Kant's Copernican discovery was 'a revolution the full significance of which is only dawning upon the world very slowly even now after the lapse of a century' (332). Ritchie traces the central point of modern metaphysics, the relativity of knowledge, to 'the main and most important doctrine of Kant – that it is only the unity of self-consciousness which makes knowledge possible' (274), while Herbert Spencer and his American disciple, John Fiske, stress the 'immense importance of Kant's views' (Fiske 1:48)[42] for science.

George Wotton is right in arguing that 'Philosophically [Hardy] inclined to the Kantian compromise between materialism [or naive realism] and idealism,' though the contemporary formulation of this was by no means limited for him to 'the "agnostic compromise"' (6–7, 107). Hardy's way of talking about the 'theory' or 'philosophy' of The Dynasts, while reminding us in a deprecatory tone that '"I have no philosophy – merely what I often explained to be only a confused heap of impressions"' (Life 441), makes more sense in the context of neo-Kantian thinking. On 1 July 1892, Hardy wrote that 'We don't always remember as we should that in getting at the truth we get only at the true nature of the impression that an object, etc., produces on us, the true thing in itself being still beyond our knowledge, as Kant shows' (Life 261–2).[43] Even the formal thought of his age ultimately meant to Hardy the 'impressions of the age' (Life 406) and all the more so when the object of thought was something like the Immanent Will.

Not necessarily far apart even in terms of their religious implications, realism and idealism formed converging lines of thought. From the point of view of scientific realism, Huxley admitted, in a famous and often repeated remark, that 'if I were to choose between Materialism and Idealism, I should elect for the latter' ('Science' 796). The more difficult choice was the one almost everyone avoided. Commenting on his attempt to reconcile appearance and reality, F.H. Bradley says 'Whether it is to be called Realism or Idealism I do not know' (485).[44] Most monists preferred to combine the two viewpoints in some way, as witness R.B. Haldane's 'concrete system of Idealism' (1:109),[45] Hartmann's 'Ideal-realism' (1:xxv), Carl Du Prel's 'Transcendental Realism' (1:77),[46] Spencer's 'transfigured realism' (First 170; Hardy, Literary 2:108), and G.H. Lewes's 'Reasoned Realism' ('Course' 321).[47] While it could be said that 'Realism in the broad sense is not antithetical to, but inclusive of, Idealism' (Caldwell, 'Epistemology' 207), it could be equally asserted that 'Idealism, when sound and healthy, is only Realism in the intensest phase of veracity' (Symonds 121).

Although finding Absolute Idealism 'in possession in so many quarters' (James, *Essays* 121), James saw 'signs of its giving way to a wave of revised empiricism' (*Pluralistic* 7). This new subspecies of monism tried to overcome the Kantian distinction between the phenomenal and the noumenal, implicit in science and explicit in monisms of the Absolute, by all but refusing to entertain the hypothesis of a transempirical reality at all. Closely allied to the new realism and pragmatism (as witness James's laudatory preface to Höffding's *The Problems of Philosophy*), critical or analytic monism also strove 'to maintain the thought of unity without dogmatizing,' realizing 'that it is lacking in the prerequisites for a complete solution' (Höffding, *Problems* 144). A cautionary tone, suitable to a novel rather than an epic, entered monistic speculation. Morgan says 'we ought not to be ashamed of stating frankly the hypothetical nature of our view' since 'analytic monism by itself is insufficient and partial' ('Three Aspects' 328, 323). Yet in their own way the 'votaries of Monism-*cum*-Pluralism' (Jones 488; Hardy, *Literary* 2:388) continued the religious concern of the British Idealists by renewing the possibility of a finite God within the context of a novelistic, 'unfinished world' (James, Preface to Höffding's *Problems* xiii; Hardy, *Literary* 2:223). While steadfastly opposed to idealist abstractions, James, as one reviewer noticed, 'is not really at issue with the idealists. Like them, he holds the cardinal doctrine that truth or reality is not a datum, but a construction.' By 1907 he had 'acquired some note as one of those teachers who provide a quasi-philosophical sanction for religious beliefs' ('Pragmatism' 10, 9).[48]

Hardy was interested enough in the relation between pragmatism and religion to quote from a letter on the subject written by an Oxford scholar to the *Spectator*. Like all the other isms, including monism, pragmatism could be considered as a generic theory 'which admits of specific variation along various lines' (Sopote 129). In one direction, made into a doctrine of truth and error, pragmatism could not serve as a foundation for theism but only because 'Theism is one of the indispensable premises of pragmatism.' The explanation, also recorded by Hardy, brings back the very Absolute which James found so repugnant: 'for minds which are not omniscient with respect to the total consequences of contemplated beliefs, the pragmatic test is useless unless they (the minds) can rely on the trustworthy guidance of an omniscient Mind' (Sopote 129; Hardy, *Literary* 2:199). 'Thus,' the letter writer continues, 'it is necessary to establish some form of theism independently of pragmatism' (Sopote 129). If the religious mind of the nineteenth century tended in the same direction as the philosophic, it was because monism held out the best hope for theism. It looked in 1901, on the eve of *The Dynasts*, that 'the great idea of spiritual monism' was the 'principal achievement' ('Spiritual' 10) of the century just past that could exercise leadership in the twentieth.

As this brief survey indicates, we cannot treat the period between Hardy's memorandum, 'Let Europe be the stage and have scenes continually shifting' (*Personal Notebooks* 15) in 1874, and the publication of Part Third of *The Dynasts* in 1908, as homogeneous in terms of monistic theory. The increasing sway of monism still left unresolved the issue between its various forms. Like Dostoevsky, Hardy had a gift 'for hearing the dialogue of his epoch, or, more precisely, for hearing his epoch as a great dialogue' (Bakhtin, *Problems* 90). He heard the reigning voices of naturalism and agnosticism and the voices, not yet fully emerged or dominant, of spiritualistic, idealistic, critical, and analytic monism. At the same time, this kind of outside context is something already inside a text such as *The Dynasts*, itself a model of Bakhtin's 'notion of the novel as a tapestry woven out of a variety of discourses' (Bové 121).

The novelistic qualities[49] of the Overworld indicate its importance for Hardy's treatment of the Napoleonic wars. While Hardy respects the uniqueness of the past, using blank verse paraphrases of 'the words really spoken or written by the [historical] characters' (Preface 4) whenever attainable, he retains contemporary reality in the form of the Overworld as a unique way of seeing the past. He does not look at the historical material as something that has already become finished; the Spirits bring it into a zone of contact with the unfolding and still unfinished character of reality in the present. Yet Hardy also gives one curious twist to the relation between early nineteenth-century history and the modern outlook of his Spirits. For the most part, the Napoleonic period unfolds before the Phantoms as if it were the present, while the historicity of their own viewpoints, the later present or more recent past from which they actually speak, remains hidden from them.

To recover this context, however, requires looking for more than a set of influences on Hardy. In many respects, *The Dynasts* represents the culmination of an intertextual mode of writing that had already become a tangled web of allusions in Hardy's late novels. As this chapter has begun to show, the context of monism consists of numerous texts even when we limit our search to the books, essays, and reviews that Hardy read. Although the significance of Hardy's reading for *The Dynasts* will always be a matter of interpretation, we can at least make better sense of the notes he kept when we see that in monism they have a common theme and one that crossed disciplines. When we approach the Overworld as a novelistic dialogue that opens out into contemporary issues rather than as an epic, hierarchical system of thought, text and context become blurred to the point where it is often impossible to say exactly where the text begins and the context ends.

In order to connect the '"ordinates"' (Hardy, Preface to *The Dynasts* 6) of the Overworld, we must now thicken our description of the Spirits' quasi-direct speech. Since one theory of monism had many voices, we may use them to reconsider the Phantom often judged to be the most important in the Overworld, and the one who 'establishes ... his superiority over his fellow-Spirits' (Orel, *Thomas* 72) – the Spirit of the Years. He often speaks as if he expects no answers but he does get replies and these come into contact with one another in the territory of the monistic theme and over issues that were not resolved by Hardy's era.

Two
_____

The Will's Official Spirit

In *The Cosmic Web*, N. Katherine Hayles does not include *The Dynasts* in her study of literary responses to scientific field theories. No explanation is given but two reasons seem clear enough and take us to the heart of our inquiry about Hardy's work. On the literary side, Hayles explores the way the field concept affects the shape of modern fiction and thus can ignore *The Dynasts* on the grounds that it is not a novel. On the scientific side, she assumes that the cosmic web was a twentieth-century creation, a revolution in world view that presumably left Hardy untouched. What Hayles fails to recognize is that the distinguishing characteristics of the cosmic web – the dynamic interconnection of all things, the impossibility of ever fully knowing the whole or of completely separating subject and object – had already become the basic tenets of various forms of monism.[1]

The range of Hardy's reading in his later years[1] shows that the writing of *The Dynasts* coincided with, indeed was made possible by, a conceptual revolution that opened monism to new stages of development. My goal in this chapter will be to examine this moment in the evolution of monistic thought as Hardy might have understood it, not to offer a master narrative of the history of monism. Many of the books and essays that he found worth quoting take a carnivalesque delight in the decrowning of the mechanical theory of the universe. In 'The Scientists and Common Sense' (1905), E. Armitage traces the speculative career of nineteenth-century science up to the comical moment when the 'Titans' of science begin 'lurching to their fall,' having constructed a universe that 'issued in a topsy-turveydom in which mind was denied all control over matter, or even over its own thoughts' (729, 728,

731). From Armitage's laughing perspective, the 'humble powers of common sense' prove able to deliver man from the 'thraldom' of the 'monsters' (728) of naturalism and their extravagent claims about the universe.

Armitage derives his argument, with its carnivalesque strategies of parody and double-voicing, from the monist he cites along the way – James Ward. As someone who wanted to clear the agnostic ground for a defence of theism, Ward shared much in common with both the idealist revival and 'the great empirical movement towards a pluralistic panpsychic view of the universe, into which our own generation has been drawn' (James, *Pluralistic* 313). We need not look any further than Hardy's reading to see how pervasive Ward's influence was during the years Hardy worked on *The Dynasts*. Originally presented as the Gifford Lectures of 1896–8, *Naturalism and Agnosticism* (1899) quickly became the most important English book in the widespread protest against the claims of science to dominate thought and culture. In a review Hardy read (see *Literary* 2:165), A.E. Taylor says 'Prof. Ward's Gifford Lectures are *the* philosophical book of the last year' (244). By 1912 we hear that *Naturalism and Agnosticism* 'has already taken its place as a classical criticism of the philosophical theories which attempt to explain experience in terms of a physical mechanism' ('Pluralism' 21).[2] Walker quotes Ward in support of a 'genuinely SPIRITUAL Monism' (15); Ritchie devotes an entire section of his *Philosophical Studies* to a favourable evaluation of Ward's book; and, in his *Concepts of Philosophy*, Ormond acknowledges his indebtedness to James Ward.

Naturalism and Agnosticism illustrates Bakhtin's contention that 'great changes, even in the field of science, are always preceded by a certain carnival consciousness that prepares the way' (*Rabelais* 49). Ward's discourse invokes the Spirit of Irony to help overturn the hierarchy established by '"the demurrer" of the scientific spirit of the age to theism altogether.' There are no neutral words in his polemic against the neutral monism of naturalism and agnosticism, 'the complementary halves of the dominant philosophy of our scientific teachers' (1:vi, 20). Ward's irreverent tone and mocking laughter did not escape Taylor's notice. We are told that Ward indulges in a 'tendency to banter,' and that his 'pleasantries at [Herbert Spencer's] expense are often heavy as well as pugnacious' (254). A repeated strategy is to bring forward many of the official and popular voices of science, especially T.H. Huxley, John Tyndall, W.K. Clifford, and Herbert Spencer, quote them at length and intact, and then dismember the quotations and subject those parts in which naturalism transgresses its agnostic boundaries to a satirical re-accentuation. In the process of exposing the latent metaphysics of 'scientific teachers [who] have trespassed unawares beyond the limits of the phenomenal' (1:136), Ward creates images of the 'language of Naturalism on the way out' (2:104).

It is important to see, for Hardy's presentation of the gaps and inconsistencies in the Spirit of the Years' outlook, that Ward does not take a position outside of monistic science; instead he shows how official science carnivalizes itself:

> In brief, taking agnostic naturalism just as it presents itself, we have found it to be really inside out. Instead of the physical world being primary and fundamental, the mental world secondary and episodic, as it supposes, the precise opposite is implicit in its own very structure. (2:229)

Neutral monism is, in reality, a species of hybrid monism, a double-voiced discourse masquerading as a monologic world view. This 'hybrid of hazy dualism and halting materialism' (2:208) affords a useful background against which to hear the vacillation of Hardy's Spirit of the Years, 'forever tossed,' to borrow Ormond's description of the agnostic, 'back and forth between the horns of affirmation and negation without the ability to get any certain hold on either' (480).

One voice, naturalism, is dogmatic and has a materialistic bias. Its tone is arrogant, its confidence unbounded, and its metaphysics reductionist. Ward keeps returning to a long quotation from Huxley on how progress means '"the extension of the province of what we call matter and causation, and the concomitant gradual banishment from all regions of human thought of what we call spirit and spontaneity."' A second voice within Huxley's own discourse, the sceptical voice of agnosticism, stems the '"advancing tide of matter"' that '"weighs like a nightmare upon many of the best minds of these days"' (1:17). Falling back on Hume's scepticism, Huxley asserts that the '"fundamental doctrines of materialism ... like those of spiritualism and most other isms"' – except, of course, the ism Huxley coined, agnosticism – '"lie outside the limits of philosophical enquiry"' (1:18–19). At this point, Ward sarcastically re-voices Huxley's word 'nightmare' so that it no longer describes the spiritual effect of materialism on theistic minds but the agnostic theory of knowledge which, like an ally turned treacherous, 'costs Naturalism ... its entire philosophical existence' (1:x).

Ward uses the term Naturalism to 'designate the doctrine that separates Nature from God, subordinates Spirit to Matter, and sets up unchangeable law as supreme' (1:186). In treating the universe as one great mechanism, naturalism relies on the theory of evolution to explain how the machine works and on the doctrine of psycho-physical parallelism to ensure that mind or spirit will not interfere with its operations. The compact with agnosticism, however, resolves the machine into a phenomenal dualism in which both matter and mind, as things in themselves, are unknowable. To mask this dualism, agnosticism shifts the unity of existence onto the plane of the Unknowable where mind and matter can be attributes of one substance. The two-aspects theory of science turns out to be an empty metaphor in which two halves are mistaken for one whole. These halves are conceived 'not as attributes of the one substance *in itself*,' as in Spinoza's monism, 'not as "ontal" attributes, but as phenomenal attributes' (2:18). With the 'eternities safely left aside' by agnosticism, the 'relativities become at once amenable to system' (1:20). Insisting on the material aspect of the Unknowable, naturalism constructs a system out of pure space, uniform time, inert mass, and invisible energy. The crowning irony is that these ultimate phenomena 'are not in themselves perceptual realities ... but abstract ideal conceptions.' They 'are not only not absolute realities, they are not even phenomenal realities' (2:154, 102).

Unwittingly, the agnostic distinction between knowable and unknowable, rather than known and unknown, brings the knower to the fore and permits Ward to question why mechanism 'all the way through' must be the 'one and only means of intelligibility' (1:120). He finds nothing neutral about the attempt to explain all experience in terms of a mechanistic scheme of unbroken laws, depending as it does on the naturalist forgetting himself and severing the world from the minds that perceive it. The advocates of neutral monism did not conduct a disinterested pursuit of truth in their struggle to redirect culture in a secular direction. Ward hears very clearly the self-serving voice of scientists proclaiming that 'there is no knowledge save scientific knowledge' (1:23) as they substituted the secular gospel of naturalism, with its 'agnoiology' (2:213) rather than epistemology, for a religious faith.

The theological epic gave way to the secular epic of science. Fiske declared 'with Prof. Tyndall, that the grandest conceptions of Dante and Milton are dwarfed in comparison with the truths which science discloses' (1:417). Many scientific thinkers did not rest content with Comte's sense of true positivism and 'substituting the Relative for the Absolute' (3:1).[3] Hardy's friend Frederic Harrison deplored the 'craving for Absolute objects of belief' ('Apologia' 673; Hardy, *Literary* 2:3), while another strict positivist, J.H. Bridges, ridiculed scientists for 'again essaying to scale the skies, and to reach that point outside them from which they may get to know how the universe was made' ('Evolution I' 871).[4]

Ward and Hardy faced the same problem: how to make speakers again of the leading interpreters of science and reconstitute their voices in an unfinished dialogue about monism. 'I do not for a moment suppose,' Ward admits, 'that the last word will be heard on these [monistic] questions in our time' (2:108). Yet he hears finality in the monologic voices of science and therefore identifies them with the speaking subjects of high or proclamatory genres, with prophets, priests, and preachers, with epic poets and tragic dramatists. In Spencer's case, he has only to repeat what some members of the scientific and philosophic community fervently proclaimed. One of Hardy's correspondents about *The Dynasts*, C.W. Saleeby, praises Spencer as the 'apostle of evolution,' a 'courageous and stupendous genius' ('Apostle' 674),[5] while Grant Allen and John Fiske rank him with 'Aristotle, Newton, Laplace' (Allen 484; Fiske 1:326-7).[6]

Spencer's grandiose survey of knowledge, the *Synthetic Philosophy,* creates for the reader/spectator a cosmic drama or 'evolutionary epic' (Ward 2:269). Unfortunately, as Ward delights in pointing out, Spencer has omitted an important act: 'Midway ... there is a transition point in the evolutional drama where the poet slides easily over from the physical standpoint to the psychical' (1:271). The two volumes missing from the *Synthetic Philosophy* constitute 'the great gap between the inorganic and the organic world' (1:8). 'And if there is one thing in Nature more worth pondering for its strangeness,' Henry Drummond remarks, in a striking passage recorded by Hardy, 'it is the spectacle of this vast helpless world of the dead cut off from the living' (61; *Literary* 1:153). This mystery was just one of many 'serious gaps *within* the bounds of science itself' (Ward 1:8). The metaphor of the 'gap' or 'loophole' became part of the rhetoric against naturalism. C. Loyd Morgan calls attention to the 'incomplete conceptions of science' and the 'gaps of existing knowledge' ('"Riddle"' 796, 785).[7] The problem went deeper than future knowledge or strictly scientific theories could solve. As Ritchie argues, there are ultimate gaps that can be bridged only by metaphysics.[8]

Ward writes his way into these spaces or vacant plots to show how

Spencer has substituted the mythology of mechanical concepts and symbols, like his 'ridiculous comparison of the universe to a spinning top' (1:8, 198), for the richness of presented reality. The more Ward uncovers what Spencer has suppressed or ignored, the more he over-states Spencer's prestige, so that it too sounds like a fiction. The 'great evolutionist's arguments' for a single and unified world view make him an example of, in Spencer's own favourite phrase, a 'pseudo-thinker' (1:231, 257). This 'pioneer of modern thought, as he is accounted to be,' this 'poet-philosopher' (1:25, 269), falls from his epic heights into the realm of the novel with its competing voices and discourses.

In Hardy's Overworld, the Spirit of the Years – the Will's 'official Spirit' as the Spirit Sinister aptly calls him – tries to speak with an epic voice, from the distant plane of acknowledged scientific truth. The only Spirit given a gender, Father Years (62; 1.1.6) identifies the ethe-real band as a 'hierarchy of Intelligences' (51; 1.1.3). It is far from the case, as Orel contends, that 'their hierarchy is not an important matter to Hardy, and should not be to his reader' (*Thomas* 73). We should attend to the patriarchal structure in which the Years, with his gift of 'bounded prophecy' (543; 3.4.2), utters the epic word that belongs to the world of beginnings. Although a Chorus of Ironic Spirits refers to themselves as 'Us Ancients' and describes how 'He of the Years beheld, and we, / Creation's prentice artistry' (173; 1.6.3), the Spirit of the Years accepts the title 'Eldest-born of the Unconscious Cause' (72; 1.2.2) and claims to be the only one present in the opening scene of the cosmic drama. His is the naturalistic assumption or 'the materialistic assertion of a self-originating world which only came to consciousness in *us*' (Hardy's emphasis, *Literary* 2:185; 'Wanted' 592).

When the Years brings the naturalistic perspective to bear on human history to explain why its dominant narrative is one of carnage and dynastic oppression, his discourse turns into late Victorian pessimism. 'The world is indeed a stage' to the Spirit of the Years 'and life is but a hollow ceremony, spontaneous enough to the eye, but wherein the actors recite speeches and follow stage directions written for them long before they were born' (Ross 740). History is a text already written by the Supreme Dynast, the 'Urging Immanence' (697; 3.7.8) whose sole interpreter the Years insists on being: 'Ere systemed suns were globed and lit / The slaughters of the race were writ' (87; 1.2.5).[9] His authori-tative word belongs to an evolutionary past that is hierarchically higher because it predetermines the present. But Hardy is careful to let the reader hear how the Years' 'truth' about the world is inseparable from his personality. His idea of the Immanent Will as the governing force that 'Rules what may or may not befall' (87; 1.2.5) is cast in his own image and mirrored, in turn, by Napoleon, that other Imperial speaker who is also addressed as father by his soldier-sons. If the Will, or the 'one flimsy riband of Its web' (After Scene 702) represented by the Napoleonic wars, become objects of controversy, the Years reminds the other Spirits, 'The ruling was that we should witness things / And not dispute them' (35; 1.1.1). The rules of discourse are 'Fixed, like all else, immutably' (87; 1.2.5).

The connection between the Years and Napoleon is one that the eldest Spirit himself makes when he tries to turn the Emperor into another prophet of the Will. 'The Emperor,' as Metternich says, is 'Imperious and determined in his rule' (366; 2.5.3) but in what sense is he determined? The Years' official attitude is that his 'acts do but outshape [the Will's] governing' (64; 1.1.6) rather than a 'self-formed force' (61; 1.1.6). When convenient, Napoleon uses a similar argument, culminating in his cry at Waterloo, 'Life's curse begins, I see, / With helplessness!' (679; 3.7.7). As the 'launching of a lineal progeny' (241; 2.1.8) becomes the dominant theme of his discourse, resulting in 'sequences of blood' (280; 2.2.6) he never expected, Napoleon increasingly speaks from the character zone of the Years. He invokes something like the 'whirlwind of the Will' (669; 3.7.4) to explain why divorce is inevitable: 'We are but thistle-globes on Heaven's high gales, / And whither blown, or when, or how, or why, / Can choose us not at all!' (281; 2.2.6). He orders Joséphine to act in the formalities of divorce 'As if you shaped them of your own free will' (358; 2.5.2), even though their private conversations show that Napoleon has another choice – the 'high heredity from brain to brain' (280; 2.2.6). Instead of allowing the Queen of Prussia to keep Magdeburg, he insists that 'Some force within me, baffling mine intent, / Harries me onward, whether I will or no.'

At this point, the Years hears his own voice in Napoleon's:

He spoke thus at the Bridge of Lodi. Strange,
He's of the few in Europe who discern
The working of the Will. (249; 2.1.8)

It is left to the reader and the other Spirits to question, or scorn as the Spirit Ironic does, the idea that '[Napoleon] is choiceless' (687; 3.7.8). As he commits his grand army to the invasion of Russia, he seems enmeshed in the Years' language, another 'bounden witness of Its laws' (39; 1.1.2). The web of determinism sounds different, however, when uttered by a Napoleon whose sudden despondency and self-questioning prevent his words from coinciding with himself:

> That which has worked will work! – Since Lodi Bridge
> The force I then felt move me moves me on
> Whether I will or no; and oftentimes
> Against my better mind ... Why am I here?
> – By laws imposed on me inexorably!
> History makes use of me to weave her web ...   (449; 3.1.1)

His repetitions – 'has worked will work' and 'move me moves me' – do not quite repeat, his exclamatory assertions seem more forced than forceful, and the silence of his pause suggests an unspoken doubt about his answers to the question the Spirit of the Pities also asks, 'Why doth he go?' (448; 3.1.1). The Years shows the anatomy of the Will to explain why and the narrator describes, without eliminating the possibility of choice, the 'films or brain-tissues of the Immanent Will, that pervade all things' (449; 3.1.1). These discourses lying side by side inevitably enter into dialogic relations even though the Spirits say nothing to Napoleon and it is not until the end of the drama that the prose narrator listens to the 'phantoms chant monotonously' (649; 3.6.8). No final answers emerge to the questions raised in world and Overworld but the dialogic context of Napoleon's speech allows the reader to hear how all words serve someone's interests. He hides behind impersonal abstractions, whether the stars, Life, History, Fate, or some mysterious force, to mask his personal ambition and preferences. In the final scene of the human drama, set in the wood of Bossu near Waterloo, Napoleon is awakened from a fitful sleep by the Spirit of the Years' words echoing his own but in 'frigid tones': 'Thus, to this last, / The Will in thee has moved thee, Bonaparte, / As we say now' (698; 3.7.9). Without incarnation, the Years initiates a brief dialogue in which his own words become subject to a crucial qualification that wrests responsibility from the 'Immanent Unrecking' (695; 3.7.8) and places it squarely on the defeated ruler of the human world. Dialogic agreement is never passive understanding that duplicates; it is responsive understanding that qualifies. Thus Napoleon replies, 'Yet, 'tis true,' then adds, 'I have ever known / That such a Will I passively obeyed!' before he surrenders to passivity and 'drowses again' (698; 3.7.9).

The Spirit Ironic also joins the conversation but with 'spectral ques-tionings,' rather than metaphysical assertions, that awaken Napoleon again: 'So I would ask, Ajaccian Bonaparte, / Has all this been worth while?' (699, 698; 3.7.9). Napoleon's answer, provoked by the unheroic epithet, 'Ajaccian Bonaparte,' draws attention to his outdated epic aspirations and discourse. His ambition had been to join the heroic lineage, literary and historical, of 'Hannibal,' and 'Nelson, Harold, Hector, Cyrus, Saul' (699; 3.7.9), and through a dynastic line to have the future remember his epic fame: 'I must send down shoots to future time / Who'll plant my standard and my story there' (348; 2.5.1). Now he realizes: 'I came too late in time / To assume the prophet or the demi-god, / A part past playing now' (699; 3.7.9). It is as if Napoleon steps out of the historical drama and enters, for the reader alert to the intertextual echo, another realm of discourse. In *Heroes and Hero-Worship* (1840), Carlyle also announces that 'Divinity and prophet are past':

> The Hero as Divinity, the Hero as Prophet are productions of old ages; not to be repeated in the new. They presuppose a certain rudeness of concep-tion, which the progress of mere scientific knowledge puts an end to. There needs to be, as it were, a world vacant, or almost vacant of scientific forms, if men in their loving wonder are to fancy their fellow-man either a god or one speaking with the voice of a god. (102)[10]

The moment of intersection is perhaps strange enough to allow for the anachronism of hearing Carlyle's prophetic pronouncements in Napoleon's voice. World and Overworld seem levelled into one, the Spirits talking directly (though, of course, their words would appear to belong to no one) without incarnation or disguise. The perspectival irony that a belief in the Will generates, or the surplus of knowledge that the Spirits gain from the 'free trajection' (Fore Scene 23) of their entities and from occasional glimpses of the Will, should not prevent us from hearing how the world's words have a way of replying to the Overworld's in a dialogic interaction that only the reader, whose mind performs *The Dynasts*, can create. If Napoleon is right about prophets, what do we make of the Years who often sounds like some latter-day Carlyle trying to open 'uninitiate eyes' (*The Dynasts* 116;1.4.5) to how 'man's whole terrestrial Life [is] but a Symbolic Representation, and making visible, of the Celestial invisible Force that is in him' (*French Revolution* 266)? One early reviewer was astute enough to ask, and with good reason, about the Immanent Will, 'is it not essentially Carlyle's "Natural Supernaturalism"?' ('Mr. Hardy's' 439). Attentive to 'Carlylean phraseology' (*Life* 473), Hardy has words made famous by Carlyle sound with a different accent in the Years' speeches.

The progress of scientific knowledge later in the century revived and revised the discourse of natural supernaturalism, itself a retailoring of German metaphysics, in a wide range of monistic theories. The key question, 'Is the Supernatural natural or unnatural?' (Drummond vi), often received a Carlylean answer. Apparently the '"*open* secret"' was no longer 'open to all, seen by almost none!' (Carlyle, *Heroes* 105). The 'living feeling of a great world-secret, the vague realisation that the natural is "supernatural,"' H.S. Chamberlain claims, 'is common to all' (1:413).

From a Christian perspective, Drummond argues that the supernatural is 'the higher natural' (281). Some theologians realized, in Höffding's terms, 'that a new and living garment must be woven for the Godhead' (*Philosophy* 181). In his sermon on 'Nature' (1876), quoted by Hardy (*Literary* 2:69), J.B. Mozley finds the distinctiveness of the nineteenth century in the way that his age has developed both principles of the natural and the supernatural. As a symbol of God, nature is 'partly a curtain and partly a disclosure, partly a veil and partly a revelation' (130). Carlyle's idea that 'in a Symbol there is concealment and yet revelation' (*Sartor* 219) could also be simplified, however. In a chapter called 'The Open Secret,' Walker claims that 'We live and move and have our being in the midst of, and by means of, a Monism in which the material is ever simply the symbol, the instrument, the expression of the Spiritual' (204).

Although endorsing Spencer's agnosticism, John Fiske also uses Carlyle's language to talk about 'the invisible Power whereof the infinite web of phenomena is but the visible garment.' Fiske felt compelled to postulate not only an Absolute, but an absolute Being: 'The "open secret," in so far as secret, is God, – in so far as open, is the World' (1:417, 424). Late nineteenth-century science was not quite so bold. Romanes, for example, did not countenance a full return to Carlyle's clothes philosophy, but he could hold open the possibility of the kind of symbolic coherence that Carlyle formulated: 'everywhere matter in motion may be the outward and visible sign of an inward and spiritual grace' (57).

For the Spirit of the Years, the symbolic means the allegorical. The surface of history appears as nothing more than a 'phantasmagoric show' in which 'The all-compelling crystal pane but drags / Whither the showman wills' (117, 116; 1.4.5). The Years reads the human 'dem-onstrations from the Back of Things' (680; 3.7.7) as Froude does the 'vast phantasmagoria' of *The French Revolution* where people are 'the mere instruments of a superior power, infernal or divine, whose awful presence is felt while it is unseen' (Froude 1:90; Hardy *Literary* 1:161).[11] When the Years illuminates the Will with 'a preternatural clearness' (172; 1.6.3), the supernatural does not shine through the natural with the same complexity as it does to reveal the 'magic-lantern figures' and 'Spectral Realities' (Carlyle 431, 150) of *The French Revolution*.

Although the phenomenal looks spectral to Carlyle, the world of appearance does not lose its dignity in contrast to a noumenal reality, as it does for the Spirit of the Years. In this respect, the Years seems closer to Schopenhauer who was also half-made by Kant. The world to Schopenhauer is 'a mere phantasmagoria of my brain' (Caldwell, 'Schopenhauer' 221).[12] The intellect shrinks into a 'hall of phantasma-gorical mystery' that 'everywhere divides actual being into subject and object' (Schopenhauer, 'Art of Controversy' 86). Time and Space are 'mere forms of our perception' and 'where the thing in itself begins knowledge ceases' (*World* 3:71, 9) – except, of course, for Schopenhauer himself. After debunking the Idea, he still promotes his own idea of the Will. This kind of arrogance and inconsistency also characterize the Spirit of the Years. The Spirit Ironic irreverently gives the Years the same title, 'Showman' (383; 2.5.6), as the Years gives to the Will, but the Years never sees his own consciousness as a magic lantern. All other viewpoints represent and falsify the world as Idea, only his own reveals the world as Will. Like Schopenhauer, he speaks of the Will as a 'real and not a hypothetical entity' but as something outside of con-sciousness, not inside, whereas Schopenhauer argues that 'the individ-ual has ... direct consciousness of will' ('Studies' 36).

In its quest for objectivity, an outward-looking science could not make Schopenhauer's inward move.[13] The Absolute may have been an 'established word' (Spencer, *First* 38)[14] for some agnostics, as it is even for the Pities (35; 1.1.1), but it was a shadowy Reality separated from the pluralism of appearance by a gulf just as impassable as that between the world as Idea and the world as Will. Clearly Schopen-hauer, and for that matter Carlyle, anticipate the difficulties of a sci-ence that 'starts out to know its world and ends by playing with the shadows of the real while the real lies beyond its grasp' (Ormond 246). If 'There is nothing that is not a content of consciousness,' the world of space and time 'might all be a dream!' (Guenther 386, 405) or, as

Tennyson thought, two dreams: 'Annihilate within yourself these two dreams of Space and Time' (Hallam Tennyson 1:171; Hardy, *Literary* 2:64).

Late nineteenth-century philosophers modified Kant to save the object from dissolving in the subject and appearance from being totally cut off from reality. They did not discredit the window theory of objects with independent existence only to embrace the idea of experience as a magic lantern picture, unreal compared to the mind which projects it.[15] Consequently, the phenomenal must be more than 'mere' appearance: 'if we decline to call anything an appearance, unless it is either perceived or perceptible, why then should we attach to it the bad sense of concealing, rather than the good sense of revealing?' (Ward 2:276). Ritchie also attacks all those monistic systems which treat the world of appearance in space and time as a world of illusion that we must leave behind us in order to discover truth: 'Appearance is the appearance *of* reality. If we know "only phenomena" we must thereby know something of that of which they are phenomena' (210).

On the other hand, appearances do not simply coincide with reality. Ward uses quotation marks to indicate how common the Kantian belief, '"reality is richer than thought"' (2:282), had become. More importantly, one kind of appearance should be distinguished from another. In Carlyle, everything phenomenal may be a show, but some appearances are transcendental and come from God, while others become doubly spectral, 'not the Phenomenon at all, but rather ... the *shadow* of it, the negative part of it,' a demonic 'red baleful Phantasmagory' (Carlyle, *French Revolution* 634, 686). Whereas such distinctions tend to be absolute in Carlyle's Calvinistic version of German metaphysics, they remain relative in neo-Kantian thought. '[W]e must distinguish,' argues Ritchie, 'within the world of appearance between those aspects of things which have more reality and those which have less reality in them' (211).

Hardy's Spirit of the Years offers the kind of monism that Ritchie attacks, the one in which 'all the phases of existence are *alike* characteristic of the All' (210–11). Except when dismissing the 'phantasmagoria' (509; 3.2.4) of the fete at Vauxhall Gardens, the Years does not distinguish between different grades, stages, or degrees of reality but, like Schopenhauer, finds the Will 'whole and undivided in every being' ('Human' 27) and therefore 'alike and identical in all things' ('Studies' 36). He obliterates the contribution of Carlyle's 'Miracle' of 'free Force' (*Sartor* 262). From the great heights of the Overworld and the perspective of the 'elemental ages chart' (701; 3.7.9), the Time-vesture of a new impersonal Absolute, there is no possibility of a human action. We might well say with James that '*as* absolute ... the world repels our sympathy because it has no history' (*Pluralistic* 47).

When the Years' monistic perspective shifts from absolute idealism to naturalism and agnosticism of the kind Maudsley endorses, the world fares little better. History is no longer the record of the achievements of great men; leaders such as Napoleon are 'Like meanest insects on obscurest leaves' (701; 3.7.9) while the people of Europe 'gyrate like animalcula / In tepid pools' (Fore Scene 27). 'Indeed,' as Maudsley explains, in words prophetic of the Overworld, 'were a regiment of soldiers on the march seen at so great a distance as to seem no bigger than ants, the spectacle would be very similar.' It is not just that soldiers can look like insects: 'There is really nothing more nor less wonderful in the intelligence of the insect's instinct than of the man's reason' (154, 150). A Schopenhauerian tone of disgust or contempt seems more appropriate for man and his human faculties, 'being the limited and shallow things they are.' If we were 'calmly to survey human history from its beginning until now, what else could be seen in it but one continued spectacle of folly and madness?' (Maudsley 2, 120).

The Years too sees only the past in the present: 'old Laws operate yet; and phase and phase / Of men's dynastic and imperial moils / Shape on accustomed lines' (Fore Scene 24). All history has a sameness that makes it the shadow, the negative part, cast by the operation of natural laws. The very fact that the Years advocates the scientific and determinate instead of the historical and contingent makes him typical of the problem that 'science has left the historical so long aside that it is beginning to forget that experience in itself is historical' (Ward 2:281). To be sure, none of Hardy's Spirits know why they speak as they do, yet there is something especially appropriate about the Years forgetting how his monologic discourse is itself historically generated.[16]

Hardy constructs the Years' philosophical discourse out of precisely those terms and expressions that were most disputed in the monistic field. At the negative pole, Maudsley agrees essentially with Schopenhauer's evaluation of consciousness: 'For what in the end is life but a dream with the eyes and other senses open? Nay, what the life of mankind on earth so far but a bad dream of nature?' (Maudsley 165). Remove the evaluative word 'bad' and substitute 'Will' for 'nature,' and this could be the Years speaking. But there was a positive pole as well. In spite of his pessimism, Hartmann does not use the phrase 'the magic lantern of consciousness' (3:122) with Schopenhauer's ridicule because for him consciousness is ultimately informed and guided by the tutelary spirit of the Unconscious. The subtext of Carlyle's language in the Years' speeches also strengthens the hints of a Divine Idea in history. If the world is a magic lantern show, the cosmic Showman may, to foreground the Years' own words, have some 'Intent' (407; 2.6.4), even a 'Plan' (414; 2.6.5).

The Years stops short of addressing the Will in Carlyle's fashion – 'O thou unfathomable mystic All' (*French Revolution* 279) – but the intertextual entanglements provide some justification for this figure. In the dialogic context of the Overworld, the Ironic Spirits appear to side with the Years against the Pities who pray to the Will. We can hear agnosticism's scornful voice – 'How pray for help in time of need to an abstraction of negations?' (Maudsley 281) – and also Carlyle's in what they say:

Semichorus II

Stand ye apostrophizing That
Which, working all, works but thereat
Like some sublime fermenting-vat

Semichorus I

Heaving throughout its vast content
With strenuously transmutive bent
Though of its aim unsentient?   (172; 1.6.3)

The highly patterned end rhymes bring the Will's artistry to the forefront, though the first three treat It impersonally and physically, while the next two emphasize thought and goal, only to be joined to 'unsentient,' a word nevertheless preceded by 'aim.' What the Spirits Ironic say does not so much settle the dispute over the Will as focus Its ambivalence. Hardy might have noticed the verb 'heaving' used in an *Encyclopaedia Britannica* article on pessimism to describe Schopenhauer's Will – the 'vague longing of the heaving World' (688).[17] From the Years' perspective, the 'Prime Volitions [...] heave throughout the earth's compositure,' 'heaving' (Fore Scene 28, 27), as the narrator also reports, the peoples of Europe in seemingly blind fashion. When the Ironic Spirits compare this heaving to that of a 'sublime fermenting vat,' the discourse becomes double-voiced. One of Carlyle's favourite metaphors introduces a note of cosmic purpose into a description of cosmic force. In *Sartor Resartus*, Teufelsdröckh apostrophizes nature as he pronounces the Everlasting Yea:

> How thou fermentest and elaboratest, in thy great fermenting-vat and laboratory of an Atmosphere, of a World, O Nature! – Or what is Nature? Ha! Why do I not name thee God? Art not thou the 'Living Garment of God'? (188)

World-History is also divinely ordered, another necessary and unconscious process of fermentation. The Years' description of the 'land's stir and ferment' (35; 1.1.2) recalls Carlyle the historian's account of how just prior to Napoleon's reign France's 'old Speech and Thought, and Activity which springs from these, are all changing; fermenting towards unknown issues' (*French Revolution* 248). This process is not without beneficial results: history means the gradual ousting of the sham by the real.

Like the discourse of Carlyle's revolutionary France, that of *The Dynasts* consists of 'So many heterogeneities cast together into the fermenting-vat' (*French Revolution* 118) and the result cannot be controlled by any one interpretive voice. Through the dialogue of the Overworld, Hardy tries to liberate the weaving Will from the 'web of categories' (Walker 197) that the Spirit of the Years' thought casts over it. Gradually a dialogic knot links together the two imperious speakers, Napoleon and the Years, and the hero of the Years' discourse, the Will's 'High Influence' (39; 1.1.2). While the 'Overking' of the human world constructs his 'Universal-empire plot' (229, 231; 2.1.6), the Years urges the other Spirits to watch how the Will's 'predestined plot' (159; 1.5.7) proceeds. The success of Napoleon's plot depends on his control over the written and spoken word. His various letters, orders, edicts, proclamations, and decrees are always 'writ in mandatory mood' (124; 1.5.1). As in all authoritarian regimes, the word is no longer free. In Part First, this control of the word is reflected in the Overworld when the Spirit of Rumour has to get the Years' permission to join the Paris crowd 'And speak what things shall come into thy mouth' (185; 1.6.7). By taking the disguise of a young foreigner, Rumour is able to reveal the other side of official truth, the news of the crushing defeat at Trafalgar. In turn, talking to a foreigner allows a Parisian street woman to reveal something else that would ordinarily be kept unspoken: "'Tis dangerous to insinuate nowadays!' (188; 1.6.7). Later we hear how 'The Paris journals flaunt – not voluntarily, / But by [Napoleon's] ordering' (310; 2.3.5). The problem of coercive speech makes Napoleon the Spirit of the Years' crowning and uncrowning double. The first reference to Napoleon is to his coronation at Notre Dame; the last view is of his solitary figure in the wood of Bossu, his fugitive soldiers passing by without seeing him, as if he too has become a Spirit. In a parallel development, the Spirit of the Years begins by ruling the exchanges of the Spirits, only to have his discourse transformed into what Metternich knows is true of any speech: 'Well – that's a point of view' (369; 2.5.3).

In the Fore Scene, the Years occupies the position of someone instructing others who are ignorant of the truth or in error. We hear a pedagogical dialogue in which he provides answers to the other Spirits' questions. The Shade of the Earth opens *The Dynasts* with 'the most prominent form of the question about the One and the Many' (Ritchie 223): 'What of the Immanent Will and Its designs?' The question of the Will provokes the Years into talking about what he admits, in a moment of self-consciousness, 'no mind can mete' (Fore Scene 21, 23). What kind of agnostic, then, is the eldest Spirit? When Huxley locates himself within an agnostic line of thought from Socrates to Kant and Hume, he says that 'it may be wise to recollect that we have no more right to make denials, than to put forth affirmatives, about what lies beyond that limit [of the phenomenal]' (*Hume* 284–5). Romanes also speaks of a 'state of suspended judgment' (59) about the existence of God or the Absolute. The theory of monism, 'which supposes matter in motion to be substantially identical with mind' (Romanes 44; Hardy *Literary* 1:174), can only lead to an agnosticism that 'leaves a clear field of choice as between Theism and Atheism' (Romanes 59).

In practice, a pure agnosticism proved difficult to sustain. John Addington Symonds explains that the term agnostic covers 'a genus including several species. According to their temperament or to their earlier associations, Agnostics lean either to Atheism or to Theism,' even though they 'agree in pronouncing the problem of the universe to be insoluble' (401). The species metaphor is appropriate, for agnosticism did, at least in terms of its reception, evolve from what was widely perceived as 'the general and most characteristic idea lying at the root of modern unbelief' (Tulloch 472)[18] to something that 'may afford a most valuable support to Theism' (Walker 15). In the 1870s agnosticism displaced materialism as 'much the more formidable philosophical form of doubt' ('Mr. Footman' 515). The reaction that followed prompted Frederic Harrison to construct a long satirical list of substitutes for the Prayer Book and the Bible, including philosophical Theism and the Unknowable. The new 'craving for Absolute objects to belief' (Harrison, 'Apologia' 673) brought Herbert Spencer's agnosticism to the forefront of the controversy about monism.

Clearly the Years leans towards the 'theology of the future' (*Autobiography* 2:247)[19] as Spencer calls his version of the Absolute. After the battle of Waterloo, the Years approves 'Your knowings of the Unknowable declared' (696; 3.7.8) by a Chorus of Ironic Spirits. Here is Bakhtin's microdialogue: various monistic viewpoints and accents in Hardy's era converged on the Unknowable, made famous by Spencer and recorded by Hardy in his 1867 Notebook (*Literary* 2:457). Leaning towards atheism, Huxley scorns Spencer's '"Absolute *redidivus*, a sort of ghost of an extinct philosophy, the name of a negation hocus-pocussed into a sham thing"' (Clodd 246).[20] In a mood of turning to the real, the Spirit Ironic also cares nothing for 'high-doctrined dreams' (698; 3.7.9) and wonders, in suitably low language, about the 'hocus-pocus' (After Scene 706) of the Will.

'I am glad to find,' Hardy told Lena Milman in 1893, 'that you are interested in "First Principles" – a book which acts, or used to act, upon me as a sort of patent expander when I had been particularly narrowed down by the events of life' (*Letters* 2:24–5). As late as 1915, corresponding with Spencer's disciple, Dr C.W. Saleeby, Hardy still confessed, '"I am utterly bewildered to understand how the doctrine that, beyond the knowable, there must always be an unknown, can be displaced"' (*Life* 400). The word unknown is more cautious, of course, than Spencer's Unknowable but the general agreement is there: 'I quite enter into Spencer's feeling – that it is paralysing to think what if, of all that is so incomprehensible to us (the Universe) there exists no comprehension anywhere' (*Letters* 3:244).[21]

Spencer stands between the kind of agnosticism identified with the 'modern spirit of negation' (Tulloch 471) and more positive, even anthropomorphic accounts of the Absolute. Ward explains that Spencer rejects 'both the Humean dictum that there is no knowledge save knowledge of phenomena and of their relations, as well as the Laplacean dictum that this knowledge is non-theistic' (1:25). In *First Principles* (1862), he breaks with his philosophic mentors, Sir William Hamilton and Dean Mansel, to argue that 'Though the Absolute cannot in any manner or degree be known, in the strict sense of knowing, yet we find that its positive existence is a necessary datum of consciousness' (98). We have a 'definite consciousness of relative reality' and an 'indefinite consciousness of an absolute reality transcending relations' (161). On the basis of this double consciousness, Spencer sees a reconciliation of science and religion: 'our consciousness of Nature under the one aspect constitutes Science, our consciousness of it under the other aspect constitutes Religion' (106).

Spencer's Absolute also represents the de-anthropomorphizing process that Hardy mentions in the Preface to *The Dynasts* (5). Content to leave his Ultimate Force shadowy and indefinite (*First* 113) Spencer came under attack from monists who refused to see the religious quest 'end in an empty agnosticism' (Höffding, *Philosophy* 384). One problem was that a belief in the Unknowable awakened little enthusiasm. 'That Unknowable Reality may be, and doubtless is, *God* ...,' says Walker, 'but a Being dwelling in such impenetrable darkness can never be to us the God Whom we need, and Whom we seek to know' (6). James Cotter Morison, whose *The Service of Man* Hardy admired (*Letters* 1:173), complains that 'The idea of God has been "defecated to a pure transparency"' (27).[22] Maudsley sees that 'Love in relation to such an impersonal absolute is love in name only' (281), or, as the Chorus Ironic asks the Spirit of the Pities, 'But where do Its compassions sit? / Yea, where abides the heart of It?' (416; 2.6.5). As the end rhyme suggests, the Will, like Spencer's 'barren postulate of an ultimate Unknowable' (Du Prel 1:xi), is both unchanging and unmoveable. The agnostic position created a dilemma: 'in order to love the infinite it must be personal, and in order to make the personal infinite it must be divested of personality' (Maudsley 282). Nevertheless, Spencer's one positive step towards the Unknowable encouraged the religious mind to approach its subject from the monistic conception of the world demanded by the facts of science.

Theodore Christlieb points out that an impersonal Absolute '*is not absolute at all*, just because It is deficient in the point of personality' (171). Bradley assumes that 'the Absolute has personality,' then adds, with characteristic distaste for the less than Ideal, 'but it fortunately possesses so much more' (153). It is, he concludes, super-personal (471). Much of his open and hidden polemic is directed against Spencer; in constructing his own first principles (1) he answers Spencer's book of the same name. He turns Spencer's objection to Mansel's idea of the infinite as a meaningless name against him: 'The Unknowable must, of course, be prepared either to deserve its name or not' (Bradley

111). Bradley goes further than Spencer to argue that we can 'gain an idea of [the Absolute's] main features – an idea true so far as it goes, though abstract and incomplete.' The incompleteness arises from the very nature of thought. Like Spencer, Bradley still insists that 'for thought what is not relative is nothing' and any 'relational way of thought ... must give appearance, and not truth' (140, 25, 28). Once started, the dialogue tended to move the Absolute away from Bradley's abstract 'outline' and closer to the 'thicket of experience' (James, *Pluralistic* 136). Haldane wonders if 'Bradley's view of thought [is] sufficiently wide?' (2:xiii), only to have his own attempt to make God more concrete questioned by Hastings Rashdall in a review that Hardy read: 'But why Mr Haldane should feel all this emotion about such an Absolute as he describes, ... I for one find it difficult to conjecture' (Review of *Stage the Second* 415).[23]

Hardy felt much the same dissatisfaction as he watched God evolve, or devolve, into the Absolute and move 'towards a consummation in which all distinction ... must be suppressed' (Bradley 409). 'I have been looking for God 50 years,' he remarked in 1890, 'and I think that if he had existed I should have discovered him. As an external personality, of course – the only true meaning of the word' (*Life* 234). The remark is not without a wry touch of humour, since fifty years places the beginning of his quest in the year of his birth! To write *The Dynasts* Hardy had to assume, as his close friend Leslie Stephen says, that 'God is not an external ruler, a part of the series of phenomena, but in some mysterious way an all-pervading essence' (*Essays* 101). Furthermore, by substituting immanence for externality, he had to modify but not relinquish the idea of personality. There were alternatives to a belief in the *'impersonal spirituality of the immanent ground of the world'* (Hartmann 3:347). Not all monists abandoned 'that interpretation which ascribes phenomena to a will analogous to the human will' (Spencer, *Principles* 1:335).[24] Ormond suffers from no agnostic loss of nerve about the validity of self-analogy as a principle for defining the Spiritual grounds of phenomena. By his monistic standards, the Spirit of the Pities' confession, 'Something within me aches to pray / To some Great Heart' (416; 2.6.5), should not be relegated to an unphilosophical 'aesthetic theology' (Ward 1:31). After all, the real motive of metaphysics, the very metaphysics the Years cannot do without, is the pressure of certain great wants of our being: 'a demand that the world at its heart shall be found akin to the feeling heart of the intelligent thing that seeks to realize it' (Ormond 334). Morgan also takes this further step and finds it legitimate to say that 'the indwelling source of the evolutionary process as a whole may be conceived in terms of a Personality transcending the limits of its manifestations in man' ('"Riddle"' 791).

In the Overworld Hardy pushes the Spirit of the Years far beyond the knowable, just as some scientists, in spite of their strict phenomenal limits, drew inferences as to what lies behind phenomena. The Years finds himself in a dialogic situation charged with the conflicts of an era, tempting him to make the Immanent Will far more than, in Hegel's memorable phrase, 'the night in which all cows look black' (Haldane 2:xiii). He speaks with his back turned to most of the Spirits but casts a sideward glance at the 'fond unbelieving Sprites' of Pity who ask the big questions, the why and whence? that agnosticism tried to suppress. Anticipating objections to his view that 'It [the Will] works unconsciously, as heretofore' (Fore Scene 21), the Years switches from an explanatory to a story-telling tone ('As one sad story runs ... / Some, too, have told' [22]) to dismiss as fictions the two fundamental articles of the Pities' 'naïve and liberal creed' (27), that men's acts are self-done and the Will conscious. The tentative, interrogatory tone belongs to Pity, who asks if suffering may focus the Will's 'consciousness' and 'wake its watch anon'; the imperative mood belongs to the Years who replies with a definitive

Nay. In the Foretime, even to the germ of Being,
Nothing appears of shape to indicate
That cognizance has marshalled things terrene,
Or will ...

The Years hides in parenthesis the way he finds his evidence: '(such is my thinking)' (Fore Scene 22). In *The Pathway to Reality* (1903–4), R.B. Haldane comments that the 'unconscious purpose' of this scientific way of seeing things is to contemplate nature 'without reference to the subject' (2:91). The Years' words have a way of turning back on himself. He cannot believe that 'By bad mad acts of severance men contrived, / Working such nescience by their own device' (Fore Scene 22). Instead he commits his own act of severance to convince the Pities that the Will's nescience is a fact that precedes consciousness, rather than thought itself being 'a most momentous part of fact' (James, *Meaning* 244).

The Years also believes that his own readings of the Unknowable have a special validity because they are the pessimistic products of the deliberate separation of head and heart: 'as for me, / I care not how they [dynastic quarrels] shape, or what they be.' The Spirit of the Pities wants the 'earth-tragedy / ... conned closelier than your [the Years'] custom is' (Fore Scene 24, 25). The Years denies that by taking on the 'feverish fleshings of Humanity' his soul will 'be won to sympathy' (41; 1.1.3): 'my unpassioned essence could not change / Did I incarn in moulds of all mankind!' (42; 1.1.3). At stake here is more than just the question of whether the Years can feel as well as think. The only Spirit whose incarnation is all mankind is the Immanent Will. The Years' preference for detached, objective viewing, for an Overworld above the human world and an impersonal truth beyond personality, is essential to his maintaining a Will 'impassible as glacial snow.' The 'Great Unshaken' (117; 1.4.5) is what he tries to be and not the final word on the nature of the Will. He reads himself into the 'wild dramas of the wheeling spheres': 'uninfluenced, unconcerned, / The systems of the suns go sweeping on / With all their many-mortaled planet train / In mathematic roll unceasingly' (60; 1.1.6). Although every philosophy may be 'a foreshortened bird's-eye view of the perspective of events' (James, *Pluralistic* 8), the Years' aim resembles the epic goal Guenther describes for science – 'to grasp the infinite all':

> It [science] gives an impulse to the human mind that bears it on to even greater heights. The vision steadily enlarges. The individual disappears; the world lies at the feet of the spectator in its broadest outlines. (426)

In this cosmic theatre, 'consciousness is nothing but a passive spectator' (Mallock 259),[25] rather than an actor or participant who supplies to the system the essential features of its objectivity.

The Years' fiction of disengagement, to 'seek that which *is*, not that which touches us' (Lewes, *Life* 358),[26] leaves out the same act as Spencer does – the transition from the lifeless to the living, in 'the wonderful drama which science has written for and presented to us' (Morgan, '"Riddle"' 783). All of the metaphors that organize the Years' discourse on the One and the many – the machine, the ruler, the puppet show, the cosmic dance, the web – are ideologically saturated, the very metaphors that spiritual or idealistic monists uncovered in the discourse of naturalism, then disputed and transformed. The more naturalism treated human agents as 'by-spectators of the show' (Ormond 170) or 'mere puppets in the hands of some over-mastering power' ('Mr. Footman' 515), the more its ostensibly neutral discourse could be made to sound pessimistic. The conscious automatons of Huxley or Clifford resembled Schopenhauer's human puppets who 'are not pulled from without, but each bears in itself the clockwork from which its movements result' (*World* 3:116). In Walker's view, 'We should be simply ... pulled by countless strings, governed by physical forces, miserably self-deceived creatures, living under an illusion of freedom, responsible for nothing, worth nothing' (326). The naturalistic universe became carnivalized, revealing a 'topsy-turveydom ... in which man was declared an automaton dancing to the pulling-strings of a giant mechanism' (Armitage 731).

The ambiguity F.R. Southerington finds in Hardy's picture of the Will, mechanistic images set against organic (158), signifies the struggle between opposing monisms. To Ward, 'It is far truer to say the universe is a life, than to say it is a mechanism' (1:180). Spiritual monists also took up the grotesque theme of the marionette, with the accent no longer placed on the puppet as the victim of inhuman force. The physical world became 'the theatre wherein the drama of purposeful conduct is enacted'; 'the actors are real persons, not merely puppets galvanised into a semblance of activity by a blind determinism' (Morgan, '"Riddle"' 794).

'People are afraid,' explains Symonds, 'lest a strictly scientific or deterministic view of human development should paralyse morality by encouraging the notion that we are only helpless cogwheels in a vast machine' (22–3). Certainly the Years encourages this notion that a Chorus of Pities exclaims, echoing some of the deepest cultural fears, 'we dare not hold' (Fore Scene 21). Pity is right in referring to the Will as the '*voiceless* Turner of the Wheel' (my emphasis, Fore Scene 22). The Years does not speak with the Will but about it, telling the other Spirits that they must not forget, 'As puppet-watchers him who pulls the strings,' the 'Prime Mover of the Gear' (Fore Scene 27). Men are 'flesh-hinged mannikins Its hand upwinds / To click-clack off its preadjusted laws.' These hypostatized laws form the cosmic web that, 'like a knitter drowsed, / ... / The Will has woven with an absent heed / Since Life first was; and ever will so weave' (Fore Scene 24, 22–3). In the universe of science, natural causality becomes 'the shuttle that runs backward and forward weaving, according to unalterable mechanical laws, the web and woof of existence' (Adler 181–2).

Not surprisingly, the Years seems satisfied that history retains its dynastic shape. His temperament is strongly inclined to a monarchical view of the Will, reinforced by Napoleon 'flushed from his crowning,' and to the juridical or civic concept of law that many Victorian scientists retained in spite of themselves. When the Spirit of the Pities suggests that 'each has parcel in the total Will,' the Years responds, 'Which overrides them as a whole its parts / In other entities' (Fore Scene 26, 24–5). The Shade of the Earth feels 'ineffectual' when contemplating how nature remains 'a thrall / To [the Will]; in all her labourings curbed and kinged!' (Fore Scene 24). By making the laws of nature much more than uniformities of coexistence and succession, the Years never has to admit, as F.H. Bradley does, 'that we do not know how the Absolute overrides the relational form' (180). Their 'terms inexorable' (*The Dynasts* 62; 1.1.6) are 'pictured as a sort of objective power ruling despotically in its domain of nature and constraining things to obey it' (Maudsley 87). The curious inversion that Ward notices in the positions occupied by the notions of cause and of law in science has also taken place for the Years: 'The more substantial causes fall out of sight, the more universal laws take on their *rôle*; and, presently, they become hypostatized as "self-existent laws"; they operate unchecked; they reign supreme, "binding nature fast in fate"' (2:248).

The clock-like laws that the Will unchecks (Fore Scene 22) are as anthropomorphic as any active causes. Even by Huxley's standards, the Years lapses into the language of pseudo-science, as if he has 'appropriated the forms of science without knowing anything of its substance' ('Scientific' 200). He does not treat laws as so much conceptual shorthand, 'true ... within their special "universes of discourse"' (Ritchie 26) but with 'no more existence outside the mind than colour has' (Huxley, 'Scientific' 199). Yet they are not finally self-existent either. The Years regards 'any sequence of natural causation as the merely phenomenal aspect of the ontological reality' (Romanes 57) of the Will. For some philosophers of science this kind of monistic thinking had an immense significance. To Romanes 'it furnishes a logical basis for a theory of things which is at the same time natural and spiritual' (58). 'No thought,' Hardy recorded, 'is so calculated to reconcile poesy and science as the thought that all our "reality" ... is only *appearance*' (Hardy's emphasis, *Literary* 1:140; 'Lange's' 900).

With 'exhaustive strain and effort only,' the Years lays bare his dynastic laws, the 'Will-webs of [Pity's] fearful questioning,' in the first of six visualizations of 'the Mode,' all designed to coerce under the guise of teaching: 'See, then, and learn, ere my power pass again.' We confront three descriptions, not one Will. In the stage directions the impressionistic narrator refers to a 'seeming transparency' (Fore Scene

27) that exhibits 'as one organism the anatomy of life and movement in all humanity and vitalized matter' (Fore Scene 28). Always sympathetic to the 'pale pathetic peoples' (559; 3.4.4), 'distressed,' as the narrative voice says, 'by events which they did not cause' (Fore Scene 27), the Pities continue to see 'bodies substantive' in the one web with its 'Strange waves ... like winds grown visible, / Which bear men's forms on their innumerous coils.' These threads are both 'irresistible,' as the Years wants the visualization to be, and flimsy 'like gossamers,' allowing the Pities to 'Deem yet man's deeds self-done' (Fore Scene 28). Felix Adler explains that 'A symbol, in the sense in which Kant employs the term, is a noumenon represented for the nonce as if it were clothed with phenomenal attributes' (175). The Years' effort to phenomenalize the noumenal while getting clear of the subject/object relation leaves the Immanent Will off stage. He must tell Pity what to see:

> These are the Prime Volitions, – fibrils, veins,
> Will-tissues, nerves, and pulses of the Cause,
> That heave throughout the Earth's compositure.
> Their sum is like the lobule of a Brain
> Evolving always that it wots not of;
> A Brain whose whole connotes the Everywhere ...   (Fore Scene 28)

The Years' treatment of the metaphysical in terms of the physiological unconscious suggests the dilemma of an agnosticism 'which cannot be materialistic and will not be idealistic' (Ward 2:107). At one point the Years gives the question that begins Chapter III of Spencer's *First Principles*, 'What are Space and Time?,'[27] the answer, 'A fancy!' (460; 3.1.3); at another, he orders the Pities to 'Speak more materially, and less in dream' (407; 2.6.4). When forced to choose, the Years usually leans to the side of subordinating the psychical to the physical.

Huxley once spoke of a nemesis in 'meddling with the unknowable' ('Science' 801). Spencer was praised for showing 'how it is possible to conceive "symbolically" that the universe may be instinct with a "quasi-psychical" principle' (Romanes 53). Inadvertently, the Years provides the Pities with the minimal conditions for a cosmic consciousness – a cosmic brain. In positing 'something hidden' that 'urged / The giving matter motion' (39; 1.1.2), the Years illustrates Spencer's belief that 'We shall always be under the necessity of contemplating [Ultimate Existence] as *some* mode of being.' But in visualizing this mode he does not, as Spencer advocates, treat his picture 'as merely a symbol, utterly without resemblance to that for which it stands' (*First* 113). We cannot always say of the Years, as one reviewer complained of Haldane, that 'The "picture" of the religious consciousness has disappeared with a vengeance' ('Unreality' 524; Hardy, *Literary* 2:159). His agnostic imagination does make the Immanent Will more than an empty signifier, a mere alias of a God who has fled. It is left to a General Chorus of Intelligences to correct the Years and teach the teacher that the phenomenal world cannot simply be identified with a cosmic brain. The Years' criticism of a Semichorus of Rumours, 'Methinks too much assurance thrills your note' (Fore Scene 26), sounds in the Chorus's warning that distinguishes between actual and symbolic conception:

> The Prime, that willed ere wareness was,
> > Whose Brain perchance is Space, whose Thought its laws,
> Which we as threads and streams discern,
> > We may but muse on, *never learn*.   (my emphasis, Fore Scene 29)

As the Years continues his efforts to instruct the Pities, using everything from fear and intimidation to pleading and cajoling, we begin to hear beneath his seemingly undivided discourse a great and unresolved thought. In one scene the human world casts a penetrating light on this interior dialogue. The Years insists that he and Pity take the form of white seabirds to impress Villeneuve with a sense of 'silent circling doom.' Irresolute and divided, the French admiral writes gloomily in private to Decrès what he 'dared ... not disclose to [Napoleon]': 'Demoralized past prayer is the marine' (71, 72, 70; 1.2.2). When Pity asks 'Why dost thou rack him thus?' the Years responds that 'I know but narrow freedom': 'We do but as we may; no further dare.' Freedom, however narrow, is something that the Years dare not officially recognize in the Will's accessories. To mask this thought, he appeals to Pity on its own ground: 'Feel'st thou not / We are in Its hand, as [Villeneuve]?' (73; 1.2.2).

If 'to *feel* the eternal (since we cannot completely know it) in the temporal, is one aspect at least of religion' (Ritchie 118), we might again ask who is the religious voice, Pity or the Years? Pity declares, in a sly dig at determinism, 'I feel, Sire, as I must!' and then turns the Years' accusation of story-telling back at him: 'This *tale* of Will / And Life's impulsion by Incognizance / I cannot take' (my emphasis, 64; 1.1.6).

What the Years asks the Pities to feel, is, by monistic standards, the goal of the religious quest: 'The supreme expression of the religious consciousness lies always in an intuition of union with the world, under whatever abstract or concrete names the infinite not-self may be hidden' (Ellis 244). The Years even sounds like a theist talking to an atheist as he explains why he must visualize the Will a second time: 'Let me then once again / Show to thy sceptic eye the very streams / And currents of this all-inhering Power, / And bring conclusion to thy unbelief' (64; 1.1.6).

The preternatural transparency that follows changes the interior of Milan Cathedral, with its outworn Christian creed, into the cosmic brain of the Years' new faith. His visualization also overlaps a deterministic scene of coercive dialogue in which 'the self-styled servants of the Highest' are 'Constrained by earthly duress to embrace / Mighty imperiousness.' Napoleon 'labours to achieve' the dynastic power that 'his active soul, fair Freedom's child' (61; 1.1.6) once overthrew; the Years struggles to achieve in a different form the theistic perspective he tries to overthrow in the Pities.

There is a way in which the Years' discourse of naturalism and agnosticism leads on in the direction Ward saw them pointing, towards a spiritual monism and the possibility that 'the First Cause of a Cosmos, to be an adequate Cause and deserve the name, must be a Supreme Intelligence' (Ward 2:269). As wary as the Years can be, ostensibly bound 'to register and watch' (Fore Scene 23), he does not wholly belong to the sceptical tradition that W. David Shaw traces in nineteenth-century Britain from Sir William Hamilton to his Victorian disciples, Mansel, Spencer, and Huxley (121). Another and later line of neo-Kantian thought also sounds in the Years' declarations about the Absolute in which 'Science and Agnosticism are ... paths whereby we are brought back to religion' (Symonds 405).

It is not just ideas or the serious exchanges with Pity that characterize the Years. What most allows us to hear his prophetic voice and elevated speech – and here we return to the carnivalization of science with which we began – is laughter. If not the fool, then at least the rogue and the clown reappear in the guise of the Spirits Ironic and Sinister who find in the Years, with his claims to impersonality and transhistorical authority, the perfect target for parody.[28]

The only Spirits to appreciate the comic aspect of the world are also the only speakers in the Overworld to use prose. The Spirits Sinister and Ironic emerge to challenge the false or narrow seriousness of both

Spirits and dynasts. In the Fore Scene Irony's one brief rejoinder insists on what the Years and Pity suppress: 'Nay, Comedy' (25). Sinister speaks twice in asides and always in blank verse, but laughter begins to sound on the edge of the philosophical dialogue. The tart Phantom's last words in the Fore Scene, spoken to Pity, transform the Years' Will into a funny monster and the abstract problem of the One and the many into a masquerade: 'Limbs of Itself: / Each one a jot of It in quaint disguise? / I'll fear all men [not the Will] henceforward!' (25).

Nothing provokes the Years' censure more than humour that breaks into the open and turns a dynastic spectacle into an object of familar contact. Sinister and Irony share the inappropriate word, 'inappropriate because of its cynical frankness, or because it profanely unmasks a holy thing, or because it crudely violates etiquette' (Bakhtin, *Problems* 118). During the service at Milan Cathedral, Sinister sees the grotesque face behind the Archbishop's mask – 'His lips with inheld laughter grow deformed' – and uncrowns the Emperor as 'one whose aim is but to win / The golden seats that other b—s have warmed.' The Years' warning, 'Soft, jestor,' brings him unexpectedly to the side of feeling: 'scorn not puppetry so skilled, / Even made to feel by one men call the Dame' (61; 1.1.6). When Sinister switches to prose for a homely parody of determinism, 'she [Nature] must cut her coat according to her cloth, as they would say below there,' Years abandons his lofty pose of neutrality and uses sarcasm in response: 'Thou Dragon of the Incorporeal world, / "As they would say below there"' (62; 1.1.6). The leading serious voices in the Overworld remain deaf to a laughter that degrades and materializes. The Years hears only an infernal voice 'We comprehend ... not,' Pity a 'Gross hypocrite!' (88; 1.2.5).

We also sense a possible personality in the impersonal Years when Irony carnivalizes the lives and wives of kings. A joke about rulers who pretend to lack ambition meets with 'Hush levities' (181; 1.6.5). A 'Hoo-hoo!' directed at Napoleon's old wife and new makes the Years sound like an earnest Victorian: 'What lewdness lip those wry-formed phantoms there?' The direct and serious word sounds in all its limitations as it becomes the laughing image of that word. 'Nay, Showman Years!,' reply the Ironic Spirits, 'With holy reverent air / We hymn the nuptials of the Imperial pair' (383; 2.5.6).

The climax of Irony's increasing boldness comes in the hilarious scenes at Carlton House that bring Part Second to a close. Nothing said in the Overworld can confine the festive evening within a framework of seriousness. When Pity suggests in verse that many guests think the loud feast almost indecent, Irony responds in a familiar tone: 'My dear phantom and crony, the gloom upon their faces is due rather to their having borrowed those diamonds at eleven per cent than to their loyalty to a suffering monarch!' (425; 2.6.7). The Years criticizes the Ironies for 'Making faint fancies as they were indeed / The Mighty Will's firm work' (432; 2.6.7) but keeps rendering low meanings in high language himself: 'Cease fooling on weak waifs who love and wed / But as the unweeting Urger may bestead!' (424; 2.6.6). 'The monological,' in Terry Eagleton's words, 'has its own unwitting humour ... Any such obsessive conversion of difference to identity is bound to be comic' ('Bakhtin' 182). The Years talks about the metaphysical Will and the human will in the same sombre way: 'There lie long leagues between a woman's word – / "She will, indeed she will!" – and acting on't' (432; 2.6.7). We are reminded of the earlier scene in the Imperial palace at Vienna when even Hardy, literally playing with history, gets in on the joke. As Maria Louisa ponders marriage to Napoleon, the narrator drily describes how 'a small enamel portrait of Marie Antoinette ... has slipped down on its face.' The Years immediately makes a great deal of 'A slight noise': 'What mischief's this? The Will must have Its way' (370; 2.5.3).

The scene gets grotesquely funny at Carlton House when the Years decides to reassert his authority by taking the shape of a 'pale, hollow-eyed gentleman.' The one person he addresses looks like his ghostly double. The Prime Minister, Spencer Perceval, is a 'pale, grave-looking man' (434, 432; 2.6.7) who 'shrinks' when the Years predicts that 'The tomb-worm may caress thee' (435; 2.6.7) before a European war begins. Next to the Will, 'my old friend Death' (621; 3.6.2) remains the Years' favourite subject. We hear him in the flesh and verse as the representative of an old and dying world, the future adding nothing new to 'the shotten years / Whose useless films infest the foggy Past' (435; 2.6.7).

Almost everything high and serious has a parodic double. The exhaustive effort needed for the Years to produce his transparencies finds a comic equivalent in the way the Ironics 'strain [their] powers unduly' for the sake of 'antics' (432; 2.6.7). In the first and exterior scene, two houses 'become transparent' (422; 2.6.6) but instead of the weaving Will, we see the distaff side of the Prince of Wales's serio-comic life. In the second scene, the Regent worries more about how his 'women will be the death o'me!' than the 'imminence of dire and deadly war' (431, 434; 2.6.7) between France and Russia. The madness and changeability of King George become the son's 'taste for change' in women who in turn 'drive me mad!' (432; 2.6.7). Irony does not have to do much to give an official feast in which 'people should sit strictly according to their rank' the structure of a carnival event. The Prince sets the tone by 'mixing up and talking unceremoniously with his guests of every degree' (431, 428; 2.6.7). Carlton House already has a 'grand entrance' and a 'covert little "chair-door"' (421; 2.6.6); the two wives aready form a contrasting pair, one 'full of jest,' the other 'Reserved, perverse' (422, 423; 2.6.6). 'There have been,' the Prince admits, 'such infernal mistakes made in sending out the cards that the biggest w— in London might be here' (431; 2.6.7). Even 'Obscure and unmissed courtiers late deceased, / ... have in name been bidden to the feast / By blundering scribes' (422; 2.6.6). As the Prince's wives steal to the fete 'With dames of strange repute,' a chorus of Ironic Spirits erupts into a loud song that pushes their difference to a carnivalesque extreme: 'A wife of the body, a wife of the mind / A wife somewhat frowsy, a wife too refined' (423; 2.6.6).

The entire action forms a series of scandals and disguises, sudden shifts and changes, mystifications and comic mix-ups, crownings and decrownings. While the Regent tries to take his father's place, Irony usurps the role of 'Father' Years, ordering the Rumours to scatter whispers that the King is dead and to impersonate the abandoned spouses, the Princess Caroline with her beastly German, and the Fitzherbert Fair with her fainting fits. One moment the carnival King-pretender hears 'Long live the King!,' the next his two ladies pour reproaches into his ears. Sweltering in the dress of a field marshal and boasting 'I was born for war,' the Prince complains about the heat of battle with the sex: 'Cursed hot here, Yarmouth. Hottest of all for me!' (436, 429; 2.6.7).

When the Years surprises the complacent politicians with his gloomy and eschatological vision of blood, fire, and confused noise in the historic future, the scene ends as it begins, in prose and with everyone mystified. Laughter returns and works both ways: while England's rulers hear themselves depicted as mouldy-minded oligarchs, the Years' verse sounds like the parody of a prophecy. 'I expected,' says the witty Sheridan, 'to see him write on the wall, like the gentleman with the Hand at Belshazzar's Feast.' Who better than Castlereagh, himself a lofty speaker, to identify the unmistakably religious tone of the Years' voice: 'His manner was that of an old prophet, and his features had a Jewish cast, which accounted for his Hebraic style' (436, 435; 2.6.7).

The unmasking of the Years as a prophetic voice recreates in comical dramatic form the decrowning of the high proclamatory speakers of monism. Even the eldest Spirit becomes subject to a carnival ambivalence in the form of reduced laughter and the novel's tendency to relativize discourses. Like that other ideologue, Angel Clare, more spirit than man, the Years is 'a sample product of the last five-and-twenty years' (Hardy, *Tess* 309) and as full of inconsistencies and contradictions. In constructing the Years' style of speaking, Hardy draws on a vocabulary already entangled in dialogic threads and on ideas already open to dispute. When we look closely at how this language actually functions in *The Dynasts*, we respond to the Will's official Spirit at the distance appropriate to irony and humour. The determinism so often mistaken for Hardy's philosophy ends up, like everything else in *The Dynasts*, as a parodic discourse, reminding us that carnivalization penetrates the very philosophical core of the menippea, inverting conceptual hierarchies and revealing that no language is unconditional or beyond dialogue.

THREE

Unconscious or Superconscious?

Historical interpretation in *The Dynasts* ranges from the simplest form, the chronicle, to the most complex and abstract form, the monistic theory of the universe. At both extremes we find the indeterminacy so important to the Bakhtinian novel. On the one hand, 'The Chronicle typically promises closure but does not provide it' (Hayden White, *Content* 6); on the other hand, the theme of the Will acquires some of the contradictory complexity of its life as an idea in the dialogue of the era. Instead of offering a single impersonal truth, with the Spirit of the Years settling all disputes (see Maynard 103), Hardy uses the novel's spirit of process and inconclusiveness to reflect the still-evolving and unfinished reality of monistic thought. In choosing his historical material, he makes it ideologically timely by a valuational connection with contemporary issues. No issue more divided monistic thinkers, became more emotionally charged, even to the point that the very fate of values seemed at stake, or pushed thought further to speculate on the unknown than the question that forms the subject of this chapter: is the Will unconscious or superconscious?

Each time the Will becomes transparent in *The Dynasts* we get a discourse that provokes rather than shuts down dialogue by giving the cosmic web the shape of the human mind. The Spirit of the Years' speeches on the anatomy of the Will with its 'Nerves, sinews, trajects, eddies, ducts' (172; 1.6.3) draw heavily on the language of physiological psychology and invoke the famous controversy over psychophysical parallelism versus psychophysical causality. Like many scientific thinkers, the Years insists on explaining conscious phenomena in terms of the material and physical. But 'physiological psychology is forced by its *own definition* to pass over into the sphere of *metaphysics*' (Hartmann 3:288). Psychophysical parallelism 'is only possible if both are derivative from a common cause' (Du Prel 2:131).

By the time Hardy wrote *The Dynasts*, Alexander Bain's monistic idea that the mental and physical proceed together as two sides of one unknown substance (see Hardy, *Literary* 2:108) was only one of several contending theories in a science that could no longer be identified with naturalism and agnosticism. In 1903 C.A. Strong summed up the alternatives this way:

> There are thus three distinct theories as to causal relations between mind and body: interactionism, asserting that the causal influence runs in both directions – in sensation from the body to the mind, in volition from the mind to the body; automatism, maintaining that it runs in one direction only – always from the body to the mind; and parallelism, denying all causal influence and holding the relation to be of a different nature. (2–3)[1]

Although both automatism and parallelism provide what the Years wants – a brain that gets along by itself without the help of mind – his position most closely resembles the conscious automaton theory of Huxley. Human consciousness is an effect of cosmic brain-events, an effect which does not in turn become a cause and react on the Will's 'automatic sense' (*The Dynasts*, Fore Scene 21).

During the battle of Waterloo, the narrator translates the last transparency in which consciousness appears irrelevant: 'The web connecting all the apparently separate shapes includes Wellington in its tissue with the rest, and shows him, like them, as acting while discovering his intention to act' (680; 3.7.7). The syntax of this passage places acting before intention in the same way that in Huxley's theory mental states 'are always a little later than the brain-events which cause them' (Strong 2). At any rate, conscious intention seems no better than a parallel phenomenon to action rather than preceding and directing it. The interior of the cosmic brain 'seems to manifest the volitions,' as opposed to ideas, 'of a Universal Will' (65; 1.1.6) and yet the faces of both French and English at Waterloo 'wear the expression of that of people in a dream' (680; 3.7.7), as if the 'films or brain-tissues' have some content, not just moving all things but creating 'inexplicable artistries' (449; 3.1.1).

'Reason or will,' says Ritchie, 'we may name the ultimate universal force, power, manifesting itself everywhere; but it makes a difference which element predominates in our conception' (244). Hardy's name for the ultimate force does not imply any simple answer as to which element predominates in his conception. His letters indicate that, like many monists, he was never quite satisfied with the word Will: 'in its ordinary sense, it is not quite accurately used in the drama' (3:113). Will usually 'implies motives, which it is absurd to imagine as acting on "the Absolute," which, if absolute, can have no wants or cravings' (Ritchie 185). On the other hand, 'an un-motivated will would be no will at all' (Walker 339). Hardy tried to escape the dilemma by using Will in a secondary sense that gradually arose in the last half of the nineteenth century to express 'that condition of energy between attentive and inattentive effort which the scientific call "reflex," "instinctive," "involuntary," action; "unconscious formative activity" etc.' (*Letters* 3:113).

Hardy's list reveals something of his strategy in *The Dynasts*, proceeding as it does from the physical to the metaphysical and a phrase reminiscent of Hartmann, who sets out to prove by numerous illustrations that reflex action depends on the unconscious intelligence. When 'physiology began to disclose that all mental processes were (mathematically speaking) *functions* of physical processes ... this was declared enough to banish for ever the conception of a Soul' (Lewes, 'Course' 325; Hardy, *Literary* 1:92). Theophile Ribot typifies the work of Bain, Spencer, Maudsley, and Lange 'in substituting for the dualistic position a unitary or monistic one' that 'connects all states of feeling with biological conditions.' At the root of the affective life is 'an impulse, a tendency, ... independent of intelligence' (112, vii, 438), the biological equivalent of Schopenhauer's 'unconscious, automatic, or reasonless will' (Hardy, *Literary* 2:107).[2]

This new physiological doctrine, in which reason is only a moment of an otherwise blind will, became part of late nineteenth-century pessimism, delivering, in E.A. Ross's estimate, the 'final blow to the old notion of the ego' (740). The Years' voiceless Will finds corroboration in the way science 'hints at the many voiceless beings that live out in our body their joy and pain, ... dwellers in the sub-centres, with whom, it may be, often lies the initiative when the conscious centre thinks itself free' (Ross 740; Hardy, *Literary* 2:49).

The growing belief that 'Everything that is really fundamental in a man, and therefore genuine works, as such, unconsciously' (Schopenhauer, 'Studies' 45–6; Hardy, *Literary* 2:29) raised an important question: should the Unconscious be understood as the antithesis or another form of consciousness? Whereas the physiologists usually answered that the Unconscious is in itself unconscious, Hartmann and Du Prel agree that it is such only from the psychological point of view in relation to individuals and for the being of senses. Those same voiceless centres of reflex action that disturb Ross remain to Hartmann 'conscious for the particular centre, but unconscious for the brain' (1:142). The 'disappearance of the cerebral consciousness,' says Du Prel, 'does not signify the disappearance of consciousness generally' (1:70). The metaphysical Unconscious, whether Hartmann's World-Soul or Du Prel's transcendental Subject, interposed between the All-One and the sensuous self, is conscious, though not self-conscious or reflective in the manner of Haldane's Absolute. The metaphysical eye can see the earthly consciousness but not itself.

In Du Prel's doctrine of soul, man is a 'monistic double-being – monistic as Subject, dualistic as Person' (1:332). The Subject-consciousness embraces and unites the empirical and transcendental egos, the two persons always divided by a moving threshold of sensibility. It is these moments when the threshold is displaced that particularly interest Du Prel: 'In dream, somnambulism, and all ecstatic conditions, an interior waking takes the place of the external sense-consciousness,' only to retire for the waking person into the Unconscious. That part of the Unconscious that awakens in sleep is 'by no means a mere remnant of the daily consciousness but a new consciousness' (1:115, 32). By being susceptible to finer influences than are received by the senses of the waking person, this soul-consciousness connects man to a transcendental world. Yet 'what is for us insensible is not therefore immaterial.' In Du Prel's natural supernaturalism, the transcendental is still in the world of sense, but beyond the threshold of the empirical ego. Somnambulism becomes 'the fundamental form of all mysticism' (2:31, 141) because the psychic faculties which come into play in this state can actually see the invisible forces of nature, in the same way that the Years can make the web of the Will appear in moments of vision.

Clearly interactionism – 'It is equally certain that the mind acts on the body' (McTaggart, *Some Dogmas* 79)[3] – comes to the forefront when the physiological unconscious gives way to the metaphysical. Du Prel replaces the unknown Substance of agnostics with the transcendental Subject as the common cause of body and mind. The soul is no longer the product but the producer of the phenomenal body and follows the 'impulse to incarnation' to experience the sufferings of conscious life because they 'are of transcendental advantage to the Subject, which has wholly different interests from the earthly person' (2:220). Much of what Du Prel says could be spoken by the Years but with the difference that the Unconscious is never merely Will. The 'hidden impulse of our actions' is a 'transcendental Ego' (2:98): 'man can be motived from the transcendental region without the mediation of his consciousness.' Du Prel might have written the stage directions for the Waterloo section of *The Dynasts*, except that now unconscious intention precedes action: 'human history is composed of acts motived by ideas and impulses transcendentally derived; while we, like somnambulists, are immovably convinced of our own deliberate agency' (2:215, 217–18).

Somnambulism seemed to confirm both the power of the unconscious life and the reality of the spiritual world. In some 'old notes written before "The Dynasts,"' Hardy did imagine a battle in which he would present an 'army as somnambulists – not knowing what it is for' (*Personal Notebooks* 58, 59). Here a battle resembles Carlyle's French Revolution, a 'singular Somnambulism' in which the participants 'Consciously ... did somewhat; unconsciously how much!' (*French Revolution* 313, 388). When Hardy thought 'that people are somnambulists,' he also meant 'that the material is not the real': what they see is 'only the visible, the real being invisible optically' (*Life* 192). In the context of war, somnambulism does not eliminate 'the difference between what things are and what they ought to be' (Hardy, *Personal Notebooks* 59) but history might be more than a blind struggle. Hartmann devotes a whole volume to the 'unconsciously impelling ideas of history' (2:6; Hardy, *Literary* 2:110) actualized through either 'the implanting an instinctive impulse in the masses' or 'the production of men of genius as finger-posts and pioneers' (2:8) whose actions lead to results that 'were quite beside the conscious purposes of such men' (2:9).

In terms of this kind of historic instinct, the Years' dreaming Will might be described as a transcendental Intelligence. The word rapt keeps occurring in his account of the Will. It is the 'Rapt Determinator' (437; 2.6.7), 'the all-urging Will, raptly magnipotent' (196; 1.6.8), creating patterns 'by rapt aesthetic rote' (Fore Scene 21). At the end of Part Second, the Chorus of the Pities' hope that 'It may wake' implies a sleeping Will, but the Years' figures have already awakened It in Du Prel's sense of an interior waking taking the place of sense consciousness. The words rapt and drowsed ('like a knitter drowsed,' Fore Scene 22) indicate a state of mind between sleep and waking, the inattention of drowsed balanced by the absorption of rapt. The ethical problem of such fixed attention on the patterns that 'seem in themselves Its single listless aim' is the 'absent heed' as to 'their consequence' (Fore Scene

21, 23, 21). Sharing Du Prel's interest in the unconscious and 'dream-dramas,' Maudsley examines the similar etymology that ecstasy and rapture share: '*Ecstasy* means literally a standing out of self ..., and *rapture* the state of one who is rapt or carried away from himself' (Maudsley 160, 288). The 'listless aim' of the Will rules out the intense delight of ecstasy and 'a Brain whose whole connotes the Everywhere' (Fore Scene 28) cannot get outside Itself except to dream an even better world. For Maudsley, 'It is beyond question that the mind can do as good work in dreams as it ever does when awake – indeed, better imaginative work' (160). Hardy too was struck by the idea that 'great talent in action – in fact genius – is a kind of somnambulism' (*Literary* 1:126). Certainly 'If each decision work unconsciously' (51; 1.1.3), the only effectual thinking is unconscious, done by the Will, 'thinking on, yet weighing not its thought' (Fore Scene 22).

'To have ideas and yet not be conscious of them': Hardy found Hartmann's exposition 'very obscure' (*Literary* 2:109, 111) but the subject fascinating enough to weave it as a sign of the times into *The Dynasts'* complex pattern of thought. Writing in 1883, one reviewer noticed a 'good deal both of fact and speculation tending to illustrate the now common doctrine of "unconscious cerebration"' ('Mr. Galton's' 1,029).[4] From the unconscious thinking of Du Prel and Hartmann to Walker's 'Unconscious Mentality' (210), a good deal of Hardy's reading moved where the dialogue of the Overworld does, on the borderline between fact and speculation. We need not make a special case for Hartmann's influence or for the sometimes curious work of the English Society for Psychical Research. Ritchie's Absolute sounds, for example, very much like Hartmann's clairvoyant, intuitive Intelligence: 'The Universal Reason works unconsciously, and in some cases *immediately.* That is inspiration' (261).

Schopenhauer may have separated Will and Idea, but the course of modern thought was to reunite them, and Hardy, with the novelist's desire to keep abreast of contemporary issues, hoped that 'my philosophy ... is much more modern than Schopenhauer' (*Letters* 4:37). Hartmann was very much a child of his time in designating 'the united unconscious will and unconscious idea "the Unconscious"' (1:4; Hardy, *Literary* 2:109). Like a magnet, spiritualistic monism aligned Will and Idea as equal poles within a unified field. Ormond discovers 'the inner being of the world' in a conception of reason 'which from one point of view is will, while from another it is idea' (14). Even Haldane, who, as an Hegelian might be expected to accentuate the

Idea, acknowledges 'the insistence of recent Psychology upon "attention," and is prepared to admit that the Ultimate Reality must be looked upon as Will no less than Thought' (Rashdall, Review of *Stage the First* 528; Hardy, *Literary* 2:166).

When applied to the doctrine of evolution, monism had the effect on the realm of the psychic of an object dropped in still water, expanding the role of consciousness out from the centre of the human cortex in a series of ever widening circles.[5] Hartmann speaks of the *vegetable* soul (2:119) and Ward claims that Aristotle's notion of a plant-soul (1:287) is tenable today. Even no less an authority than Darwin provided supporting evidence in a review article by R.J. Mann that Hardy quoted (*Literary* 1:139). 'Uncertaintly, by fits, the Will doth work' (219; 2.1.3) like the way plants advance with 'a fitful and uncertain, and not with a steady, pace.' Yet in neither case does uncertainty imply blindness. Plants 'are endowed with a keen faculty of discrimination, and, in a certain sense, of perception. Dr. Darwin, indeed, seems inclined to regard them as possessing almost the attributes of a vegetable brain' (Mann 255–6, 258). Hardy commented that the 'theory of consciousness in plants is an arresting one: but I have always known it intuitively, and hate maiming trees on that account' (*Letters* 3:331). Unexpectedly, the Chorus of Years expresses a similar concern when it initiates the lyrical account of the fauna of Waterloo field on the eve of the battle. If 'Life ... is the same in the worm as in the man' (Goldwin Smith 723), the Years has some reason to report how 'The worm asks what can be overhead' or to worry that the ears of corn will be 'Trodden and bruised to a miry tomb' (651; 3.6.8).

Monism also extended at least the rudiments of consciousness far beyond the living world. In Clifford's view, 'we are obliged to assume ... that along with every motion of matter, whether organic or inorganic, there is some fact which corresponds to the mental fact in ourselves' (266).[6] Hartmann did not exaggerate when he observed that 'Already the most distinguished natural philosophers recognize the interior, psychical side of atoms' (3:240). Since his pantheistic substance has two attributes, matter that is phenomenally knowable, and energy or spirit that is unknowable, Haeckel can speak of even the atom having a 'universal "soul" of the simplest character' (225; Hardy *Literary* 2:418), just as the Spirit of the Years juxtaposes atoms and souls in talking about men. They subsist as 'atoms of the One' (Fore Scene 28); these atoms when dead 'are snuffed-out souls' (480; 3.1.9).

Like the Years, Clifford denies God, freedom, and immortality but postulates that 'Matter is a mental picture in which mind-stuff is the thing represented' (286). While Ward saw nothing more in Clifford's wild speculation than 'the atom renamed' (2:15), Hardy found this a very attractive idea. The problem remained, however, that 'you cannot find the link (at least I can't) of one form of consciousness with another' (*Letters* 1:262). Mindstuff means that '*if* matter has a consciousness it is an atomistic consciousness, and between the consciousnesses of the several atoms no *communication* is possible' (Hartmann 2:183). We can now see better why the Years seems compelled to image/imagine a cosmic brain. In naturalistic versions of panpsychism, 'Consciousness cannot exist without a brain; and the only rational conception of an intelligent Deity would oblige us to suppose the whole universe to be a brain' (Mallock 251).

Hardy wondered 'how much complication is necessary to produce consciousness' (*Literary* 1:174). Many thinkers could dispense with the physiological model of a brain as a prerequisite to cosmic consciousness. Among the scientists, Romanes points out that:

> For aught that we can know to the contrary, not merely the highly special-ized structure of the human brain, but even that of nervous matter in general, may only be one of a thousand possible ways in which the material and dynamical conditions required for the apparition of self-consciousness can be secured. (49–50)[7]

Hardy also read how August Weismann 'grants, and even seems to contend, that there is ... a mind-stuff for the whole, as there is a mind-stuff for the parts, – the interior view of which may correspond, more or less, closely to the general conception of a ruling intellect' ('Mr. Justice' 655).[8] The most microscopic of evidence could become charged with the same macrocosmic significance. In another article that interested Hardy, Andrew Wilson moves from a consideration of the amoeba or protoplasm as the basic unit of consciousness to a startlingly broad conclusion built on the final, theistic words of the *Origin of Species*: '"There is grandeur," to quote Darwin's words, "in this view of life," which, whilst it satisfies the demands of scientific faith, leaves behind it no doubt of the existence, at the source of law, of a controlling, all-directing Mind' (435).[9]

Hardy was struck by the way science itself tends to establish the conviction that everything is part of one mind-penetrated unity. Even Spencer, for all his silence about the Unknowable, finds 'the spiritualistic conception of the external world, as consisting of something essentially identical with what we call mind' (*First* 559), justified. It is little wonder that Symonds saw the scientific theory of the cosmos as 'pregnant with a new metaphysic and a new theology' (127). Huxley's scientific researches, for example, 'were on the very border where science and theology meet and led directly to some fundamental problems' (Stephen, *Studies* 210) of the kind that Hardy explores in the Overworld. The exchanges between the Pities and the Years should not be heard as two mutually exclusive monologues but as a dialogue that reveals 'the inevitable point of contact between Science and Religion' (Symonds 16). A review article on the New Theology forms one of the entries in Hardy's 'Literary Notes III' and occasioned his parenthetical remark, 'Very like the "Immanent Will" of the Dynasts' (*Literary* 2:353). According to Reverend R.J. Campbell, quoted at length in the article, 'The starting point of the New Theology is belief in the immanence of God and the essential oneness of God and man' ('"New Theology,"' 7; Hardy *Literary* 2:354). The demand within science for metaphysical grounding became 'a datum for the formation of the idea of God because it everywhere leads toward a spiritualistic conception of the world' (Ormond 606). Fiske, for one, does not hesitate in preaching that 'The existence of God ... is the fundamental postulate upon which Cosmism bases its synthesis of scientific truths' (1:184).

In turn, the demand for a scientific theology was welcomed as an important step in the remoulding and renewal of religion. Spencer leads the way when he asserts that 'the beliefs which Science has forced upon Religion, have been intrinsically more religious than those which they supplanted' (*First* 104). 'The tendency of scientific ideas,' Symonds believes, 'is to spiritualize religion' (9). As monism evolved past its negative or neutral stage, 'the reign of [to borrow Maurice Maeterlinck's striking phrase] the *positive sublime*' seemed destined to be overthrown. Many speculative thinkers shared his feeling that a 'spiritual epoch is perhaps upon us' (32, 25).[10] The antagonism between science and religion is swept away in Fiske's cosmism, as is the opposition between theism and naturalism in Hartmann's philosophy of the Unconscious.

The future of the novel looked to Hardy much like the future of philosophy to Hartmann. The fate of both genres seemed very much tied to a naturalism in the process of making 'an historical transition from the prior shallow Materialism to a complete and whole Ideal-realism' (Hartmann 1:xxv). About 1903, Hardy said that spiritual naturalism 'nearly defines my own old idea of the principle of novels of the future' (*Literary* 2:48). This old idea, 'approximately carried out ... in the supernatural framework of *The Dynasts*,' dates back to a series of notes made in 1886 when Hardy felt 'Novel-writing as an art cannot go backward. Having reached the analytic stage it must transcend it by going still further in the same direction. Why not by rendering as visible essences, spectres, etc. the abstract thoughts of the analytic school?' (*Life* 183). In the novel of the future, the substance and the shadow would change places in a new monistic sense of the real and man would be caught in the cosmic web revealed by the Spectres of abstract thought:

> The human race to be shown as one great network or tissue, which quivers in every part when one point is shaken, like a spider's web if touched. Abstract realisms to be in the form of Spirits, Spectral figures, etc.
> The Realities to be the true realities of life, hitherto called abstractions. The old material realities to be placed behind the former, as shadowy accessories. (*Life* 183)

These notes directly reflect the transformation of monism by the 'neo-Kantian movement of the past thirty years' (Masterman 8; Hardy, *Literary* 2:148) of the nineteenth century. The Overworld is very much the result of Hardy going still further in the direction of making thought itself the subject of a new novel. Like Goethe's *Faust*, *The Dynasts* has 'as much reflection as action in it; but the reflection itself is made dramatic' (Lewes, *Life* 454) or, as Bakhtin would say, dialogic.

Spiritualistic monism did not necessarily lead on to theism unless, like Symonds, the monist was bold enough to say that all form is fundamentally a mode of mind. Our mind is not coextensive with the universe; yet we may reasonably infer from its presence in ourselves that 'there is mind in the universe below us and above us' (12) in the form of a Universal Mind. The meaning of the above/below distinction in *The Dynasts* becomes crucial as laughter in its reduced forms of irony and sarcasm forces the Years to defend the 'World-Soul's way' (172; 1.6.3) in language that reflects the spiritual dimension of monism and transforms the cosmic brain into a cosmic mind. The Spirit Sinister's casual scorn brings the Years to the verge of 'trying to prove that there is any right or reason in the Universe' and of wishing that 'I could move [the Will] to enchain thee.' Hearing its own voice in the Years' wish, Pity responds, 'Would thou couldst! / But move That Which is scoped above percipience, / It cannot be!' (62; 1.1.6). If the Will is above sympathy, then 'out of tune the Mode and meritless / That quickens sense in shapes whom, thou [Years] hast said, / Necessitation sways!' (147; 1.5.4). The Years tries to defend the indefensible and in the process hints at a mind that in being like the human below might be above a cosmic brain:

> Nay, blame not! For what judgment can ye blame? –
> In that immense unweeting Mind is shown
> One far above forethinking; prócessive,
> Rapt, superconscious; a Clairvoyancy
> That knows not what It knows, yet works therewith. –   (147; 1.5.4)

These double-voiced lines condense the contradictions within monism into a catalogue of attributes separated by commas or semi-colons, coexisting without being pushed into harmonious connection. The idea Hardy often entertained of a Will that is no more 'than an unpurposive and irresponsible groping in the direction of the least resistance' (Life 398) still haunts the Years' speech. The cosmic Mind may be inferior to the human, incapable of judgment and forethinking, prócessive[11] rather than purposive. But another possibility sounds of a superconscious mind that is in some mysterious way above the human, a Clairvoyancy capable, as a Semichorus of Ironic Spirits later says, of unconscious planning (696; 3.7.8). In terms of Symond's positive Agnostic creed, only 'it may be, is your limit' (405). The Years seems to reach this limit to affirm that God's knowledge is intuitive. Under the heading 'God as super-conscious,' Hardy paraphrased Hartmann's explanation of the superiority of the 'unconscious clairvoyant intelligence' to 'the halting, stilted gait of the discursive reflection of consciousness' (Hartmann 2:247; Hardy, Literary 2:111). Hartmann explains the paradox of a clairvoyant Will as follows: 'this seeing can never be aware of its own vision, but only of the world, and without the mirrors of the individual consciousnesses can also not see the seeing eye' (Hartmann 2:246–7).

Clearly a crack divides the mirror of the Years' consciousness. A novelistic inconclusiveness that seeks some valorized support in the future emerges from his epic voice with its emphasis on the deterministic past:

> Nay, nay, nay;
> Your hasty judgments stay,

Until the topmost cyme
Have crowned the last entablature of Time.
O heap not blame on that in-brooding Will;
O pause, till all things all their days fulfil!   (148; 1.5.4)

The Years does not remain neutral about a Will whose brooding repeats with difference, inwardness replacing outwardness, the thoughts
of Milton's Holy Spirit which 'Dove-like satst brooding on the vast
Abyss' (*Paradise Lost* 1:21). Like philosophers of the Absolute, he asso-
ciates the Will with a totality which, as James points out, is 'considered
to carry the further attribute of *perfection* in its train' (*Pluralistic* 50).
Faced with the irrationality of a perfect timeless whole being made up
of at least some imperfect historical parts the Years makes time a
means for preserving the belief that 'all are overruled in that final
whole that perfects them' (Bradley 404). To be consistent, however, 'No
attribute connected with succession can be applied to it [the Absolute],
for it is all at once and wholly what it is' (James, *Pluralistic* 39).

We may bring the Years' vacillations into sharper focus by hearing
them against the monistic alternatives provided by W.K. Clifford and
George J. Romanes. Although Clifford sees the whole universe as com-
prised of mind-stuff, he concludes that the universe as a whole is
mindless when measured by human standards of consciousness. In
'The World as an Eject' Romanes attacks Clifford's position for claiming to be the only possible one. Like the Spirit of the Years, he imagines
'the visible siderial system compressed within the limits of a human
skull' and then asks how much of the cosmic brain does scientific
monism sanction us in calling mental, not just the raw material of
mind? He points out that an impersonal world eject or inferred cosmic
subjectivity 'does not tend to show that it is of lower psychical value
than conscious personality: on the contrary it tends to show that it is
probably of higher psychical value.' Monism provides a provisional
support for the conclusion that '*if* the ultimate constitution of all things
is psychical, the philosophy of the Cosmos becomes a "philosophy of
the Unconscious" only because it is a philosophy of the Superconscious' (51, 53, 54).

Hardy, on the other hand, owned to a mistrust of metaphysic on the
basis of probability:

It ultimately comes to this – such and such things *may* be. But they will
ever be improbable: and since infinitely other things may also be, with

equal probability, why select any one bundle of suppositions in preference to another. I prefer to relegate such thoughts to the domain of fancy.
(*Letters* 1:261)

After reading Bergson's *Creative Evolution* in 1914, Hardy relegated the
theory of an *élan vital* to the realm of fancy. Since the conflict between
creative and mechanical evolution recalls the Romanes versus Clifford
controversy, we may gather from Hardy's criticism of Bergson what he
might have asked of any theory of cosmic purpose to grant it some
validity or 'truth' value. First, Bergson's theory (in Hardy's view) of 'a
sort of additional and spiritual force, beyond the merely unconscious
push of life' seemed 'much less probable than single and simple determinism, or what he [Bergson] calls mechanism.' Second, 'If nature
were creative she would have created painlessness, or be in process of
creating it' (*Letters* 5:84). In other words, the Pities' wish at the end of
Part Second of *The Dynasts*, 'Yet It may wake and understand' and
'With knowledge use a painless hand' (437; 2.6.7), would have to be
more than just another agnostic 'may be.' Finally, on the grounds that
presumably monism is more convincing than dualism, Hardy also
objected to Bergson's philosophy as 'only our old friend Dualism in a
new suit of clothes' (*Letters* 5:79). Hardy knew, however, that scientific
monism, while preserving determinism, was open to the same charge.
To Armitage, the scientists' 'characteristic attitude in our time is not a
monistic one, such as Haeckel boasts, but it is the frank dualism of the
vulgar' (736).[12] We should remember that, while Hardy favoured
determinism over Bergson's creative evolution, he made a choice
between two fancies. The determinist fancy (*Letters* 5:79), as he called
it, is superior because more probable. The ideal had to have at least
some foundation in the real or, as Bradley puts the matter, 'The possible itself would not be possible, if it were not more, and if it were not
partially real' (344).

At the close of the nineteenth century, Bergson and Ward were more
the exceptions than the rule in demanding contingency and indeterminacy to justify the universe as a realm of ends or spiritual purposes.
'Either the universe,' says Ward, 'is mechanical or it is teleological; it is
not likely to be a mixture of the two' (2:63). Ritchie's response was typical: 'May not the universe be both at once, through and through
mechanical when regarded in its material or spatial aspect, teleological
when regarded in its spiritual aspect' (109).[13] By trying to overthrow
determinism, the aspect of Christianity he most disliked and saw reap-

pear in secular guise, Ward leaves 'no environment for an ultimate and universal mind to act against, and thus, if "God" is really all and mechanism nothing, "God" can be neither active nor passive' (Taylor 258).

Hardy may not have found some forms of spiritualistic monism as 'clumsy and confused' (*Letters* 5:84) as Bergson's vitalistic monism, especially those that address the issue of probability.[14] For Romanes, as for Hardy, it was a matter of great moment to determine the probability of the psychological superiority of the world eject. The social organism provided the evidence closest at hand for something larger than the individual brain. Many monists advanced towards an affirmation of the universal Mind through the intermediate stage of the collective social personality that, like the Shade of the Earth, 'may feel the throes of war and famine' (Romanes 51).

To move from this collective to a cosmic consciousness meant thinking in terms of the relation between the parts and the whole. In a letter to Caleb Saleeby, Hardy defended the idea of freedom in *The Dynasts* on the grounds that the whole cannot be totally present in and therefore cannot completely govern any given part: 'The nature of the determinism embraced in the theory is that of a *Collective* Will; so that there is a proportion of the total will in each part of the whole, and each part has therefore, in strictness, *some* freedom' (*Letters* 5:69). As Ormond says, 'The many has its rights' (525).[15] It was only in the most extreme forms of absolute monism that 'the world is no collection, but one great all-inclusive fact ... represented as an absolute mind that makes the partial facts by thinking them' (James, *Pluralistic* 36). Sometimes the Years thinks in exactly this way, even when he speaks of a conjunctive Will in which the parts constitute the whole. Watching the massacre at Borodino, he sees

A Will that wills above the will of each,
Yet but the will of all conjunctively;
A fabric of excitement, web of rage,
That permeates as one stuff the weltering whole.   (467; 3.1.5)

His emphasis on the web of collective rage illustrates the 'tendency of communities to be more completely under the control of impulse than are individuals' (Ormond 316). The one Will may mean the conjunction of many wills; the result is still something above the will of each.

Monism brought the notion that parts and whole are only two names for the same thing under close scrutiny. Romanes finds that social phenomena 'cannot always be explained by regarding them as the sum of the thoughts and actions of its constituent individuals' (52). 'There is thus,' James insists, 'something new in the collective consciousness' (*Pluralistic* 188). The Pities believe that this something new can be insight rather than rage: 'The pale pathetic peoples still plod on / Through hoodwinkings to light!' (559; 3.4.4). Although 'The world-movements transcend and defy the ideals and guidance of all human agents' (Ormond 329), they are not simply the blind human welterings that the Years finds in Europe's madding movement (264; 2.2.3). James believes 'that new qualities as well as unperceived relations accrue from the collective form. It is thus superior to the distributive form' (*Pluralistic* 173). Romanes sees 'clear indications of the great fact that the high order of complexity which has been reached by the social organism *is* accompanied by evidence of something which we may least dimly define as resembling subjectivity' (51). In pessimistic thought, the possibility of a general consciousness became the salvation of the future. Hartmann dismisses Schopenhauer's outdated asceticism and all endeavour after individual negation of will, stressing instead 'the collective *inner spiritual* evolution of humanity.' Although 'only the UNCONSCIOUS for ever rules' (2:10, 243), Its redemption depends on the conscious and collective will of humanity.

The politics of monism changed as the evolution of the many unsettled the rule of the One. Whereas Schopenhauer prefers monarchies to republics as the form of government natural to man (see 'Human Nature' 48), Hartmann advocates a 'right mean between democratic anarchy and centralized autocracy' (3:276). In Germany at the close of the nineteenth century, monism left a choice between democratic and aristocratic constitutions (see Haeckel, *Riddle* 8–9). As we might expect, monists elsewhere saw the democratic implications of an Immanent Will. James connects the rise of pantheism with science and politics:

> The vaster vistas which scientific evolutionism has opened, and the rising tide of social democratic ideals, have changed the type of our imagination, and the older monarchical theism is obsolete or obsolescent. The place of the divine in the world must be more organic and intimate. (*Pluralistic* 30)

When God becomes immanent in everything, the result is a 'democratic philosophy' (Symonds 245). High thinking now went with plain perception. Monists such as Ritchie and Haldane, himself a member of

Parliament, address the intuitions of the 'plain man' (Ritchie 95; Haldane 1:241) with respect. Thought was conceived in democratic terms, including the new equality between reason and emotion. Maudsley compares the workings of the brain to a council or parliament: 'while one member speaks the rest are silent.' This interior 'confederation of organs' (77) has its ideal equivalent in a 'Federation of the World' (Fiske 2:228). Pessimists and optimists agreed that historical progress depends on the 'evolution of the living sentiment of human solidarity' (Maudsley 313).

Monists did not stop at a personification of humanity and 'the relative Religion animated by the Positive Spirit' (Comte 3:355). Instead of one world movement they found a plurality of social forces. Moreover, 'it is the exceptional social movement that is altogether, or even in the main, the result of prevision and purpose' (Ormond 315). Hardy, who once remarked that 'I am not a Positivist' (*Letters* 3:53), reached a similar impasse:

> You may call the whole human race a single *ego* if you like; and in that view a man's consciousness may be said to pervade the world; but nothing is gained. Each is, to all knowledge, limited to his own frame. (*Letters* 1:262)

Some 'old notes written before "The Dynasts"' reveal that he had considered another substitute for God rather than the Immanent Will: 'We – the People = Humanity – a collective personality ... The intelligence of this collective personality Humanity is pervasive, ubiquitous, like that of God' but what it witnesses, as do the Spirits, is '"our" getting into a rage for "we" knew not what' (*Personal Notebooks* 58, 59). Something was gained from thinking about this kind of collective consciousness but, unlike his friend McTaggart, Hardy did not get 'rid of the difficulty of minds within a Mind by frankly admitting that the universal Mind is only a name for the organised society of individual minds' (Rashdall, Review of *Stage the First* 528–9; Hardy, *Literary* 2:167). The model or analogy of a social eject, with its own probability, led on to the possibility of transcending the limitations of a world ego restricted to humanity. For Ormond, 'The final metaphysical implication of sociology seems to point to an eternal consciousness in which the world-movements as a whole are conceived and purposively directed to a unitary end' (332).

James calls this consciousness, in a phrase that Hardy recorded, the

superhuman consciousness (*Pluralistic* 310; *Literary* 2:201). Many thinkers felt with him that 'the drift of all the evidence we have seems ... to
sway us very strongly towards the belief in some form of superhuman
life which we may, unknown to ourselves, be co-conscious' (309).[16] The
evidence provided some degree of probability and the arguments were
at least plausible, which was all Hardy finally asked of the philosophic
basis for *The Dynasts*: 'whether it were true or false, little affected his
object, which was a poetical one wherein nothing more was necessary
than that the theory should be plausible' (*Life* 343).

For a more confident tone, such as the Years often displays, than the
'seems' and 'may' of provisional conclusions, Hardy had to turn to
speculative or absolute idealism. To Symonds, 'the venerable conception of Spirit immanent in the Universe has acquired a fuller certainty
... [a] foundation of probability' (289), from the discoveries of physical
science. Hartmann's epistemology, combining the inductive results
of science with insights mystically gained, allows him to speak with
even more certainty. The world process is purposive, guided by the
'inweaving' of the '*immanent* God' (2:26, 27) whose 'mode of thinking
is, in truth, *above* consciousness.' Negatively defined, the cosmic mind
'is unconscious, vaguely but positively defined superconscious' (2:247,
258).

It was easier for theologians to accept an Idealism that made consciousness central to the truth of the Absolute. Walker could look for
support from philosophy as well as science because 'Modern Idealism
affirms that there must be a Universal Consciousness in order to give
meaning to the Universe beyond ourselves' (30). Bradley, for example,
argues that 'Every element of the universe, sensation, feeling, thought
and will, must be included within one comprehensive sentience.' Sentience was reassuring, but in the consummation of Bradley's 'super-
personal' (140, 471) Absolute, 'thought has certainly been so transformed, that to go on calling it thought seems indefensible.' It is
beyond the divisions of self-consciousness and beyond the ideal God
of religion. The way the Absolute 'stands above, and not below, its
internal distinctions' (152, 472) sounds much like the way Hartmann's
'God in his absolute intuition is raised far above all reflection' (2:263).
With Haldane, however, Hegelianism is a religion in which 'God is ...
at all events self-conscious' (Rashdall, Review of *Stage the Second* 411):
'God means Absolute Mind conscious of itself as completely realising
the highest ends' (Haldane 2:117).

Faced with such a plurality of monistic voices, Hardy wondered with William James in *The Meaning of Truth*, 'Whose is *the* true idea of the Absolute' (Hardy, *Literary* 2:241)? In the era itself he heard 'the competing claims of agnostic naturalism and a speculative idealism' ('Professor' 171; Hardy, *Literary* 2:165) but in *The Dynasts* he does more than approximate voices that were deaf to one another or in opposition. When the Spirit of the Years speaks, we hear some unsuspected affinities. The arrogance of naturalism and the confidence of absolute idealism both fall within his character zone, as do their appraisals of the ethical status of nature and the Absolute respectively. Hardy knew from science that 'nature is *unmoral*' (*Letters* 3:231) but he also suspected, as he wrote to the Hegelian philosopher McTaggart, that in a way the Absolute is not much different: 'As a mere empiricist I have the common-place feeling that the Timeless Reality knows no difference between what we call good and what we call evil' (*Letters* 3:329). Indeed, Bradley's perfect Absolute knows no such relative distinction: 'in relation to the Absolute, there is nothing either bad or good.' But 'the real problem,' Bradley admits, 'is to show how appearance and evil ... are compatible with the Absolute' (363, 143).

Hardy confronted this same problem while apparently considering the question of *The Dynasts* in 1886:

> May. Reading in the British Museum. Have been thinking over the dictum of Hegel – that the real is the rational and the rational the real – that real pain is compatible with a formal pleasure – that the idea is all, etc. But it doesn't help much. These venerable philosophers seem to start wrong; they cannot get away from a prepossession that the world must somehow have been made to be a comfortable place for man. If I remember it was Comte who said that metaphysics was a mere sorry attempt to reconcile theology and physics. (*Life* 185)

Whatever Hardy may have been reading in the British Museum, his evaluation does not reflect any first-hand encounter with Hegel's Absolute Idealism. Hidden within Hardy's own direct words, and helping to form the axiological position of the passage above, are phrases from an *Encyclopaedia Britannica* article on pessimism. Hardy read how 'The double-faced dictum of Hegel, that the real is the rational and the rational the real, was often understood to justify the principle that, whatever is, is right' (687). It was, however, the antithesis of this principle that Hardy copied into his 'Literary Notes I': 'the central principle of pessimism asserts that in the order of nature, i.e., so long as the will to live remains unbroken, happiness in the true sense is impossible. Life as life necessarily involves misery' (*Literary* 1:203). The two great precursors of monism thus stand in a relation of pure opposition: nineteenth-century optimism derives from Hegel, 'for in idealism we find the true home of optimism'; nineteenth-century pessimism starts with Schopenhauer who 'dethroned reason.' Whereas 'real pain is compatible with a formal pleasure' ('Pessimism' 687) in Hegel's system of thought, pleasure is only the negation of pain in Schopenhauer's. The article does not attempt to mediate these two extremes but does make pessimism sound more in tune with the ongoing thought of the world. We can perhaps see why Hardy makes Hegel sound outdated by identifying him with the comfortable prepossessions of venerable philosophers. In terms of the encyclopedia article's historical perspective, pessimism, while far earlier than optimism as a mood, is much more recent as a philosophy. Hegel represents merely a return to idealism with its optimistic interpretations; Schopenhauer and Hartmann give theoretical voice to the natural and instinctive pessimism of the race.

The word pessimism appeared only three times in the second edition of *The World as Will and Idea*. It was not until 1866 that pessimism 'began to show itself in books which discuss [Schopenhauer's] views' ('Pessimism' 689). Numerous magazine articles on Schopenhauer appeared throughout the 1870s and in 1883–6 *The World as Will and Idea* was translated into English. Ralph Goodale concludes that by 1879 'every person alive to the developments of the day must have heard of him; and by 1883 an educated man could not think of pessimism without thinking also of Schopenhauer' (242). Hartmann also enjoyed, as E.A. Ross observed at the time, a brilliant success:

> In twenty years Hartmann's 'Philosophy of the Unconscious' has reached its tenth German edition, entered all the great languages of Europe, and called forth a vast literature of its own. Thoroughly in touch with modern culture and gifted with a striking style, Hartmann is to-day, perhaps, the best read philosopher on the continent. (Ross 741)

Hartmann undoubtedly appealed to the pessimistic temper of the age but, as the article on pessimism explains, he also gave the reading public what it wanted to know, 'the metaphysical inferences to be gathered from the recent advances of scientific theory,' and gave them in terms of the most popular literary genre by paying the 'tribute of imitation to the naturalistic tendency and sensationalism of the contemporary novel' ('Pessimism' 689). Like the ship and the iceberg in 'The Convergence of the Twain,' *The Dynasts* and the *Philosophy of the Unconscious* seem, in retrospect, to have been bound on paths coincident. Hardy owned the 1893 edition and, according to J.O. Bailey, had read Hartmann for sure by 1897, the same year he began work on *The Dynasts*. A much deeper convergence underlies this coincidence, however. The Coupland translation of Hartmann appeared in 1884, just two years before Hardy formulated his idea of the novel of the future. In some respects, Hartmann provides a model for the spiritual naturalism of *The Dynasts*. His aim is to create 'an idealistic philosophy beside and above the mechanical cosmic theory of the Sciences of Matter' (1:xxiv). The choice of prepositions is revealing. There is both the novelistic encounter between two opposing philosophical voices that stand beside each other in the world of culture, and the epic desire that Hardy resists to create out of these opposing voices one monologic viewpoint above idealism or naturalism. In 1888, and still thinking about the novel of the future, Hardy wrote that 'A "sensation-novel" is possible in which the sensationalism is ... not physical but psychical' (*Life* 213). Again, Hartmann had preceded him, for in his universe of 'spiritualistic Monism' (3:194) the psychical is always the underlying cause of the physical. He constructs a lurid story of the suffering and pain necessary to bring about a cosmic negation of the Will. Ultimately the naturalism and sensationalism of the novel are transformed into a metaphysical and religious drama that shares the pretensions of men of science 'to frame a world-philosophy within the scope of which all things in heaven and earth shall fall' (Armitage 728).

In the relativist culture at the close of the nineteenth century, pessimism, like optimism, denoted a composite state of mind. Hartmann admits the positivity of pleasure but still gives weight to the misery of the world. Bradley, on the other hand, finds a balance of pleasure over and above pain. For Hardy, too, pessimism was really only a relative term and he insisted on being called a meliorist, not a pessimist (*Letters* 1:262; 5:278). Yet in spite of their 'supercilious regard of hope,' Hardy lists 'Schopenhauer, von Hartmann, and other philosophers ... who have my respect' (*Personal Writings* 58). The thought that pessimism has had its day was comforting but false (*Literary* 2:55). For one thing, the appeal of pessimism, in some ways the end result of the Kantian philosophical scepticism, was made all the more powerful because it continued the Christian emphasis on the ethical value of suffering.

'The truth is,' Hardy remarked, 'that in ethics, Kant, [Schopenhauer] etc. are nearer to Christianity than they are to [Nietzsche]' (*Letters* 5:51). In a striking sentence that Hardy recorded (*Literary* 2:48), Ross also suggests that the transition from Christianity to pessimism is a repetition with difference: 'And so, as the altar lights of the old worship of sorrow grow dim, there arises the legend of a suffering unconscious' (743). The incarnation of Christ finds its equivalent in the immanence of Hartmann's Unconscious, 'a God who descends into our breast and dwells therein' (2:253), but instead of redeeming, It needs redemption from the bondage of finite existence. Turning towards Nirvana was part of a wider movement that Jerome Buckley calls the revolt from reason (185). We can hear this revolt often in Hardy. 'As some philosopher says,' he wrote to Edward Clodd in 1902, 'if nothing at all existed, it would be a completely natural thing; but that the world exists is a fact absolutely logicless and senseless' (*Letters* 3:5). Hartmann agrees: 'I conclude with Schopenhauer from the misery of existence, that the creation owes its first origin to an *irrational* act, i.e., to such an one in which reason has had no part' (3:13).

Pessimism did not constitute the final word to Hardy, but its truth was one he heard suppressed by the counter ideology of optimism when idealism revived as a form of monism. In Bradley's reformulation of Hegel, 'pain, after all, might be compatible with harmony and system' (474). Less cautious, Haldane asserts that 'Evil has no direct relation to God any more than nature has' (2:133). Hardy might well have shared McTaggart's exasperated response to Ormond's view of the cosmic mind: 'how can he [Ormond] deny that God's purposes are not to some extent defeated?' ('Review' 435). James quotes McTaggart in support of his contention that the '*ideally* perfect whole is certainly that whole of which the *parts are also perfect.*' The Absolute 'introduces a speculative "problem of evil" ... and leaves us wondering why the perfection of the absolute should require just such particular hideous forms of life as darken the day for our human imaginations' (*Pluralistic* 123, 117).

The Pities wonder the same about the Absolute when measured by 'A world so ill-contrived' (343; 2.4.7) but their occasional desire for Nirvana arises as much from the dialogic as from the historical context. The Years' replies often leave them in the position of the grieving mother whom Frederic Harrison imagines Spencer consoling with, '"Think on the Unknowable"' (Spencer, 'Last' 832).[17] Confronted or affronted with this kind of (dis)comfort and the inescapable fact of pain, the Pities prefer to think with Schopenhauer that 'our whole existence is something which had better not have been' ('Counsels' 7): 'Better than waking is to sleep' (411; 2.6.4). The Shade of the Earth also sees that 'A juster wisdom his who should have ruled / They [massed mortalities] had not been.' The Years responds, though in a voice tinged with agnostic doubt, that the Will's 'coils / Are, maybe, good as any' (39; 1.1.2). Hartmann argues that this is the best of all possible worlds, but he makes the crucial distinction that 'the *best possibility* of a thing does *not* say anything whatever as to its goodness' (2:362–3).[18] As long as the word good lingers in the Years' attitude towards the cosmic web, Pity persists in asking 'But why any?' (39; 1.1.2).

Pity's question is still backward-looking, to the origin of things, but as all the Spirits gather together in the After Scene Hardy completes the shift from past to future. It may be 'the on-going – i.e., the "becoming" – of the world that produces its sadness' (*Life* 210), but time is the only aspect of appearance that might make God superior in goodness to man. At least the Will becomes indisputably a Mind in the Epilogue. The Years does not correct Pity's summation of his position, 'Thou arguest still the Inadvertent Mind' (703). The Years' static argument doubles his view of the unchanging Absolute. Like Ritchie or Bradley, he cannot admit the 'conception of the Absolute as Becoming' (Ritchie 228). By asking 'shall blankness be for aye?' (703), Pity assumes the absolute reality of time and change. The important question for both Spirits, as for McTaggart, 'is not whether there is a God, but what sort of nature he, or it, possesses' (*Dogmas* 187).

Hardy noticed that 'Fifty meanings attach to the word "God" nowadays.' Like Hartmann, he speculated on 'a fundamental ultimate Wisdom at the back of things' (*Life* 406, 398) but without denying that the world, to alter Schopenhauer, seems 'like a half-expressed, an ill-expressed idea.' In a conversation with William Archer in 1901, Hardy, commenting on the incompleteness of alleged manifestations of a spirit world, explained how the problem of evil is inextricably tied to the limitations of God:

> Do you know Hartmann's Philosophy of the Unconscious? It suggested to me what seems like a workable theory of the great problem of the origin of evil, – though this, of course, is not Hartmann's own theory, – that there may be a consciousness infinitely far off at the other end of the chain of phenomena, always striving to express itself, and always baffled and blundering, just as the spirits seem to be. (Archer 316)

In Hardy's thinking, time is stretched out in terms of space; it becomes, in effect, dominated by space. With God infinitely far off, his striving in time is only doomed to repeat the first thing, the origin of evil. God has good intentions but remains the '*Invariable Antecedent*' (*Life* 235; emphasis added), trapped in the absolute past, 'always baffled and blundering.'

In the *Life* we are told that 'This idea of a limited God of goodness, often dwelt on by Hardy, was expounded ably and at length in McTaggart's *Some Dogmas of Religion* [1906] ..., and led to a friendship which ended only with the latter's death' (317). Hardy recorded (*Literary* 2:206) McTaggart's definition, 'By God I mean a being who is personal, supreme, and good.' The rest of the paragraph that Hardy omits makes clear, however, that these are relative attributes. In McTaggart's doctrine of non-omnipotence, God 'has that awareness of his own existence which I have of my own existence' but he is 'more powerful than any other being' and 'of such a nature that he would be rightly judged to be more good than evil' (186).

McTaggart, Ward, James, Höffding: the last monists Hardy read all agree that 'if we are to use the term Absolute for the Whole, God is not to be identified with the Absolute' ('Pluralism and Theism' 21). Like Hartmann, they all make an imperfect God the postulate of the religious consciousness. McTaggart thinks that the world must be a Unity but there is no Mind that knows the whole. Hardy also read how 'Absolutism is as antipathetic to Professor Ward as it was to William James, whose phrase the "block-universe" he repeatedly uses to characterize and condemn the standpoint.' Ward tries to preserve the monistic standpoint by making the limitation of God a self-limitation and therefore 'not to be identified with the pluralistic idea of "a finite God"' ('Pluralism and Theism' 21). The latter idea was, of course, J.S. Mill's and one that James renewed while still allowing for the possibility of the Absolute. If the absolute exist, James says, 'then the absolute is only the wider cosmic whole of which our God is but the most ideal portion.' The advantage is that by 'having an environment, being in time, and working out a history just like ourselves, he [God] escapes from the foreignness from all that is human, of the static timeless perfect absolute' (*Pluralistic* 125, 318).

The answer to the Spirit Ironic's question, 'What is [the Will's] shape? Man's counterfeit?' (416; 2.6.5), may, after all, be yes. In determining the Will's shape, the Years chooses two parts of the human anatomy to oppress the other Spirits. One might be called the idealist's nightmare in which man becomes the unconscious and automatic thoughts of a cosmic brain or mind. The other might be called naturalism's nightmare in which man is reduced to something less than a hand: 'So the Will heaves through Space, and moulds the times / With mortals for Its fingers!' (265; 2.2.3). To be either 'the puppets of Spirit' or 'the puppets of Matter' (Walker 375) inspires fear but this can be overcome by lending a bodily substance to nature and the cosmos. Bakhtin explains that in the grotesque mode of representation, the body 'can merge with various natural phenomena, with mountains, rivers, seas, islands, and continents. It can fill the entire universe' (*Rabelais* 318).

While the Years goes no further than to treat the Will occasionally as a cosmic body, the narrator implies that Europe has a human shape. One reviewer had no doubts about the identity of the figure and even hinted at the tradition of grotesque realism to which the description belongs: 'This presentation of Europe as a huge man and the human beings as a sort of blood-corpuscles in which the pulsing of the Immanent Will is visible has certainly originality and a touch of the gruesome poetic' ('Mr. Hardy's' 432). The effect of the narrator's impression is to weaken the limits between man and nature: 'The nether sky opens, and Europe is disclosed as a prone and emaciated figure, the Alps shaping like a backbone, and the branching mountain-chains like ribs, the peninsular plateau of Spain forming a head.' There is the additional human touch of clothing: the broad and lengthy lowlands that stretch from the North of France and across Russia look like a grey-green garment (Fore Scene 27). The description is repeated in the After Scene but now 'The lowlands look like a grey-green garment half-thrown off, and the sea around like a disturbed bed on which the figure lies' (702). The grotesque body has become ambivalent, its clothes no longer adequate. On the negative side, it is prone in position and emaciated in shape; on the positive side, it is a body still in the act of becoming. The garment might also be a bed-covering and since it is half-thrown off the sleeper might be about to awake. Something has disturbed the sleeper as well as his bed, now partly uncovered, and that something may well be suffering. When Hardy thought in melioristic terms, he reached the idea of a collective consciousness through the physical image of the body:

Altruism, or The Golden Rule, or whatever 'Love Your Neighbour as Yourself' may be called, will ultimately be brought about I think by the pain we see in others reacting on ourselves, as if we and they were a part of one body. Mankind, in fact, may be, and possibly will be, viewed as members of one corporeal frame. (*Life* 235)

In so far as the grotesque body represents the Will, it helps transform the timeless Absolute into a chronotope, a spatial image marked by time and change and one that (pre)figures the Pities' hope of the awakening Will. The later monists took the static spatial metaphors of the Absolute's immanent and transcendent relation to its parts and made God the most ideal changing part of the unknown whole. The Pities, in turn, take the Years' Will and imagine a future in which the whole gradually evolves into two fully conscious areas, the human and the superhuman(e). God will not be fully God, nor man wholly man, until this process is complete, perhaps not until 'far-ranged aions past all fathoming / Shall have swung by, and stand as backward years' (After Scene 703). It is as if the Pities activate Romanes's monistic metaphor of concentric circles. The fact of individual consciousness and worth centres a circle of inferred human subjectivities that might become a collective consciousness, but this circle falls within the largest one of the cosmic mind whose higher psychical value might one day be ethical. Fechner's special thought that appealed to James helps explain the relationship between one circle of consciousness and another: 'the more inclusive forms of consciousness are in part *constituted* by the more limited forms. Not that they are the mere sum of more limited forms' (*Pluralistic* 168).

Reading *The Dynasts* as by and large a poetic version of Hartmann's ideas, J.O. Bailey says 'the idea that the Unconscious may develop consciousness in itself as a whole is suggested all through the *Philosophy of the Unconscious*.' Oddly enough, the only point Hardy escapes from the net of Hartmann's supposed influence is at the end of *The Dynasts*: 'In Hardy's concept, the Mind grows conscious indeed, but only as informed by Its conscious parts – not apart from these parcels of Itself' (Bailey 157, 179).[19] What Bailey offers is a double misreading. Hartmann believes that 'the will itself can *never* become conscious, because it can never contradict itself' (2:96) and thus, as T.R. Dale rightly concludes, 'Hardy's presentation of an unconscious will gradually becoming conscious is ... directly and essentially opposed to von Hartmann's teaching' (101).

What happens in the Overworld also characterizes *The Philosophy of the Unconscious* precisely because Hartmann makes change and becoming necessary for the redemption of the world-process. In his vision of the future, the argument grows more tentative as he speculates on how some finite parts might outweigh the Absolute whole. First he has to hope that 'one day the major part of the actual volition or of the functioning Unconscious Spirit may be manifested in humanity,'

> for only when the negative part of volition in humanity outweighs the sum of all the rest of the will objectifying itself in the organic and inorganic world, only then can the human negation of will annihilate *the whole actual volition of the world without residuum*, and cause the whole kosmos to disappear at a stroke by withdrawal of the volition, which alone gave it existence. (3:135–6)

The difficulty of achieving the 'collective feeling in every individual' leads to a qualification. Only a part of humanity needs to be filled with the necessary pessimistic consciousness, 'provided that the spirit that is manifested in it be the larger half of the active spirit of the universe' (3:137, 139). In his 'Literary Notes II,' Hardy paraphrased Hartmann's idea of 'The God,' then added his own comment on how there is no conclusive conclusion:

> It appears that the author does not commit himself absolutely to this conclusion; asserting that, [should] any believe in a future happiness of the world by evolution etc. ([which] he has called the [third] stage of illusion) the principles remain just as valid for those thinkers, since the final goal of the world-development may be conceived positively or negatively. (*Literary* 2:113)

In Hardy's After Scene, the Will Itself is novelized, caught up in the process of 'becoming,' the very word Hardy emphasized to explain the one idea he added to the dialogue of the era: 'I think the view of the unconscious force as gradually *becoming* conscious: i.e. that consciousness is creeping further and further back towards the origin of force, had never (so far as I know) been advanced before The Dynasts appeared' (*Letters* 5:70). Here the spatial movement of a slow crawl combines with a paradoxical temporal movement. While the future unfolds, consciousness creeps back towards the origin of force, as if one day it will arrive at a new start that should have been the old beginning. Since 'the Unconscious Will of the Universe is growing aware of Itself,' the cosmic mind will be self-conscious, not just super-conscious in the reflectionless way of Hartmann's All-One. Hardy arrived at this idea by reflecting on the probable implications of the monistic metaphor of the parts and the whole:

> What has already taken place in fractions of the Whole (i.e. so much of the world as has become conscious) is likely to take place in the Mass; and there being no Will outside the Mass – that is, the Universe – the whole Will becomes conscious thereby; and ultimately, it is to be hoped, sympathetic. (*Letters* 3:255)

Hardy does not, of course, express this idea directly in *The Dynasts*: it arises out of a specific context of dialogic relations in which change and becoming catch the Spirits before they do the Will. In the Fore Scene, the Shade of the Earth asks Pity, 'And who, then, Cordial One, / Wouldst substitute for this Intractable?' (23). In the After Scene, the Spirit of the Years asks the same question: 'What wouldst have hoped and had the Will to be?' (703). While he safely places the subjunctive mood in the past tense, the Years indicates an openness to change by finally asking a question. For their part, the Semichorus of the Pities begin their reply in an old form of discourse, the hymn, suited to the traditional theistic idea of the moral ruler of the universe. The opening of their Chorus is based on the Magnificat and a traditional trust in Providence (see Pinion, *Commentary* 266), the Pities speaking of the past, indeed even the Years' confessed past, as if it were the present they still want. The peculiar tense shifts foreground the importance of time. The thought of 'times ... when the mortal moan / Seems unascending to Thy throne' (703) and of 'Why suffering sobs to Thee in vain' pushes their discourse out of the Christian past towards the theology of the future. The Pities' new hope is commensurate with pure agnosticism as Romanes understands it: 'We hold that [the Will's] unscanted scope / Affords a food for final Hope' (704). Since 'Men gained cognition with the flux of time / ... wherefore not the Force informing them' (703)? The effect on the Years of the Pities' hymn to a 'Wellwiller' whose 'means the End shall justify' (704) is startling:

> Something of difference animates your quiring,
> O half-convinced Compassionates and fond,
> From chords consistent with our spectacle!
> You almost charm my long philosophy

Out of my strong-built thought, and bear me back
To when I thanksgave thus ... Ay, start not, Shades;
In the Foregone I knew what dreaming was,
And could let raptures rule! But not so now.
Yea, I psalmed thus and thus ... But not so now!   (705)

The hesitation indicated by the ellipses and the intensified convincing
tone in the repetition of 'but not so now' indicate that the Years is only
half-convinced himself. The Years sounds like a mentor, but he has
himself as well as the other Spirits to convince. His external voice, like
Napoleon's 'loud career' (61; 1.1.6), is a rejoinder from his own interior
speech, addressed to himself in a persuasive accent. The verbs thanksgave and psalmed point to a Christian context for the Years' past and
suggest that the shadow of religion persists for him, as it did for many
agnostics. In his biographical sketch of Clifford, Mallock makes the
point that the emotions he expresses about the nobleness of humanity
'are not the result of his scientific observations or of his later experiences, but they are the echo or the survival of emotions that had been
ingrained in him at his mother's knee or under the arches of Exeter
Cathedral' (262). The difference is that the Years is not satisfied with a
religion of humanity. His nostalgia is for the Absolute.

In the Fore Scene the Year's opposition to any blessed Hope is more
than a matter of his dislike for an unfinished universe. The Spirit of
the Pities speaks as if the Will were conscious and consequently the
Years does not find it meet to have the problem of waking posed in
terms of what might focus a distracted or averted Mind. In the After
Scene, the Spirit Ironic's reply, 'I know / 'Tis handsome of our Pities
so to sing / The praises of the dreaming, dark, dumb, Thing' (705)
goes unanswered for the very reason that the Pities construct their
new idea of waking out of the Years' monism. The mechanistic universe still exists in the 'rhythmic roll' of the 'systemed suns' (704).
There is still Spencer's universal 'rhythm of evolution and dissolution'
(*Autobiography* 1:554), the 'vast order of cosmic involutions, evolu-
tions, and dissolutions' (Maudsley 140) that make all human events
seem so small to Maudsley. In their hymn, the two Semichoruses of
the Pities reluctantly let go of the link between this cosmic order and a
personal God. The mortal fingers of the Years' cosmic body belong to
a 'Thee'; the stars 'ride radiantly' only to be 'darkened by Thy Master-
hand!' When their song reaches its climax of 'Exaltant adoration,' God
becomes a strange other, 'The Alone, through Whom all living live, /

The Alone, in whom all dying die' (704). The closing speeches of the Pities then effect one final transformation: the It of agnosticism displaces the Thee of theism who now inhabits the future. At the same time, mechanism is given the kind of idealistic reinterpretation that spiritual monists gave it. By viewing mind, in the sense of consciousness, as a specific emergent of the evolutionary process, the Years prepares the way for the Pities to see this emergence monistically as a characteristic of the whole. Bradley's criticism of naturalism applies equally well to the Years: 'Thus to assert that, in the history of the Universe at large, matter came before mind, is to place development and succession within the Absolute' (252). It is precisely this idea of development that the Pities seize upon to see the whole universe as a striving towards deity.

Yet Hardy does not set up a hierarchy of Intelligences to overthrow it for a new one, as Ward does in constructing an either/or argument to replace a neutral with a spiritualistic monism. The dialogue of the Spirits ends with prediction, not prophecy, and with a vision of the future that sounds more like Höffding's 'Critical Monism' (*Problems* 136; Hardy, *Literary* 2:385) than the monism of science or of Absolute Idealism. The Chorus of the Pities hears that future as if it were already part of the present, inarticulate sounds gaining a voice that turns the epilogue into a new prologue:

> But – a stirring thrills the air
> Like to sounds of joyance there
>   That the rages
>   Of the ages
> Shall be cancelled, and deliverance offered from the darts that were,
> Consciousness the Will informing, till It fashion all things fair!   (707)

There is more here than the 'forlorn hope of the irrational Pities' (Brennecke 144). In the first place, as Maudsley admits, 'it is not quite foolish to suppose that there are deep *thrills* of feeling in man's being which have a more apocalyptic cosmic meaning than the achievements of his conscious thoughts' (29; my emphasis). More importantly, the Pities' lines reflect the common view that monism 'is the only theory of things which can receive the sanction of science on the one hand and of feelings on the other' (Romanes 58). Monism allows Symonds, for example, to turn his speculative thought into emotional utterance in verses that celebrate a God 'which permeates the living whole, / Alike in sentient clay and senseless clod' (406).

In the Pities' new design, good as well as beautiful, consciousness informs the Will and the Will consciousness in an interplay that crosses the boundary, 'ever ... the stronghold of Agnosticism' (Ward 2:275), between appearance, the Years' 'weird phantasma' (65; 1.1.6) of nature and history, and his unchanging Absolute. To the Pities, such an absolutely unchangeable ground of continuous growth is unthinkable. Their vision of God asserts the reality of time. The Unknowable may be in the 'grip of becoming' (Höffding, *Philosophy* 88), struggling, like the religious consciousness itself, 'into more continuous and better shape' (James, Introduction to Höffding's *Problems* xiii; Hardy, *Literary* 2:223).

Bakhtin offers the paradoxical insight, useful in considering the way *The Dynasts* ends, that the closed world of the epic can remain incomplete, while the absence of internal conclusiveness increases the need for a formal and external ending in the novel. Given his epic orientation towards the absolute past, the Spirit of the Years remains indifferent towards endings and new beginnings: now is the same as evermore and the whole cosmic web is repeated in each strand such as the Napoleonic wars. Nevertheless, events lose the finished quality essential to the world of the epic (see chapter 7) and we do get an external ending, with Napoleon defeated and the Spirits offering their last comments on the Will. Their dialogue, ending as it does with a glimpse of a possible new future, leaves us in the state of not knowing characteristic of the novel. The contact between the Spirits and the inconclusive context of monism helps make a novelistic world where 'there is no first word ..., and the final word has not yet been spoken' (Bakhtin, *Dialogic* 30).

Four

Poetry and Prose

We have seen that very little of the dialogue about the Will can fairly be called 'Hardy's home-made theology' (Brooks 295) or 'an odd piece of home-made metaphysic' (Stewart 35). Instead of being a 'private language' (Hynes, *Pattern* 164), much of the 'esoteric vocabulary' (Carpenter 192) of the Spirits, 'a language full of strange words and abstractions' (Halliday 162), belongs to the thinking world. We might say that the Overworld constitutes a new home for monistic thought, but the house itself remains populated, almost over-populated, by the voices of others. Why then have critics persisted in treating its dialogue as a unitary language even when they recognize that it does not promote any single world view? The answer is simple enough: whatever Hardy had to say or intended to say, his Spirits converse in 'the language of poetry' (Orel, *Thomas* 18).

It is one thing to bracket the way the Spirits Ironic and Sinister increasingly and openly speak in prose, but the larger stylistic project cannot ignore R.J. White's comment that at least one-third of the poem is in prose. This has the look of calling attention to something important. We notice, however, that *The Dynasts* remains a poem and precisely for the reason that the other two-thirds is in poetry. This way of counting the prose only ensures that it can never really count, even when we 'remember that some of the best lines ... are in prose' (Wright 94). We also cannot ignore that since so much of *The Dynasts* is in blank verse, 'it stands or falls, as poetry' (Gittings 110). Some of the lyrics and 'weird linguistic gargoyles' (Hawkins 182) of the Phantoms may be worthy of praise, but from the early reviews on most critics have found the blank verse stiff and cumbersome. They end up wishing for another *Dynasts*: '[George] Meredith's comment that the work would have been "more effective in prose" is damaging but not unfair' (Page 179).

The reason the blank verse does not work for so many readers has a great deal to do with the way it seems to move on the borderline between poetry and prose. The prosaic verse at once suggests that Hardy was more at home in prose and definitely not at home in the form of verse common to the epic and the drama. Evelyn Hardy reaches this conclusion by way of the rough draft of Part Third, acts 1 to 4. The discovery that Hardy initially set down his thoughts in prose shows that he was not instinctively at ease in blank verse. Evelyn Hardy fails to mention, however, that even the lyrics of the rough draft are the result of Hardy reworking prose passages. Unless we assume, as Meredith did, that Hardy felt uncomfortable in any kind of verse, we may consider the possibility that Hardy's poetry owes more to prose than could simply be erased through conversion. It is hardly surprising that a novel created out of numerous prose genres contains 'many kinds of poetry and prose which express a world of multiple reality' (Brooks 297). Instead of exploring this context, including the generic dialogue between verse and prose, critics have viewed *The Dynasts* as a kind of awkward half-way house, the blank verse of the Persons of the drama tied too closely to historical records, the poetry of the Spirits too dependent on the technical vocabulary of monism. It is as if *The Dynasts* never successfully emerged as a poetic genre from the prose works which inform so many of its speeches: from historical, philosophical, theological, and scientific writings, from reviews and speculative essays, and, as the signpost 'W&P' (for Tolstoy's *War and Peace*) left standing in the rough draft indicates, from the novel as well.

All prose or pure poetry: the case against Hardy's language often comes down to his mixed materials, especially 'the lengthy passages of ill-disguised prose and only partially versified transcription' (Orel, 'What' 123). We are told that 'a good deal of Hardy's verse ... is not verse at all but spoilt prose' (White 124). The wooden blank verse never achieves the privileged status of poetry and has lost the vitality of the prose from which it emerged. In many evaluations, poetry and prose switch places in a damaging way, the verse 'stiffly prosaic' (Page 179), the prose 'far more poetic than the poetry, far more dramatic than the drama' (Gittings 114). If the real heart of the epic can be found only in the stage directions and dumb shows, it is difficult to see how *The Dynasts* 'triumphs over its faults' (Orel, 'What' 123) of language. We are nearing the final solution and absurdity of concluding, as E.A. Horsman does, that 'the poem succeeds in spite of its language rather than because of it' (16).

Clearly any defence of *The Dynasts'* language has to get clear of the kind of logic that construes the relation between poetry and prose only in quantitative or qualitative terms. William Rutland concedes that the 'rough blank verse ... cannot be called poetry,' only to assert that 'it was never meant to be' (321). 'Written as prose,' he argues, '[*The Dynasts*] would cease to give the illusion of a play' (322). The question remains, however, why Hardy gives so many important prose lines to dynasts and Spirits. As we shall see, his prose may be easy to appreciate on its own but has proved difficult to explain in relation to the verse.

Critics who followed Rutland took the important step of bringing language, now conceived as a 'set of contrasting speech-conventions' (Southerington 179), back into the sphere of thought. Beginning with Samuel Hynes (1963) and continuing with Jean Brooks and F.R. Southerington (1971), different styles of diction become different levels of awareness in an epistemological hierarchy. Hynes discovers two groups of speakers with two corresponding kinds of language: 'the Spirits of the Overworld employ poetic diction, while humanity speaks the language of common speech' (*Pattern* 164). The distance between the 'blind leaders of humanity' and the 'lofty vision of the Overworld' (166, 167) generates and justifies the contrast between the 'flat, unvarying speech' of the dynasts and the 'rich and various language' (166) of the Spirits. Blinded by his own pattern, Hynes makes metaphor the valorized way of knowing and its relational, as opposed to merely descriptive, knowledge the exclusive property of the omniscient Overworld. Far below the ideal consciousness of the Spirits, 'Men speak without metaphor' and, so we are told, without imagery as well, about a world they 'cannot know' (166).

Hynes introduces one potentially disruptive feature into his meticulous binary pattern. In passing, he finds it necessary to subdivide the language of common speech into the formal standard English of the dynasts and the more colloquial English of the common people. In Brooks and Southerington these two relative varieties separate into distinct styles of speech in a tripartite view of language in *The Dynasts*. Since the Spirit-language continues to be ranked above the blank verse of the dynasts, we might ask where the prose of the commoners finds its place if 'Knowledge, or the lack of it, is often the key to changes of style in *The Dynasts*' (Southerington 183). Brooks is silent on this matter but clearly admires the way 'The humble ranks speak in the humorous half-poetic prose of the novels' (297). At the start of his analysis, Southerington goes further by giving this group of speakers a higher status than the dynasts before the Will. The dynastic leaders are almost completely subject to the Will; even their monotonous way of speaking is inevitable. The only true characters are the rustic and anonymous figures who 'speak a racy, convincing prose, full of vigour, and often with humour.' In its freedom and conviction, this 'language of equilibrium' (179) seems poised somewhere between the dynastic style and the visionary style of the Spirits.

It turns out, however, that Southerington's main agenda of countering deterministic/pessimistic readings of *The Dynasts* is at odds with the idea of a speech hierarchy borrowed from Hynes. We hear this difficulty most clearly when knowledge displaces freedom as the measure of speech value: 'Broadly speaking, we might say that prose ... is a symbol of ignorance – in the case of the rustics it might even be blissful ignorance – verse is a symbol of knowledge, and metaphorical verse a symbol of knowledge with added perception' (183). The hesitation and approximation are there for good reason. The only way ignorance and freedom can converge in prose is to argue that ignorance is not so much bliss but a kind of freedom. Thus when Wellington speaks in prose in the first half of the scene following the battle of the Nivelle (3.3.6), he 'momentarily ceases to be a part of the Will, and is in a position to make an unfettered – because uninformed – decision.' While there can be no exit from the Spirit of the Years' Will, often described, we recall, in metaphorical verse, characters step in and out of Southerington's Will in the most surprising ways. When Wellington knows why the French fought so poorly, he speaks with purpose and in verse, his 'pledge to the Will bringing him back into his normal dynastic style' (184) and presumably making him a puppet again. The fetters of knowledge and the freedom of ignorance make knowledge and freedom incompatible, even though both are necessary for the evolution of consciousness. The downfall of Napoleon depends on freedom from the unconscious Will and on mature knowledge overtaking the popular consciousness. As the peoples' knowledge develops, we would expect to hear some 'elevations into verse' in their speech; instead we find 'sudden lapses into prose' (183) by the dynasts. Unable to demonstrate that these were carefully planned, Southerington decides that 'How far Hardy intended shifts of diction to illustrate his meaning is an open question, but not a particularly fruitful one' (186).

The shift from prose to poetry in the scene at Wellington's quarters has nothing to do with knowledge. What Wellington hears from the French officers during the meal only 'bears out / What I but lately said' (535; 3.3.6). We expect to hear prose voices as 'wine is passed freely, and both French and English officers become talkative and merry' but the prisoners gloomily report the disaster at Leipzig in the official terms of the Imperial *Gazette*. Blank verse suits minds not yet freed from the memory of past glory. The French officers feel that 'France's fame / Is fouled' and recall scenes of once valiant victory and a bridge that 'had rung so oft / To our victorious feet!' (534, 535, 536; 3.3.6).

The very attempt to save *The Dynasts* from stylistic evaluations in which the prose, though quantitatively inferior, fares much better than the poetry produces functional evaluations in which poetry is symbolically or metaphorically superior to prose. Placed at the bottom of the hierarchy of seeing, the prose in turn unsettles the whole ladder of speech reaching from world to Overworld. Unruly and intrusive, prose links the highest speakers, who sometimes use it, to the lowest, who almost always use it, and both groups to the narrator of the stage descriptions who could scarcely be called ignorant.

Not surprisingly, it is only when this narrator comes to the forefront of interpretation that the prose achieves a visionary stature that approaches its stylistic importance as good writing. Susan Dean (1977) continues the emphasis on poetic vision in *The Dynasts* but in a way that allows her to change the position of prose from a form of speech that scenes and characters drop or lapse into, to a type of vision on the edge, side, or circumference of what she still considers to be a poem. Although the narrator's prose contributes to all four perspectives in Hardy's poetic vision, the one she calls (and devotes a whole chapter to) the periphery of vision finds its full expression only in prose, especially the stage directions 'where most of the peripheral phenomena are presented' (283). These phenomena also include the marginal characters who speak in prose and who, as a collective and humourous voice, have more than a marginal importance.

Dean finds freedom exactly where Southerington does, for the same reasons, and at the same price of dispensing with Hardy's avowed monism. The freedom that sets off the prose speakers from the dynasts begins as a relative difference – 'Life does have degrees of freedom' – and ends as an absolute distinction, the dynastic speakers reciting their lines by rote, 'while half-remembering a long-ago time when they were free from such compulsion' (259). Meanwhile, on the edge of the drama, humourous life proceeds 'outside the web that interweaves the people in the Napoleonic drama, and outside the web being woven out of ourselves' (268). The edge or margin to Dean has a number of meanings but one coincides with the way Southerington uses 'fringe.' Clearly involved in events, the dynasts 'possess little will of their own, while the remaining rustic and similar figures are merely on the fringe of events, or not involved at all' (Southerington 182). In Dean's view, freedom is not achieved so much *within* a monistic Will as *from* 'the historical currents of the Will' (247). The cosmic web shrinks to the one compacted whole of the big historical events, such as battles and the movements of armies, where the Will concentrates its energy, while 'on the circumference, at a remove from the central impulse, impulsion is to some degree relaxed' (257–8) or even absent when characters are on the outside, not involved at all in the war against Napoleon, and thus 'simply free' (273). 'Here,' Dean suggests, 'on the drama's margin, "Life" seems a better word for "Will."' Indeed, the perspective of the periphery 'testifies against [Hardy's] own statements in the poem about the "Monistic theory of the Universe"' (257, 261).

We come now to the other meanings of periphery. It is not only a perspective situated on the edge of the epic-historical world but also the peripheral phenomena seen as a consequence of the mind entering a 'realm of experience that is beyond the reach of the Will's pulsations' (Dean 275). The freedom of the viewer does not free the phenomena viewed; they are 'gratuitous' in another sense, because they do not serve Hardy's theme of monism and hence 'cannot be defined as functional.' The other perspectives take the idea of a single Unconscious Energy as 'their common theme and testimony.' The fourth perspective, a kind of fifth column, is 'trained upon distinctions, irregularities, and texture' (265, 247, 267). To keep the peripheral vision separate from the Spirits and their monism, Dean has to argue that the Phantoms cannot really see phenomena at all, in spite of the many concrete descriptions offered from the viewpoint of the Overworld. What the abstract perception of the bodiless Phantoms misses is available to the peripheral characters who together make up the 'universal *body* of human nature.' In the stage descriptions, Hardy as narrator also keeps close 'to "raw," i.e., unfiltered, sensory fact' (259, 241), recording what the fleshly characters overlook when distracted by the pressure of events and making the details available to the attentive reader.

We need not dispute the skill with which Hardy unobtrusively registers in prose the 'beauty and individuality of things that are near and familiar' (Dean 284), but the question remains whether this peripheral vision of the prosaic is opposed to monism as Dean claims. The opposition she maintains can be restated as the problem of the One and the many that all theories of monism address. If we think in terms of contending theories of monism, instead of one theory, then the world of her unifying perspectives sounds very much like the block universe of absolute monism, while the 'distinctness, quiddity, uniqueness of each thing' (41) in her peripheral perspective recalls 'the phenomenal world in all its particularity' (James, *Pluralistic* 175) that radical empiricism tried to rescue from the abstractions of monistic idealism. At least 'Pluralism, in exorcising the absolute, exorcises the great de-realizer of the only life we are at home in' (*Pluralistic* 49).

We can better understand now why the separation of oneness from manyness leaves the prosaic vision of freedom (or the freedom of the prosaic vision) on the periphery of *The Dynasts* as a work of art. Outnumbered three to one in Dean's perspectival count, and with the centre of the drama preoccupied by 'its urgent vision of unfreedom,' the periphery of vision is left to the side of the poem. To her credit, Dean does not marginalize it, but the best she can do is elevate it from an inferior to a secondary or subordinate perspective, a 'counter-element to the primary and tragic one in Hardy's vision' (277).

All the accounts of language as vision line up speakers like great blocks of Napoleon's old, middle, and young guard and contrast types of speech as if they were opposing armies before the battle that is always a messy affair. In our actual readings of *The Dynasts* we confront the mixing of languages, all of which do not lie on the same plane. We constantly move from the high and straightforward plane to the comic plane of parody and travesty. *The Dynasts* is full of parodic doubles and laughing reflections of the serious word and official truth in all their generic forms.[1] Like the halos of light that never desert the head-shadows of Hardy's midnight revellers in *Tess*, the corrective of laughter is never far from the lofty direct word of both Spirits and Persons.

While prose is not the exclusive domain of laughter – we also hear it expressed, for example, in low forms of poetry – it often accompanies the prose and, as one might expect, suffers much the same fate in critical assessments. Everyone admires it but on the margins of world and Overworld and not as a link between them. On balance, the humour forms only 'a single bright thread in the dun fabric of *The Dynasts*'

(Carpenter 190), its sole function to supply some much needed light relief in an otherwise sombre drama.

In spite of the hierarchical thinking of critics, the humour or comedy does not remain sealed off in a separate and subordinate position. It enters into dialogic relations with prevailing truths and authorities and reveals the false face of unities based on hierarchy. The laughing word and its prosaic vision help provide the corrective of a contradictory multi-sided reality that cannot be confined within the narrow frame of any high genre, language, style, or voice. In monistic terms, the unofficial voices of *The Dynasts* renew the tension between the One and the many that prevents any philosophical theory, Imperial vision, or tragic perspective from permanently constituting the centre or heights of truth. From the point of view of the many and the world's second truth, all rulers and official Spirits, in politics and interpretation, world or Overworld, eventually turn into pretenders to the throne of vision and power.

In the rest of this chapter, we will concentrate our attention on a series of scenes apart from the battlefield that illustrate Bakhtin's idea of the stylistic variety of all genres that enter the realm of the serio-comical. The mixing of prose and verse in and across scenes shows how carefully Hardy constructed *The Dynasts*. The gaps in his chronicle allow him to bring people and events separated in historical space and time closer together with carnivalesque effect. The specifically carnival nature of the laughter gives the scenic construction an inner logic that helps bind the historical drama together. Hardy also reaches out, however, through his 'complex sense of intertextuality' (Neill 14) to other contexts of poetry and prose, incuding his own novels, that further emphasize the different language levels and the continual exchange between the serious and the comic. As we shall see, one way of understanding the carnivalesque world of *The Dynasts* is through its strong relation, explicity signalled in a comic scene, with *The Mayor of Casterbridge*.

Most of the scenes in which critics find it 'difficult to determine ... why Hardy chose verse or prose for dialogue' (Garrison 205) occur in Part Second where we go behind the walls of the dynasts and into their elite gatherings or private meetings. In Bakhtinian terms, we can best understand the relation between prose and verse as 'a system of intersecting planes' (*Dialogic* 48). Whenever Hardy wants to display the official attitudes or one-sided seriousness, the lofty pretensions or unconditional intentions, of his historical speakers, we get elevations into blank verse with all its high generic associations.[2] The so-called dynastic style is both the means of representing hierarchical or centripetal discourses and an object of representation bounded by the prose, including the prose of the dynasts themselves.

In Part First, Parliament is already a serio-comical world where the opposition mocks the government's war measures act as 'Mr. Pitt's new Patent Parish Pill' (42; 1.1.3). Nevertheless, parliamentary eloquence, as a form of elevated speech, belongs in verse. In Part Second, we enter a club in St James's Street where such rhetoric becomes reported in prose and turns into the laughing image of parliamentary speech. Even the 'brilliant peroration' of young Peel 'was all learnt beforehand' and sounds in the club like a parody of patriotism: '"the fiery glance of freedom which flashed incessantly from the indignant eyes of the British soldier!"' (374; 2.5.4). While some club members snore and others stagger in drunk, the prose voices report all seriousness as a mask, Castlereagh 'Donning his air of injured innocence,' Canning speaking gravely 'with bits of shiny ornament stuck on – like the brass nails on a coffin' (376, 377; 2.5.4).

When prose displaces verse, the dialogue no longer sounds on the distant plane. Hardy keeps placing thought and speech under such conditions that the official world reveals its hidden side, like the Prince of Wales's 'sly' and 'private wicket' (422, 423; 2.6.6). Historical events receive a second, carnivalistic plane or unfold in a novelistic zone of contact. Inside Carlton House, majesty combines with a joke. The Regent 'provisionally throws a regal air into his countenance' (426; 2.6.7) and tries to sound in verse like one of the scions of the ancient lines. The royal conversation then jumps from the death of kings to a discussion of sheep in prose and how the Duke of Bedford's sheep-shearing dinner almost made him late for the crowning feast. We continue to hear prose speakers, whether the Prince cursing his wives or two lords calling their host Prinny and the King of Rome a feeble brat (428; 2.6.7), until the Prime Minister enters with his grave news about war.

Hardy also leaves most of the earlier scene at the Marchioness of Salisbury's in prose. The Viscount de Materosa refers in verse to some official writings, but the conversation is mainly about unofficial doings, from messengers sent in secret and the Bourbons flying secretly, to Fox's interview with an assassin and Godoy hiding in the garrett (267, 269; 2.2.3). We begin with the narrator's description of the lofty symbols of the new alliance: at one end of the reception-room 'an elaborate device, representing Britannia offering her assistance to Spain, and at the other a figure of Time crowning the Spanish Patriots' flag with laurel.' Then the Prince of Wales enters, the dialogue begins, patriotism becomes just another topic of prose conversation, and British assistance sounds on the physical level: 'We'll whack him [Napoleon] and preserve your noble country for 'ee' (264, 269; 2.2.3). What Bakhtin says of Myshkin applies equally well to the Prince: 'the constant *inappropriateness* of his personality and his behaviour impart to him a certain integrity, almost a naiveté; he is precisely an "idiot"' (*Problems* 173). With his foppish speech – 'By Gad,' 'Dash my wig,' 'O dammy' (266, 267, 270; 2.2.3) – and crude manners, Hardy's ninny usually manages to turn a grand room into a carnival square for scandal and disclosure. Materosa finds himself recounting the scandalous behaviour of his decrowned royal family: 'they all threw themselves upon Napoleon's protection. In his presence the Queen swore that the King was not Fernando's father! Altogether they form a queer little menagerie.' Romantic and political intrigue instead of 'pure disinterestedness' (269, 270; 2.2.3) link England and Spain. When Don Diego asks about the Princess of Wales, he discovers 'Ladies a little mixed, as they were at our court. She's [Mrs Fitzherbert] the Pepa Tudo to *this* Prince of Peace?' Mr Bagot admits that in England virtue is two-sided: 'you sin with naked faces, and we with masks on' (268; 2.2.3).

The laughing truth also accompanies the Prince of Wales in the Brighton scenes, where he adopts the language of official pronouncements and banquet speeches to glorify the vast victory at Talavera and the great expedition to the Scheldt. While the Prince plays the bard of war, giving a place 'long unsung, / ... the crest and blazonry of fame,' Sheridan sings an irreverent couplet sotto voce that unmasks the victory celebration as an occasion to '"drink little England dry!"' (339; 2.4.6). The chorus of cheers that surrounds the Prince does not include the prose voices in either scene. The narrator mentions how the Prince and his brothers swagger out of the banquet hall. Sheridan privately offers his mock praise for a 'poet born' (339; 2.4.6), then has to tell him what to say. In a prose aside, a noble lord hears another's speech in the Prince's verse: 'Prinny's outpouring tastes suspiciously like your brew, Sheridan. I'll be dammed if it is his own concoction.' Transposed into a prosaic key, the official news becomes thoroughly materialized. 'I give the recipe,' Sheridan replies, 'and charge a duty on the gauging' (343; 2.4.7). Both the emphasis on drinking and the imagery of the Prince's speech parody the actual conditions of war in the not so 'jaunty, jocund land of Spain' (342; 2.4.7). In the jarring scenic construction, Brighton falls between Talavera where the heat is so intense that both armies drink from the same stream, and Walcheren where the moan of a dying army replaces the cheers of the fashionable crowd.

The Prince, who hopes to 'shine our country's gracious King' (341; 2.4.7), goes out in a 'blaze of wax candles,' making his final and ironic bow to the people in the grand setting of an opera house. What should be a crowning moment, the Regent taking his place as one of the Allied sovereigns, becomes a command decrowning. From the start, a carnival atmosphere threatens the state occasion. The house is 'crowded to excess, and somewhat disorderly'; the noise is such that 'scarcely a note of the performance can be heard.' The dialogue's first voice takes on the sound of the marketplace and throws confusion into the royal box: 'Prinny, where's your wife?' (573; 3.4.8). All of the sovereigns expose themselves in prose. The Prince has to pretend that the gallery's abuse is a compliment to the Emperor of Russia. When the rulers disagree about the downfall of Napoleon, an official celebration of peace turns into a petty squabble about their enemy's career. The Prince may not believe that the ex-Emperor is now an object of ridicule on Elba, but he hears one of his own subjects call out, 'Shall we burn down Carlton House ... and him in it?' An evening that begins for him with 'God save the King!' ends with 'Long Life to the Princess of Wales!' (578; 3.4.8). The Princess who feels like 'Punch's wife ... when Punch himself is present' (576; 3.4.8) gets crowned by the crowd and the Prince, who thinks his wife a damn fool, becomes the laughing-stock he fears. The sovereigns go up and down in a comedy of errors, bowing to the Princess, and she to them, while the Prince tries to explain that 'We were supposed to rise to the repeated applause of the people' (577; 3.4.8). By the last act of the tragic opera, he is in a carnival hell where nothing high matters: 'Oh, damn the peace, and damn the war, and damn Boney, and damn Wellington's victories! – the question is, how am I to get over this infernal woman!' (578; 3.4.8).

Hardy pairs the decrowning of the Prince on the comic plane with the decrowning of the King on the serious, the pitful scene at Windsor Castle leading directly to the farce at Carlton House. A king 'Mocked with the forms and feints of royalty' is a carnivalized king in spite of the sombre tone. Even his apartment is a mockery, in reality a padded cell but 'overlaid with satin and velvet, on which are worked in gold thread monograms and crowns' (414, 411; 2.6.5). The theme of the official lie appears in the dialogue as well and helps to explain the 'odd intermingling of verse and prose in the scene' (Garrison 205). Verse is Sir Henry Halford's mask, prose the visitors' true faces. Except for the first attendant, Halford is the only one we hear speak directly to the King and he continually pads the truth, pretending that Albuera is a 'glorious victory you [the King] have won' and that 'We arrive / But to inquire and gather how you are' (415; 2.6.5). When Halford switches to prose we hear his real motives:

> Well, we must soften [the news] down a little, so as not to upset the Queen too much, poor woman, and distract the Council unnecessarily. Eldon will go pumping up bucketfuls, and the Archbishops are so easily shocked that a certain conventional reserve is almost forced upon us. (418; 2.6.5)

At the end of the scene, all the prose speakers are more concerned with parties or food than with their King.

The King himself is two-sided but, unlike Halford, who wears the room's false front, he is a genuinely ambivalent figure, combining reason and madness, blindness and insight, rage and humility. As a prose speaker he is still on the verge of the 'fourth great black gulf' in his life, so lost in time that he has to ask an attendant what month it is. His life outside of life leaves its mark on the verse he suddenly uses to address the physicians. Madness and suffering make him express a grim version of carnival's life turned inside out. Its characteristic inversions even sound when he quotes St Paul to sum up his life in moral terms: '"The good that I would do I leave undone, / The evil which I would not, that I do!"' His eyes may be defective but he sees through Halford's flattery: 'When will the speech of the world accord with truth, / And men's tongues roll sincerely!' (413, 419, 416; 2.6.5). While England celebrates the victory at Albuera, the King experiences the festive time as a bitter carnival. He hears the 'cruel indecency' of a band playing 'boisterous music' (415; 2.6.5) supposedly in his honour. His degradation is not simply a negative process: it is 'As if the madman were the sanest here!' Caught in the pathos of death and renewal, the King appears in a moment of unfinalized transition. The loss of his daughter humanizes him and helps him see the 'fearful price for victory' on the battlefield. Yet his 'vast aversion ... to bleeding' (416, 420, 413; 2.6.5) does not make him want to stop the blood-letting in Europe. His deeper affliction, the one he shares with the mad assailants at Albuera, remains the war itself.

Nothing ever loses touch with laughter in *The Dynasts* but laughter has many gradations. There is a resonance between the suffering image of the King in Part Second and the laughing image in Part First. Some Wessex spectators talk about him as 'a very obstinate and comical old gentleman' presiding over a military review where 'one fool makes many.' To their prose intelligence, the world is a place of carnivalesque extremes: 'And what a time we do live in, between wars and wassailings, the goblin o'Boney, and King George in flesh and blood!' (79, 77, 78; 1.2.4). The King reads the signs of the times very differently, hearing in the crowd's cheers for Nelson 'Heaven's confidence in me and in my line, / That I should rule as King in such an age!' At the end of his interview with Pitt in Gloucester Lodge, he shifts to prose to discuss matters far below 'Our just crusade against this Corsican' (103, 101; 1.4.1). Although the King describes the stage created for his entertainment as a type of all the world, he does not think of the curious structure as including himself. What he explains at a distance to Pitt, and that seems to have no bearing on his sacred war, *is* the carnivalesque world of *The Dynasts*: a place where combat and humour occupy the same stage and laughter literally leads to blows – 'four guineas the prize for the man who breaks most heads' (105; 1.4.1). The logic of folk humour escapes the King, but Hardy lets us know through his Wessex spectators that the people are not just mocking each other in their grinning matches. If the King 'were nabbed' by Boney, they would have nobody to 'grin at through horse-collars' (79; 1.2.4). The image of the King made prisoner, 'snapped up in a moment, like a minney by a her'n,' begins as a 'joke' (78; 1.2.4) in the folk conversation and ends with the grim irony of George a captive in his own castle, deprived of divine authority and no longer interested in 'whatever entertains my subjects' (105; 1.4.1).

Hardy does not forget that 'All the acts of the drama of world history were performed before a chorus of the laughing people. Without hearing this chorus we cannot understand the drama as a whole' (Bakhtin, *Rabelais* 474). We hear the laughter – and the despair and lamentation – of voices that have 'passed to where History pens no page' (484; 3.1.10). Popular laughter in *The Dynasts* retains some of the freedom and frankness Bakhtin identifies with the culture of carnival folk humour. There are many carnivalesque uncrownings and often in settings that recall the public square or marketplace. A deep distrust or suspicion of official truth ebbs and flows through the prose conscious- ness of the people, no matter what their nationality. Where there is incomprehension, there is also the possibility of 'prose intelligence, prose wisdom.' The novelistic Hardy uses a 'failure to understand lan- guages that are otherwise generally accepted ... to perceive them phys- ically as *objects*, to see their relativity, to externalize them, to feel out their boundaries' (Bakhtin, *Dialogic* 404). The various low figures in *The Dynasts* express laughter's 'interior form of truth' (Bakhtin, Rabelais 94). They often grasp better than anyone else the incompleteness of all truths and unmask the pretensions of authority to speak for the good of the whole nation.

On Rainbarrows' Beacon, Egdon Heath, prose incomprehension can 'be sharp enough in the wrong place as usual.' The comical dialogue about geography ends up saying more about the location of words than places. When young James Purchess explains how he learned the world is round in church, he also reveals how truth can depend on the distinction between up and down:

'Twas the zingers up in gallery that I had it from. They busted out that strong with 'the round world and they that dwell therein,' that we com- mon folks down under could do no less than believe 'em. (82; 1.2.5)

Old John Whiting also seems impressed with words that come from the top, only to admit that military speech is just 'A form o'words, ... no more' (83; 1.2.5). The rank and file have a second life in which bodily pleasures have more importance than military rules. The initial concern for where Napoleon might land quickly gives way to the satis- faction of knowing that eighty tubs landed at Lullwind Cove the night before. Old Whiting's desire to taste a drop while on duty recalls the second spectator's confession during the military review: 'I've took to drinking neat, for, says I, one may as well have his innerds burnt out as shot out, and 'tis a good deal pleasanter for the man that owns 'em' (79; 1.2.4). The consequences of going dry make a strong case for drinking:

They say that a cannon-ball knocked poor Jim Popple's maw right up into the futtock-shrouds at the Nile, where 'a hung like a nightcap out to dry. Much good to him his obeying his old mother's wish and refusing his allowance o'rum! (79–80; 1.2.4)

The report about Popple incorporates the same folk humour as the comments about Napoleon's eating habits. The thought of Boney having 'rashers o'baby every morning' is enough to make Keziar Cantle 'laugh wi'horror at the queerness o't ... He should have the washing of 'em a few times; I warrant 'a wouldn't want to eat babies any more!' (85; 1.2.5). Before a shot is fired in *The Dynasts* we see war through the grotesque realism[3] of prose voices. The Wessex scenes do more than provide comic relief; they also introduce the principle of degradation that organizes Hardy's representation of the European conflict (see chapter 5).

We get a different impression of the drama as a whole when, instead of reading *The Dynasts* vertically from the Overworld down, we listen to the unofficial truth as expressed through what survives of the laughing and abusive chorus of the marketplace. The reverse or underside of established truth is an essential ingredient of prose style and always breaks through when the high and the low, the serious and the comic, are juxtaposed within a single scene or from one scene to another in a dialogic interanimation of languages.

On the French side, the voices of servants bring out the laughter in the decrownings and reversals that occupy the serious minds. On her death-bed, Joséphine looks back in grief at how 'I grew to be the captive, he [Napoleon] the free.' While Hardy gives due weight to her 'heart-break and repinings' (571, 568; 3.4.7) in verse, we also hear what two servants think in prose of her divorce. The first has every right to speak about the Empress in familiar terms for she too is little more than an obedient fellow servant: 'So, poor old girl, she's wailed her *Miserere Mei,* as Mother Church says. I knew she was to get the sack ever since he came back.' The high speech formula continues to be used in a comical way as the second servant adds the perspective of Father Time to Mother Church, concluding that it is droll when someone's downfall means sombody else's turn. Before Napoleon re-enters and the dialogue returns to verse, the laughter spreads to the Emperor who to found a new dynasty must act 'like the meanest multiplying man in Paris' (359, 360; 2.5.2).

In 1814, just before Napoleon's abdication, we again move inside the Tuileries where the prose of the servants parodies the fears and indecision of Marie Louise in verse. In the fluid realm of familiar speech, 'all that is sacred and exalted is rethought on the level of the material bodily stratum or else combined and mixed with its images' (Bakhtin, *Rabelais* 370). The laughter that degrades and materializes overcomes the fear expressed by the first servant: 'Sacred God, where are we to go to for grub and good lying to-night? What are ill-used men to do?' (549; 3.4.3). God is invoked not for spiritual sustenance but for the body's needs and when the third servant points out that 'Now there will be a nice convenient time for a little good victuals and drink, and likewise pickings, before the Allies arrive,' he adds, 'thank Mother Molly' (550; 3.4.3), not 'Sacred God.' Laughter removes the question of whether to leave or stay – a burning question for the Privy Council and the Empress – from the lofty and serious plane. To dissuade his equals from leaving, the third servant plays with a high form of wisdom 'in good society' (550; 3.4.3). First he asks, 'Dost know what a metaphor is, comrade?' The answer is a typical prose failure to understand and one that lowers this kind of truth to the material stratum: 'A weapon of war used by the Cossacks?' (549; 3.4.3) 'It happens,' explains the third servant, 'to be a weapon of wisdom used by me.' We finally get the metaphor: 'The storm which roots the pine spares the p–s–b–d' (550; 3.4.3). Down in the fertile pissbed and brimming with metaphors 'at this historic time' (549; 3.4.3) the third servant offers the kind of humour that uncrowns the high in order to regenerate the bodily roots of the world. Here is a wisdom that the other servants can share, a truth that celebrates the relativity of all prevailing truths: 'Good! Your teaching, friend, is as sound as true religion! We'll not go' (550; 3.4.3). Although Marie Louise's carriages carry away the Imperial treasure, the servants decide that 'True worth and abundance are ... only in the lower stratum' (Bakhtin, *Rabelais* 369) of the body with its food and drink.

The resourceful third servant has no need of weaving new white cockades; he has never got rid of the old and may safely stay. He knows that 'There's rich colours in this kaleidoscopic world' of contradictory becoming and that white will do as well as any where power makes the established order profitable to serve. This is why he answers the request, 'Hast got another?' by disclosing that 'Ay – here they are; at a price' and proceeds to make a profit as the others purchase cockades. Armed with the 'rich' colour of white, the servants can appreciate the 'comedy in all things' (551; 3.4.3) and the gay relativity of events. Even the capitulation of Paris represents 'Another glorious time among the many we've had since eighty-nine' (551–2; 3.4.3).

Outside, in the public square, 'the people of Paris are glad of the change' too. For a brief time after the collapse of Imperial rule, a carnival atmosphere reigns in the city. The people turn into the festive chorus of the marketplace, mocking and deriding a monument to military power. 'They have put a rope,' says the fourth servant, 'round the neck of the statue of Napoleon on the column of the Grand Army, and are amusing themselves with twitching it and crying "Strangle the tyrant!"' (551; 3.4.3).

The political turnover is not simply the result of superior invading forces. The Emperor should know that 'things like revolutions turn not back, / But go straight on' (552; 3.4.4). Earlier the Spirit of the Pities recalls a Napoleon who 'Professed at first to flout antiquity, / Scorn limp conventions, smile at mouldy thrones, / And level dynasts down to journeymen!' (61; 1.1.6). The revolutionary Napoleon is infused with the carnival spirit: he flouts, scorns, smiles, and levels 'To throne fair Liberty in Privilege' room.' Having 'turned man of mere traditions' (Fore Scene 23), he in turn becomes subject to the popular laughter and downward movement of another upheaval. The problem with revolutions is that they follow the position of carnival too closely. Their reversal of hierarchic levels is only a temporary suspension, though on a much larger time scale, of the official system. The carnival turned political is followed by the fears and oppression of everyday life and a return to the very hierarchy it subverts. A scowling, sardonic Napoleon crowns himself in 1805 and 'Ney's manner shows / That even he inclines to Bourbonry' (555; 3.4.4) in 1814. Revolutions do have a way of turning back instead of going straight on, or rather, of doing both at once. Directed against Napoleon, the ideal of popular revolt is no longer Liberty. The people 'see the brooks of blood that flowed forth; / They feel their own bereavements' and thus 'Rapturously / They clamour for the Bourbons and for peace' (553; 3.4.4).

The restoration of the Bourbons does not escape the people's laughter and the logic of carnival in the stage narrator's prose. Following Napoleon's abdication, the scene switches to Bayonne where both the Peninsular army and the French soldiery are drawn up in ranks awaiting something. What we see suddenly transfers high ceremonial gesture and ritual to the material sphere. The ceremony begins with the firing of a signal-gun, followed by the lowering of the tricolor down the flagstaff; but before the official salute can take place the stillness of the scene is broken by a raucous and unexpected laughter. The royal object on the top of the pole quickly becomes decrowned: 'there shoots up the same staff another flag – one intended to be white; but having apparently been folded away a long time, it is mildewed and dingy.' Just as the Bourbon standard is raised as a symbol of hierarchical unity, the touch of grotesque realism lowers it to the grave as a decaying material object. The scene ends as it begins, with the image of military power that supports the Bourbon regime, but in the midst of this serious and official frame we get the ambivalent coupling, reminiscent of carnival's praise/abuse, of the spontaneous 'Ha-a-a-a!' that joins all the regiments 'unconsciously' with the 'Hurrah-h-h-h!' (562; 3.4.5) that is expected of them.

Hardy chooses the outskirts of Avignon, the city where popes were once crowned, as the setting for Napoleon's uncrowning encounter with people liberated from the Imperial point of view. Here Napoleon is arraigned before the people's court. The exchange between the two postillions parodies the legal system as they consider the crowning case of Joachim Murat, 'him that's made King of Naples; a man who was only in the same line of life as ourselves.' The vivid bodily awareness of traditional folk humour runs through their dialogue. When the second postillion reaccents the question 'We Kings?' in a scoffing way, he reminds the first that 'if we hadn't been too rotten-fleshed to follow the drum' we would have been 'Kings of the underground country ... by this time.' No final judgment is reached except that, breaking with the procedure of an official court, the second postillion comically agrees to 'think over your defence' (563; 3.4.6).

The news of how Napoleon and his escort are threatened by the mob turns out to be much closer to the humorous insults of the carnival tradition than to real physical violence: 'they have strung up his effigy to the sign-post, smeared it with blood, and placarded it "The Doom that awaits Thee"!' (564; 3.4.6). When the people of Avignon rush out to confront Napoleon, Hardy makes their abusive style of speech a more potent weapon than the sticks and hammers they carry. The collective voice of the 'Populace' degrades him with a series of scornful titles: 'Ogre of Corsica! Odious tyrant! Down with Nicholas!' (565; 3.4.6). There is an element of respect as well as abuse in these names. The people recognize far better than the commissioners the 'Strange suasive pull of personality' (165; 1.6.1). One old woman lifts her voice into blank verse, punctuated by an oath, to challenge the assurances of Sir Neil Campbell and Count Schuvaloff: 'How do we know the villain mayn't come back? / While there is life, my faith, there's mischief in him!' (566; 3.4.6). It is the flesh-and-blood Napoleon she fears and by the body she judges him in prose: 'Give me back my two sons, murderer! Give me back my children, whose flesh is rotting on the Russian plains!' Napoleon's patriotic appeals to family take on a concrete reality he never intended as the populace also orders him to 'give us back our kin – our fathers, our brothers, our sons.' Even his vow to see his own family drowned in the Seine rather than captured by his enemies turns back on him scornfully: 'We'll pitch him into the Rhone!' (565; 3.4.6).

Hardy still grasps the dialogic possibilities of a trial that intensifies into a murder case. The curses of the mob sound against the laughing truth and prose wisdom of a market-woman who would 'show mercy to [Napoleon].' Distrustful of authority, even the Virgin Mary, 'as 'a called herself,' she has 'not much pity for a man who could treat his first wife as he did ... He might at least have kept them both on.' Napoleon is simply a man, his two wives poor women, and half a husband is better than none to someone who thinks in terms of the body and its sustenance. There is nothing abstract about the market-woman's grounds for mercy: it is preferable to having 'my stall upset, and messes in the streets wi' folks' brains, and stabbings, and I don't know what all!' (564; 3.4.6). The dismembered flesh of soldiers and horses makes the Napoleonic battlefield sufficiently like a butcher shop, without having the marketplace turned into a battlefield.

History may dictate that the whole scene teeters on the brink of violence, but Hardy also emphasizes the way the barriers between speakers comically break down. Looking out of the carriage, Bertrand reprimands the populace – 'Silence, and doff your hats, you ill-mannered devils!' – as if their unofficial truth were nothing more than a few indecent expressions. The comic mixup he receives for a reply, 'Listen to him! Is that the Corsican?,' is entirely appropriate for a marshal whose career remains tied to Napoleon's. The speaking situation changes after a stone breaks the carriage window and 'One of the mob seizes the carriage-door handle and tries to unfasten it' (565; 3.4.6). The Commissioners of the Powers jump out of their coaches and try persuasion on an equal footing. Prose incomprehension forces them to explain their lofty 'pledge to Europe for [Napoleon's] safety.' It is not so much his life as the whole dynastic system that the mob threatens. When Campbell refers to Napoleon as the ex-Emperor, he means of France. Napoleon is still a dynast with the official title of Emperor and Sovereign of the Isle of Elba and a royal residence at the Palace of the Mulini in Ferrajo. As such he is 'in the Allies' sworn care'; not even 'a zealot for the Bourbons' will brook any 'wanton breach of faith' (566; 3.4.6) against him.

When Napoleon finally puts his head out of the carriage window, he appears 'haggard, shabbily dressed, yellow faced, and wild-eyed.' He is so physically shaken that he tells Bertrand, 'I'll mount the white cockade if they invite me!' (566, 567; 3.4.6). Any change, however, is merely the necessity of disguise. The people are right in addressing his curst ambition (565; 3.4.6). Inside the carriage, he continues to speak in the blank verse of epic aspiration. He has to convince himself that 'In Europe all is past and over with me. / Yes – all is lost in Europe for me now!' and just when he reaches this conclusion he adds, 'But Asia waits a man, / And – who can tell?' (567; 3.4.6).

The trial of Napoleon at Avignon brings into the open the decrowning image implicit from the very start of his crowning relationship with Marie Louise. In the prose scene of Courcelles, we hear Napoleon 'chuckling good humouredly' about 'How we have dished the Soissons folk' and their 'stately ceremonial to match' (381; 2.5.6). The absence of the folk does not mean that he escapes their humour. The Emperor ends up the fool, rushing across the muddy street from church to inn only to hear his 'dearest spouse' exclaim, 'Ah, heaven! Two highwaymen are upon us!' (383, 382; 2.5.6). Murat cannot help laughing silently at the eager bridegroom and his shrinking bride, while the Chorus of Ironic Spirits add their 'Hoo-hoo!' in an irreverent song that makes the women in Napoleon's life a carnival pair of extremes: 'First 'twas a finished coquette, / And now it's a raw ingénue' (383; 2.5.6).

The carnivalized image of the Emperor as outlaw persists and what begins as a funny mistake eventually turns serious and official. Returning from Russia as a fugitive and outlaw, Napoleon has 'to show [his] face / In a fierce light' (490; 3.1.12) before gaining entry to the Tuileries. The Spirit Ironic wonders whether Marie Louise almost faints with fright or joy when she sees her 'tramp-like' spouse dressed in the 'shabbiest and muddiest attire' (490, 489; 3.1.12). Their serio-comic reunion looks back to Courcelles and on to the Hundred Days when the Emperor officially becomes an outlaw and the once raw ingénue takes Count Neipperg as a lover, betraying the husband who abandoned his first wife.

It is only after Napoleon's escape from Elba that the 'official minds' (587; 3.5.2) identify him, like the mob with its public-square words, as a dangerous and illegitimate voice, in Castlereagh's opinion, as 'one who is loud to violate / Bonds the most sacred, treaties the most grave!' (604; 3.5.5). Metternich does not risk tampering with the 'solemn Declaration' of the Congress of Vienna; he reads it word by threatening word:

> By breaking the convention as to Elba
> Napoleon Bonaparte forthwith destroys
> His only legal title to exist,
> And as a consequence has hurled himself
> Beyond the pale of civil intercourse.
> Disturber of the tranquillity of the world,
> There can be neither peace nor truce with him,
> And public vengeance is his self-sought doom.   (592; 3.5.4)

This piece of judicial writing, assuming, as it does, a dynastic world united in lawful tranquillity, locating all difference in the figure of Napoleon, reminds us of the pompous and monumental tone of the Spirit of the Years who speaks as one invested with full power to represent the Absolute. The plenipotentiaries repudiate Napoleon in such a way that he cannot answer, placing him 'Beyond the pale of civil intercourse' and making him in extreme fashion a threat to the whole world.

The Declaration at Vienna spreads everywhere in an attempt to limit and direct thinking about Napoleon. We hear from the Emperor Francis how the 'Allies have papered Europe' (592; 3.5.4) with it. In its original form, the joint Declaration wears the diplomatic mask of circumlocution and euphemistic expression. Napoleon is not a public enemy but a 'Disturber of ... tranquillity.' The Allies do not openly declare war on him, though 'There can be neither peace nor truce with him.' They do not directly tell anyone to murder him: 'Public vengeance is his self-sought doom.' It is worth following the path of this official discourse down from its impersonal, proclamatory heights through different speakers and interpreters, until its evasive speech gets unmasked in the realm of laughter and prose.

The actual meaning of the Allied response to Napoleon depends on who speaks and under what conditions. In the Old House of Commons, Castlereagh tries to defend the Government's military preparations while not appearing to be against peace. He wears the mask Shelley gives him in 1819 at the time of the Manchester Massacre:

> I met Murder on the way –
> He had a mask like Castlereagh –

Very smooth he looked, yet grim;
Seven blood-hounds followed him ...   ('The Mask of Anarchy' 5–8)

'Very smooth ... yet grim' is the way Hardy's Castlereagh sounds. He introduces the subject of Napoleon's 'plot' by intensifying the rhetoric of the Declaration to a crisis pitch and elevating the parliamentary debate to an epic level where 'Few things conceivable / Could more momentous to the future be / Than what may spring from counsel here to-night' (599; 3.5.5). We can see why it takes Castlereagh to identify the Spirit of the Years in one of his incarnations as 'an old prophet' (435; 2.6.7). Nothing short of prophecy, the 'auguring mind,' is needed to effect 'Deliverance from a world-calamity / As dark as any in the dens of Time' (599; 3.5.5). Whether Castlereagh knows his Milton well enough to remember Moloch's description of Hell as 'this dark opprobrious Den of shame' (*Paradise Lost* 2:58), he does present Napoleon in Miltonic and epic terms as the fallen leader 'Dropt down so low, that he has set at naught / All pledges, stipulations, guarantees' (599; 3.5.5). Satan, 'with ambitious aim / Against the Throne and Monarchy of God / Rais'd impious War in Heav'n' (*Paradise Lost* 1:41–3); Napoleon 'calls himself most impiously / The Emperor of France' to extend his sinister influence over a band of fallen men 'Who have shared his own excitements, spoils, and crimes' (599; 3.5.5).

Since everything Castlereagh says is in the name of '"GOD, AND KING, AND LAW!"' (Shelley 37) – even his motion is conceived as 'an address unto His Royal Highness' (600; 3.5.5) – we begin to suspect that Shelley's mask of anarchy fits him as well as Napoleon. Indeed as the solemn Council of 1815 proceeds, Castlereagh's own voice sounds against the background of Pandemonium and the rhetorical manipulation of the supreme 'Anarch' (*Paradise Lost* 2:988). Satan tries to limit the great consult in Book Two to the question of 'open War or covert guile' (41), as if he favours neither choice and free speech will decide the issue. Castlereagh proposes that the wise choice 'Must lie 'twixt two alternatives, – of war / In concert with the Continental Powers, / Or of an armed and cautionary course' (599; 3.5.5). Does 'twixt' mean that one of the two alternatives must be chosen, or that some position between the two military options must be found? Speaking for the opposition, Sir Francis Burdett comments that 'It seems to me almost impossible, / Weighing the language of the noble lord, / To catch its counsel, – whether peace or war' (600; 3.5.5).

Confronted with 'that mystery of phrase / Which taints all rhetoric of the noble lord' (603; 3.5.5), the opposition shifts its attack to the calculated ambiguity in the Declaration itself. 'If words have any meaning' to Whitbread, 'the [Declaration] incites'

> To sheer assassination; it proclaims
> That any meeting Bonaparte may slay him;
> And, whatso language the Allies now hold,
> In that outburst, at least, was war declared.   (603; 3.5.5)

In spite of Castlereagh's guile, the opposition suspects that, like Milton's Moloch, the foreign minister is for open war and sanctions murder. Predictably they get nothing but denials from him. At least in Hell matters get decided. In England the House of Commons divides along predictable lines and nothing is resolved at the level of official debate, though we do end with the pandemonium of 'Opposition Cries' and 'excited calls' that 'The question is unanswered!' (605; 3.5.5).

One scene later and we are back on the public square where laughter, especially in the form of gallows humour, is a living tradition. The setting is Durnover Green, Casterbridge, and the great crowd gathered there has no doubts about the meaning of the ruling classes' legal judgment against Napoleon: 'a rough gallows have been erected, and an effigy of Napoleon hung upon it.' As if hanging is not enough, 'some soldiers have been riddling the effigy with balls' (605; 3.5.6) and under it are faggots of brushwood in preparation for a kind of burning at the stake.

We may approach the controlled violence of the three forms of mock execution on Durnover Green by way of the skimmity-ride in *The Mayor of Casterbridge* (1886), the two effigies of Henchard and Lucetta tied by their elbows back to back on a donkey in a spectacle that is at once a 'Daemonic Sabbath' and a 'great jocular plot' (353, 342). In the *Mayor of Casterbridge*, the suburb of Durnover forms the geographical low point of the county town and contains 'much that was low' in other senses as well, including a pair of bridges where 'all the failures of the town' (378, 296) gravitate. All that is high and respectable finds a parodic double in the lower part of town. Moreover, the hierarchical structure of the town as a whole is mimicked and mocked by the doubleness and obvious duplicity of the suburb itself. It has its picturesque upper part and seedy lower lanes. In Mixen Lane, the 'honest' streetwomen wear spotless 'white aprons over dingy gowns.' The inn called

Peter's Finger, 'the Church of Mixen Lane' (330), has a clean and respectable appearance and a stock of polite speech formulas, but the front door is always shut and customers enter by way of a narrow, unofficial door halfway up the alley. We can imagine which direction Peter's Finger is pointing. Even the names from the low part of the town have a mocking resonance. The old Roman Durnover hints at the carnival turnover and in Mixen Lane, Mixen being the dialect word for a dung heap, the high and the low do get mixed: 'amid so much that was bad needy respectability also found a home.' At least in this 'hiding-place' the other side of official truth can be opened. Jopp reads aloud passages from Lucetta's love letters and the carnival spirit in the person (and name) of Nance Mockridge declares in proper tones, '"I say, what a good foundation for a skimmity-ride"' (329, 328, 332).

The foundation of the skimmity-ride is suppression, not just 'the secret which Lucetta had so earnestly hoped to keep buried' (332) but also the ten-year ban on the ride itself. The displaced recurrence of the past has the look and sound of a carnival event: first 'the passage of the Royal equipages' and the consequent '"great elevation"' (351, 342) of Lucetta and Farfrae, then the lurid procession of the torch lit effigies that moves to 'rude music' and 'roars of sarcastic laughter' (353). As Simon Dentith points out, the skimmington is a carnivalesque ritual descended from English versions of charivari (74). When the suppressed erupts in illegal form, the universal spirit of Bakhtin's carnival disappears. The skimmington is a performance with footlights: '"the funniest thing under the sun"' (334) to its participants brings the shock of scandal to its spectators.

The '"good laugh"' from Mixen Lane is both a full laugh and laughter transformed into a narrow moral meaning. Carnival's moment of absolute reversal, when the master and the slave switch positions, provides one of the instigators, Jopp, the chance to humiliate his former employer, Henchard, who once snubbed him, and to shame '"One [Lucetta] that stands high in this town."' For Jopp 'at least, it was not a joke, but a retaliation' (335, 333, 342). Hardy does not play down, as Dominick LaCapra says Bakhtin does, 'the element of scapegoating that might appear in carnival itself' (*Soundings* 27). For the representatives of one-sided seriousness, laughter now has the power to kill or revive, not in a symbolic but in a frighteningly literal way. Lucetta dies in childbirth from an epileptic fit and Henchard refrains from suicide only by confronting his uncrowning effigy floating like a corpse in Ten Hatches Hole. The distinction between comedy and tragedy is no longer total or pure: the intended victims of the bitter and mocking side of carnival also become the sacrificial scapegoats in a tragedy of revenge.

Clearly one of the doors through which carnival enters *The Dynasts* is Hardy's own fictional prose. Even one of the rustics from *The Mayor of Casterbridge*, Solomon Longways, for whom the skimmington is '"too rough a joke"' (340), reappears on Durnover Green in *The Dynasts* to comment on the mock execution of Napoleon. Back in the hands of all the laughing people, from local inhabitants and villagers to county yeomen and volunteers, the spectacle functions as a critique of the scapegoating of Napoleon by official authority and a comical uncrowning of the man who would be Overking of Europe. Hanged in effigy outside of all hierarchical values and reduced to the skeletal essentials of his popular nickname, 'Boney,' Napoleon acquires a peculiar relief, a full, material nature. We get the carnival transfer of known objects to an unexpected use in one woman's explanation of how 'This is only a mommet they've made of him': 'His innerds be only a lock of straw from Bridle's barton.' Laughter brings Napoleon up close and peers inside of him, turns him into a scarecrow dressed in an incongruous mixture of peace and war. 'He's made ...,' continues Longways, 'of a' old cast jacket and breeches from our barracks here. Likeways Grammer Pawle gave us Cap'n Megg's old Zunday shirt that she'd saved for tinder-box linnit' (606; 3.5.6).

The detailed description is an attempt to enlighten a rustic who has heard that '"Boney's going to be burned on Durnover Green to-night"' and has rushed all the way from Stourcastle thinking that the chaps who told him meant Boney himself. The literal-minded rustic proceeds to the right conclusion about the wrong people when he laments that 'there's no honesty left in Wessex folk nowadays at all!' His outburst against 'false deceivers' (606, 607; 3.5.6), while comically redundant, suggests that there might be a truth that deceives.

Christian or not, the dynasts would find it most convenient if someone did kill Napoleon. The other, true face behind the cant of their Declaration now arrives in prose by way of a guard on a mail-coach from Piccadilly: 'You have heard, I suppose, that he's given up to public vengeance, by Gover'ment orders? Anybody may take his life in any way, fair or foul, and no questions asked.' No one has to ask whether the Allies now mean war. The guard also announces in the blunt and comical accents of the street what the Government would not admit in the lofty tones of blank verse: 'And there are to be four armies sent against [Napoleon] – English, Proosian, Austrian, and Roosian' (608, 609; 3.5.6).

With war on the way, the prevailing truth can profit by the carnival inversion of Napoleon's authority. The mail guard recalls that 'just as we left London a show was opened of Boney on horseback as large as life, hung up with his head downwards. Admission one shilling; children half-price. A truly patriot spectacle!' The words of the advertisement indicate one way that official Power 'circulates' in the nation. The London show promotes itself as a patriotic spectacle, and in turn it sells patriotism. On the other hand, the politics of carnival are not quite so simple on Durnover Green as the guard's patronizing comparison, 'Not that yours here is bad for a simple country-place' (608; 3.5.6), suggests.

To be certain, patriotism is at work on Durnover Green, but Hardy also leaves us with a disquieting sound that sets off the deep play with the scarecrow of authority in Wessex from the city's patriotic show. A keeper with the carnival name of Tricksey has 'emptied his powder-horn into a barm-bladder, to make [Napoleon's] heart wi'' (606; 3.5.6). When the flames reach the gunpowder, the effigy is blown to rags. Having lived for years with the threat of invasion, the country folk see Napoleon as more than an effigy, and the explosion as more than just patriotic fireworks. They do not need any news of slaughter from London to know that either Napoleon will be killed or there will be another war in which bodies, perhaps some of their own, and gunpowder will be needed to stop him.

As if to confirm the popular point of view, the narrator opens Act Sixth with a long description of the Imperial army as a body with 'three limbs' (612; 3.6.1) massed on the Belgian frontier to take the offensive against Wellington and Blücher. In spite of 'the shadows that muffle all objects,' there is nothing spectral about the writing, with its emphasis on the way more and 'more bodies move' (611; 3.6.1). When the French seize Charleroi, the point of observation descends so we can follow what Napoleon reads while sitting in a chair near the Bellevue Inn. The proximity to the public inn signals another uncrowning moment as 'His listless eye falls upon a half-defaced poster on a wall opposite – the Declaration of the Allies.' Now the meaning of the Declaration as the licence to murder is directly and unequivocally registered as the effect of prose on Napoleon's body, the word made flesh: 'His flesh quivers, and he turns with a start, as if fancying that some one may be about to stab him in the back' (612; 3.6.1).

In many respects, Hardy's Napoleon belongs to the same generic world as the character whose rise to power also depends on his 'one talent of energy' – Michael Henchard. At one point in *The Mayor of Casterbridge*, the narrator explicitly compares the shape of their respective careers, calling the dinner at the King's Arms 'Henchard's Austerlitz: he had had his successes since, but his courses had not been upward' (*Mayor of Casterbridge* 293, 206). Most critics agree that Henchard's story has a tragic, even epic stature[4] and that Hardy found in the Napoleonic era 'the last possible epic story' (Hynes, 'Mr. Hardy's Monster' 227),[5] one that comes close to a five-act tragedy (see Wright 190; Hopkins 432). Hardy's chronicle may have narrative gaps, but it is a story with more than chronology as an organizing principle.[6] Events in *The Dynasts* unfold on a grand scale with Napoleon as the epic hero, either the 'typical villainous over-reacher of the English epic tradition' (Giordano 36), or the 'drama's leading "old" hero' (Dean 172) who falls back on an 'outmoded epic pattern' (Brooks 285). Even as a 'low-mimetic protagonist,' he remains part of an 'epic literary structure' (Buckler, 'Thomas' 224). Even as a puppet of the Will or Cosmic Mind, he is an illustration of the very 'high-doctrined dreams' (698; 3.7.9) that Hardy's Spirit Ironic disclaims.

Like Henchard, however, Napoleon cannot be explained just in terms of 'high seriousness' (Orel, Introduction xxv), nor can *The Dynasts* be called 'the supreme expression of those ideas which had inspired the Wessex novels' (Urwin 16), unless by ideas we include the carnival view of the world. By seeing Henchard within the carnival tradition, we may illustrate the deep continuity between his struggles in the marketplace and Napoleon's on the battlefield, a continuity that shows how Hardy the poet could be as much a novelist as Hardy the prose writer.

Three aspects of Henchard's life – his relation to laughter, to the crowd, and to time – anticipate the representation of Napoleon in *The Dynasts*. What the narrator calls 'Time, the magician' – as if time belongs with the 'thimble-riggers, nick-nack vendors and readers of Fate' (101, 72) at the fair – makes the plot of *The Mayor of Casterbridge* more strange than tragic. By opening the story on Fair Day, the first of many festive occasions, Hardy indicates that events will unfold in carnival and mystery time. Henchard and family enter the fair as its traditional carnival licence makes the crowd grow denser, 'the frivolous contingent of visitors, including journeymen out for a holiday, a stray soldier or two home on furlough, village shopkeepers, and the like, having latterly flocked in' (72). The 'preponderance of pivotal scenes which take place in public' points to the carnival spirit of communal performance more than to the way Henchard fits Bakhtin's 'model of the public man of classical biography' (Moses 225, 226). All of the crowning and uncrowning moments in Henchard's life, as in Napoleon's, take place before the crowd and with at least a trace of ambivalent laughter in the scene. Instead of tragic catastrophes, we get a series of surprising shifts and reversals, so many turns and complications that Joseph Warren Beach compares the plot to a movie.

The crowd scene in the furmity booth establishes the generic ambivalence of the novel as a whole. The main features coincide with a carnivalized menippea: the slum naturalism (with antiquated slop, smuggled rum, grotesque drinkers, and a presiding hag), the scandal of a wife-selling, a person's ultimate and decisive words and acts on public display, the sharp contrasts, the lofty theme of 'youth's high aims and hopes' sounding in the midst of the low company, Henchard's abuse met by the 'unexpected praise of his wife' (74, 75). Most of all, the narrator calls attention to the way the scene develops on the borderline between tragedy and comedy. Henchard starts drinking in a jovial mood, then quickly turns argumentative and quarrelsome. The spectators see a 'piece of mirthful irony carried to extremes' (78) and ready to pass over into its opposite. After Henchard first offers to sell his wife, Susan warns him that '"A joke is a joke, but you may make it once too often, mind!"' While matters are getting serious for her, the company responds 'with a laugh of appreciation' (76), one anonymous voice offering a comical bid of five shillings.[7] When Newson suddenly appears in the doorway and bids five guineas, the proceedings cross the threshold from jovial frivolity to lurid seriousness: 'Up to this moment it could not positively have been asserted that the man ... was really in earnest' (78). Yet gestures that have an air of finality never appear quite final. Even with the sale a reality, 'some of the guests laughed' and instead of revealing an epic or tragic wholeness Henchard shows a look of concern 'as if, after all, he had not quite anticipated this ending' (79).

The theatrical quality of events inside the tent, people dividing up into spectators and chief actors (78), extends to the outside. As the sun sets, all the world looks like the cosmic stage of The Dynasts: 'To watch it was like looking at some grand feat of stagery from a darkened auditorium' (80). On this stage, the laughing word always accompanies the serious. In the scene of Henchard's wedding, as Leonora Epstein shows, the ceremony 'moves into a carnival atmosphere' and 'descends into comic grotesquerie' (53, 54). Close to the chief actors, the groomsman Farfrae can appreciate only the 'serious side of the business.' It takes the special genius of the Casterbridge folk 'to enter into the scene in its dramatic aspect' (154) as something staged. From the outside, the solemn wedding looks both funny and sinister, a carnivalesque misalliance of a '"skellinton"' wife and a '"bluebeardy"' husband (155, 156). Paired with the opening scene, the wedding creates an ambivalence that resists interpretation as pure tragedy or comedy.

A carnival sense of the world, with its roots deep in the culture of folk humour, determines the selection of events and the way characters and scenes pair up to uncover such surprising connections as the sale beneath the sacrament of middle-class marriage. Right from the start, we get a carnivalistic shift of positions and destinies: the end of one marriage marks the beginning of another, and 'a start in a new direction' (85) for Henchard. The reference to his 'Life and Death' in the full title of the novel does not mean that Hardy's interest lies in biographical time. Henchard lives like Napoleon in carnivalized time. The tragical crisis at Weydon Fair turns out to be the first in a series of scenes that all seem to require change and rebirth, death and renewal. The chronotope of crisis and break in life works both within and across scenes, especially the eighteen-year gap between the first two chapters and the rest of the story. While the missing years seem to bring crime and punishment closer together, time also moves with a carnival logic. The uncrowning of Henchard in the furmity tent seems to coexist with the crowning occasion of the great public dinner at the appropriately named King's Arms. Everything high in the story has a side that faces the public square. Lucettta's High-Place Hall overlooks the *carrefour* and marketplace; the King's Arms Hotel has a bow-window that projects into the street, the shutters left open while Henchard and the town's elite dine. The charge of bad bread brings crisis time into the official banquet and again Henchard appears in a moment of unfinalized transition, his mood suddenly changing the way Napoleon's does so often in *The Dynasts*. First we hear his loud laugh of triumph, then we see his face darken with the temper which 'had banished a wife nearly a score of years before.' The outspoken word that mocks and provokes him comes from the open space of the street where a crowd of all classes feels 'none of the restraints of those who shared the feast' (104).

Henchard keeps meeting strangers at crucial moments in his life:

first Lucetta, then the sailor in the furmity tent, and finally Farfrae whose new idea for saving the grown wheat changes the direction of Henchard's life as much as Newson. The strangest meeting of all, literally a matter of life and death, gives saving the appearance of an 'appalling miracle' (372). The ambivalence of the skimmington ride does not fully emerge until Henchard sees what looks like his double in Ten Hatches Hole and decides not to commit suicide:[8] '"That performance of theirs killed her, but kept me alive!"' The circular pool is a chronotopic image, time made visible in a space 'formed by the wash of centuries.' It is as if we see the plot as well as Henchard's effigy 'floating round and round there' (374, 372, 373). A plot with so many surprising turns is also like the ventilator wheel in one of the windows at the Three Mariners: it 'would suddenly start off spinning with a jingling sound, as suddenly stop, and as suddenly start again' (119–20).

The turn in Henchard's fortunes comes as suddenly as a movement of the wheel. The scene at the Town Hall begins comically with the old furmity dealer on trial for pissing against a church wall. Her irreverence prepares the way for the carnivalesque reversal that follows: the accused becomes the accuser and the judge and criminal change places. The accusation of wife-selling muffles the satirical laughter but the police court becomes the equivalent of the carnival square where there is no difference between the great man and the poor woman: '"I'm no better than she!"' Already a public event, the scene of scandal and uncrowning quickly includes the chorus of the laughing people from Mixen Lane. Henchard leaves the court only to pass through 'a group of people on the steps and outside that was much larger than usual' (275). Again the narrator emphasizes the abrupt carnivalistic change in Henchard's fate and appearance. The velocity of his descent is so rapid that it appears as strange as his rise to power over the narrative gap. Carnivalized time brings everything that looks disunified and distant close together. In Henchard's case, the years between past and present incidents go unperceived and thus 'the black spot of his youth wore the aspect of a recent crime' (291). In the larger historical perspective, the Roman past turns out to be more like the Casterbridge present than respectable citizens assume. The gulf in time 'too wide for even a spirit to pass' (140) closes up in space. The Roman amphitheatre survives as the Casterbridge Ring and just a foot or two below the surface of a field or garden can be found a dead soldier of the Empire. Public hangings and 'pugilistic encounters almost to the death [that] had come off down to recent dates' (141) make the history of the amphitheatre a sinister continuation of the bloody games originally played there. The popular view confirms that '"Casterbridge is a old, hoary place o' wickedness,"' with even '"the best o'us hardly honest sometimes"' (121).

The old tragedies in the Ring have their grotesque and funny side when they become part of folk tradition. The description of the woman (Mary Channing) hanged and burned in 1705 belongs to serious history but tradition reports how after 'her heart burst and leapt out of her body' not one of the thousands present 'ever cared particularly for hot roast after that' (141). No matter how grim the event, it still wears the look of the mask above the arch of the old back door of High Place Hall. The original 'comic leer' (212) can still be discerned, but generations of stone-throwing have given the mouth a ghastly expression. As Norman D. Prentiss explains, 'we see the comic and the tragic mask together, awkwardly coincident, occupying the same physical space' (68). Although Henchard has to throw himself into 'a mood of jocularity,' he sees that switching places with Farfrae has the structure of a joke. Henchard's rapid descent accentuates the '"biting undertones"' that his speech shares with the 'caustic words' (299, 310, 121) of the Casterbridge folk. During the Royal visit, he becomes a '"fearful practical joker"' (308) in the manner of Mixen Lane. He carnivalizes the official greeting, staggering into the space in front of the Royal carriage and 'blandly' holding out a hand to the 'Illustrious Personage' (340) in mock familiarity.

The '"turn and turn"' and '"up and down!"' (299) of Henchard's ambivalent career reflect the market prices during the period before free trade. 'Prices,' the narrator comments, 'were like the roads of the period, steep in gradient' (257) and dependent on a turn of the weathercock. When the weather seems to promise a good harvest, prices do not simply drop: they rush down. Henchard tries to retrieve his fortunes in the marketplace in much the same way Napoleon tries to recover from the disaster in Russia: both characters become reckless gamblers. What the narrator says of Henchard applies equally well to Napoleon on the eve of his last battle in the wheat fields of Waterloo: 'He was reminded of what he had well known before, that a man might gamble upon the square green areas of fields as readily as upon those of a card-room' (260–1). Henchard feels himself on the threshold, backing bad weather, his investments the stake, his heavy losses another decrowning. His experience of love is no different. The lie he tells Newson to keep Elizabeth-Jane, like the story Napoleon spreads about Grouchy's arrival at Waterloo, represents 'the last desperate throw of a gamester' (402).

In his preface to *The Mayor of Casterbridge*, Hardy explains how the story arose from three historical events: 'the sale of a wife by her husband, the uncertain harvests which immediately preceded the repeal of the Corn Laws, and the visit of a Royal personage' (67). As we can now see, these three seemingly unrelated events are deeply connected on the carnivalistic plane. In turn, *The Dynasts* grows out of Hardy's fictional world of prose and laughter, a world that already seems to mix history with carnivalized time.

The striking similarities between the *Mayor* and *The Dynasts* show that Hardy did not change careers when he became the chronicler of the Napoleonic wars instead of the chronicler of Wessex. In her useful summary of things that impede access to *The Dynasts*, Susan Dean lists 'its apparent singularity among Hardy's writings' (9). Yet in Bakhtinian terms, Hardy did not leave novel writing behind him. If 'there exist excellent novels in verse' (Bakhtin, *Dialogic* 9), *The Dynasts* is certainly one of them. The contempt Hardy sometimes expressed towards the novel, describing himself, for example, as merely a good hand at a serial, was directed more at contemporary expectations than the possibilities of the genre itself. The novel remained for Hardy, as for Bakhtin, a developing genre. In this respect, *The Dynasts* represents a new kind of novel, not the last great epic. We recall Hardy saying that novel writing as an art should go forward. Although he never abandons the old material realities in *The Dynasts*, he does create through the Immanent Will and the Spirits a spectral dimension to reality only glimpsed in his novels. It is as if *The Dynasts* magnifies the moment in the *Mayor* when Henchard sees his ghostly double floating in Ten Hatches Hole and has his sense of the supernatural, already strong, turned into frightening belief.

What is 'novel' about *The Dynasts* also constitutes a reworking of the old. The ancient menippea, one of Bakhtin's predecessors of the novel, is a flexible enough genre to include the fantastic as well as the naturalistic and to assimilate poetry in a way that makes it one voice among many. In *The Dynasts*, poetry and prose form the broadest divisions in the novelistic layering of language. While the blank verse, the style of all who hold power, pursues the goal of oneness, the prose often participates as a decentralizing force in the carnivalesque unmasking of power. What results is not a single language but a dialogue of languages. In crossing the border between poetry and prose, Hardy incorporates speakers from his novels who intensify the speech diversity of *The Dynasts* and contribute in their own comical way to the verbal and ideological decentring of the dynastic world. What we have briefly considered in relation to the *Mayor of Casterbridge* will now become the subject of the remaining chapters as we explore in detail the connections between carnival, war, and the mass actions and novelistic heroes of Napoleonic history.

FIVE

A Carnivalesque Picture of Carnival

To explain the way Dostoevsky leaps over space to concentrate action on the threshold or the public square, Bakhtin looks back on a fundamental difference between carnival life and carnivalized literature. If 'in essence [carnival] was limited in time only and not in space,' in practice 'its central arena could only be the square' (*Problems* 128). When carnival left this 'highly specific, extremely important area' (*Dialogic* 159) during the seventeenth century, it lost the 'authentic sense of a communal performance' (*Problems* 131) and ceased to exert a powerful and direct influence on literary genre. This decline did not mean, as Dominick LaCapra suggests, that literature then 'sought surrogates for the former public meeting place.' Dostoevsky's 'conversion of drawing rooms and thresholds, which are supposed to be chambers of intimacy, back into squares for carnivalesque scenes of public disclosure and uncrowning' (*Rethinking* 302) belongs to a very old generic tradition. In carnivalized literature, places other than the actual square 'can, if they become meeting- and contact-points for heterogeneous people – streets, taverns, roads, bathhouses, decks of ships, and so on – take on [an] additional carnival-square significance' (*Problems* 174, 128).

While not intended to be exhaustive, Bakhtin's list of examples seems to share his tendency to turn 'his eyes from bloodletting' (LaCapra, *Soundings* 27). Missing is one of the places in life and literature, in *War and Peace* and *The Dynasts*, for example, where people from various positions, classes, and nationalities come together on a massive scale. Since the carnival square, like Hardy's Immanent Will, can 'glimmer' through the actual fabric of almost any naturalistic scene of familiar contact (*Problems* 133, 145–6), why not through the battlefield?

Commentators agree that Bakhtin 'does gloss over the negative aspects of carnival' (Gardiner 140),[1] especially 'the dangers of carnivalistic violence and antinomian energy' (Morson and Emerson, *Mikhail* 470) that, we may add, a battle also unleashes. Easy to overlook, however, is his remark that 'images of a social, historical, and natural catastrophe' can be 'represented as a carnival with its masquerades and disorderly conduct' *(Rabelais* 234–5), a point that Hardy's Spirit Sinister seems to grasp in referring to 'pestilences, fires, famines, and other comedies' such as 'my Lisbon earthquake, ... my French Terror, and my St. Domingo burlesque' (30; 1.1.1). In passing, Bakhtin mentions Rabelais's prognostic of how 'Men will change their dress so as to cheat others, and they will run about in the streets like fools and madmen; nobody has yet seen such a disorder in nature.' Bakhtin calls this prophecy a 'carnivalesque picture of carnival' *(Rabelais* 234), as if carnival's benevolent upheavals can themselves be overturned in a terrifying way.

In *The Dynasts*, the 'Great Historical Calamity, or Clash of Peoples' (Preface 3) allows Hardy to use carnival's 'way of sensing the world as one great communal performance' (Bakhtin, *Problems* 160) to organize the mass movements of armies and crowds. Strung out as a series of historical ordinates in a 'chronicle-piece' (Hardy, Preface 6), the Napoleonic battles are also tied together by carnival's logic of decrowning and debasement. 'The "swing" of grotesque realism, the play of the upper with the lower sphere, is strikingly set into motion' (Bakhtin, *Rabelais* 163) by the violence and disorder of a battle or the panic and confusion of a retreat. Yet the serious historic struggle has its laughing side, in the sounds, for example, 'of popular rejoicing at Wellington's victory [at Salamanca]. People come dancing out from the town, and the merry-making continues till midnight' (460; 3.1.3).

Two other scenes in Spain also have a popular character and carry much more weight in Hardy's chronicle than in the fuller records of the Peninsular War. In the first, the plundering of the immense wine vaults of Bembibre during the retreat of Sir John Moore's army provides the historical basis for a carnivalesque interlude. The disgust of the military historian at the disgrace (Napier 1:323) of hundreds of inebriated soldiers is just one voice in Hardy's prose scene. 'It is,' says one anonymous officer, 'the worst case of brutality and plunder that we have had in this wretched time!' Hardy constructs the scene as a grotesque counterpoint of sober and drunken speakers. On the road, fear of the pursuing French and of a 'Commander-in-Chief ... determined to maintain discipline' (287; 2.3.1) gradually restores order. The downward thrust of the procession in the mud – a horse collapsing from exhaustion, a prisoner shot for pillaging, the dead dropped from wagons – leads to the underground of the cellar, a topographical lower stratum where the motley figures bury themselves in straw to save their lives.

The carnivalesque 'Hell!' of the deserters has 'all that man can wish for here – good wine and buxom women' (289, 284–5; 2.3.1). People and objects have an inverted relation to the outside world and everyday life. The abundance of wine flows into 'extemporized receptacles' (284; 2.3.1) and into the willing mouth of a deserter who literally turns on his back to let the wine run down his throat. In war's earthly retreat, respectable women become willing, bawdy songs appear under the romantic guise of 'lifting up' a tune from back home, the 'eternal 'Ooman and baby' take the place of a 'proper God A'mighty' (289; 2.3.1), loud snoring turns into 'snoaching,' a combination of sleep and poaching, and as dangerous as stealing when a dead woman is 'the only one of us who is safe and sound!' (285, 288; 2.3.1). The sharp orders of a dying sergeant above ground are echoed incoherently by a deserter who talks in his sleep like a recruit. The only command in the underworld is 'Shut up that!' (288; 2.3.1) to the sleep-talker, the only blow a shoe thrown at him, and the only dispute a comical weighing of 'Bristol Milk' versus 'barbarian wine,' the paradise regained of Spain's 'open cellars' (285; 2.3.1) versus the paradise lost of England's 'Adam and Eve' (289; 2.3.1) tavern.

When water replaces wine the situation is more serious but still carnivalesque. The thirst of the soldiers on the second day at Talavera is powerful enough to interrupt the fighting and so unexpected that Pity begins to see life in its droll aspect, pleading the 'wryness of the times':

> What do I see but thirsty, throbbing bands
> From these inimic hosts defiling down
> In homely need towards the prattling stream
> That parts their enmities, and drinking there!
> They get to grasping hands across the rill,
> Sealing their sameness as earth's sojourners.   (335; 2.4.5)

For a moment, the 'grotesque shape' of 'Life's queer mechanics' has a positive pole. The brotherhood of drinkers is the true carnival crowd embodying the life of the people outside of military duty. The soldier undergoes a crisis of splitting on the field of battle, wishing for friendship but ordered to kill. The contradictions in the scene cannot be resolved and thus laughter is reduced to Irony and redirected in prose at the Will: 'The spectacle of Its instruments, set to riddle one another through, and then to drink together in peace and concord, is where the humour comes in' (336; 2.4.5).

Transposed to the context of Napoleonic war, what Bakhtin calls the primary carnivalistic act – 'the *mock crowning and subsequent decrowning of the carnival king*' (*Problems* 124) – has a different look. Before each battle, the persons crowned or their representatives are already seriously in place. While the initial display of colourful uniforms looks like a carnival masquerade, a battle does not immediately or inevitably suspend all hierarchical difference, nor does it always turn into a pageant without footlights. Those in command, including royal or aristocratic incompetents, usually occupy, and sometimes remain in, the elevated and detached position of spectators.

In the scene of Vimiero, the battle, like carnival, seems to be life organized as a kind of game, with Sir Arthur Wellesley and Marshal Junot the chief players: 'The battle is begun with alternate moves that match each other like those of a chess opening' (282; 2.2.7). The separation between players and pieces, and the hierarchical difference between pieces themselves continues but the left/right moves of chess give way to the up/down movement that the Napoleonic battle so often shares with carnival as the French climb the hill against the English centre, only to be driven back down the slopes. On the English left, the same see-saw pattern unfolds twice in the struggle for a ridge. What emerges through the extreme concentration of the Dumb Show, a two-day engagement condensed into five short paragraphs, is the way the movements dictated by the typical Napoleonic battlefield of heights and hollows mime the vertical structures of dynastic power.

Just as the English are about to settle the fortunes of the day, a message arrives that strengthens the connection between distance and official power. The word that prevents the battle from giving birth to a decisive English victory comes from a 'distant group' higher than Wellesley whose position in a 'group of heights' (283, 282; 2.2.7) is not yet supreme but still far enough above the action to necessitate a telescope for close viewing. The word that, for the reader at least, seems to belong to no one, points beyond direct military commands to the politics of war. Hardy could have identified the sender of the message. He knew from his copy of Sir William F.P. Napier's *The History of the War in the Peninsula* that 'scarcely had [Wellesley] sailed when he was superseded' and 'reduced to the fourth rank' (1:130) in the army of Portugal, below Sir Hew Dalrymple, the new chief commander, Sir Harry Burrard, and Sir John Moore. Having just come ashore when the battle of Vimiero opened, Burrard refused to allow any further offensive operations at its close.

We do not see Wellesley again in *The Dynasts* until after Napoleon decides to hand over the pursuit of Sir John Moore's army to Marshal Soult at Astorga and leave Spain (January 1809). 'More turning may be here,' warns the Spirit of the Years, 'than he designs. / In this small, sudden, swift turn backward, he / Suggests one turning from his apogee!' (296; 2.3.2). The small turn gains momentum until Napoleon's fortunes swing like a gambler's with sudden carnivalesque reversals, while Wellesley's steadily rise. The same age as Napoleon, and with a large nose that recalls the caricatures of Boney, Wellesley is the Emperor's double in the pursuit of power, eventually facing him as the first Duke of Wellington on Mont Saint Jean, with its crowning position and sacred name. Along the way, and after each successive victory, Hardy carefully registers the dynastic implications of his growing military reputation. On the field of Talavera (27–8 July 1809), 'Sir Arthur Wellesley has seated himself on a mound that commands a full view of the contested hill' (336; 2.4.5). Created viscount after Talavera, he is referred to as Lord Wellington by Foy and Masséna before the lines at Torrès Védras. In 1812–13 Wellington takes the offensive against lines and hills instead of defending them. The plain of Salamanca (22 July 1812) lies under the view of the opposing commanders with Marmont on the top of the Greater Arapeile and Wellington on the Lesser. Again a battle that begins with lateral movement, the French 'extending to the left in mass' (455; 3.1.3), becomes focused on the highest point. The English must go down in order to climb up. The action concentrates in the middle hollow where Wellington descends from his detached hill, until by nightfall the English stand alone on the crest once crowned by French artillery.

In another sense, the greater height still belongs to Marmont as the Duke of Ragusa. Whether real or honorific, the titles of the French marshals – Soult, the Duke of Dalmatia, Ney, the Prince of Moscow – remind us that they also play 'the unfinished game of Dynasties' (214; 2.1.3). Through his marriage to Caroline Bonaparte, Murat even receives a crown under the Empire. Yet before Napoleon crowns anyone else he crowns himself and begins the transformation of the Empire into a dynastic system, 'Each for himself, his family, his heirs'

(181; 1.6.5). From the start of *The Dynasts*, the Spirit of the Pities regrets how, 'turned man of mere traditions,' he allows his considerable talents to 'sink to common plots / For his own gain' (Fore Scene 23). By 'advancing swiftly on that track / Whereby his active soul, fair Freedom's child, / Makes strange decline,' Napoleon 'labours to achieve / The thing it overthrew' (61; 1.1.6). This inward turn and descent, as strange as any in his outward career, leads straight on to his coronation at Milan cathedral (1805). Just as the Heralds proclaim him 'crowned and throned' the Spirit of the Pities reminds Napoleon in a whisper of the time when he was only Lieutenant Bonaparte fighting for 'fair Liberty' (63; 1.1.6).

The Lieutenant who 'Professed at first to flout antiquity' (61; 1.1.6) turns into the King and Emperor who embraces it in the person of Marie Louise. Even 'starched and ironed monarchists cannot sneer at a woman of such a divinely dry and crusted line as the Hapsburgs!' (393; 2.5.8). By rejecting Joséphine's wish that 'The second of his line be he who shows / Napoleon's soul in later bodiment' (281; 2.2.6), he sets the example for the elite of Imperial society to follow. In the Salon-Carré, they literally follow Napoleon and his bride, one dynast after another. The Spirit Sinister remembers that there would be no persons of distinction under the Empire if carnival had not made the transition from play to revolutionary upheaval in the streets of Paris. 'It may be seasonable,' Sinister suggests, 'to muse on the sixteenth Louis and the bride's great aunt, as the nearing procession is, I see, appositely crossing the track of the tumbril which was the last coach of that respected lady ... It is now passing over the site of the scaffold on which she lost her head.' When the heralds finally enter we are not sure whether the Bourbon past or Bonaparte present has arrived: it passes before us, another of history's hierarchical processions, its spectators also 'ranging themselves in their places' (390; 2.5.8) like the illustrious personages behind the new dynast and the old. At the height of the Empire, merit looks to a future of privilege. The Imperial dignities 'won by character and quality / In those who now enjoy them, will become / The birthright of their sons in aftertime' (391; 2.5.8).

The one notable absentee from the processional, Napoleon's brother Joseph, the King of Spain, turns out to be Wellington's next opponent in the last of the Peninsular battles Hardy selects for *The Dynasts*. 'The Chief' (495; 3.2.1), as one officer refers to him, is now the Marquis of Wellington about to fight the battle of Vitoria (21 June 1813) that will make him 'Field-Marshal' (505; 3.2.4). With each move up, however, he faces someone above him in dynastic rank. 'On some high ground ... may be discerned the Marquis of Wellington's tent' (494; 3.2.1) but even higher is 'the French King Joseph stationary on the hill overlooking his own centre' (499; 3.2.2). If Napoleon levels old 'dynasts down to journeymen' (61; 1.1.6), Wellington helps 'Europe's mouldyminded oligarchs / Be propped anew' by toppling a new King and sending an Emperor, the 'rawest Dynast of the group' (435; 2.6.7), into exile. In battle, as in carnival, crowning and uncrowning remain inseparable. 'To down this dynasty' always means to 'set that one up' (38; 1.1.2), the crowns of Kings literally depending on the crests of hills. In Joseph's case, the heights are all abandoned and, in effect, a kingdom lost as the English 'ultimately fight their way to the top' (499; 3.2.2).

The highest of struggles, the battle of the Emperors at Austerlitz (2 December 1805), turns on the abandonment of the Pratzen heights by the centre divisions of the Austro-Russian army even before the fighting begins. On the eve of the battle, Weirother proceeds to defend his plan to move down from the heights in order to turn the French right, while Langeron, speaking in one of the genres of reduced laughter, sarcasm, points out the possibility of a disastrous reversal. The comical figure of old Field-Marshal Prince Kutúzov, who keeps 'nodding, waking, and nodding again' (166; 1.6.2) during the proceedings, wakes up at this point, though not enough to order anything different. We expect that under the serious conditions of a council of war, laughter will be reduced to a minimum but it still leaves its track in the structure of the scene and in what follows. Just as 'there begins a movement among the Russians, signifying that the plan ... is about to be put in force,' the narrator also hears the carnivalesque 'noises of drunken singing arise from the Russian lines at various points elsewhere' (168; 1.6.2). The next morning, with the shape of the battlefield accentuated by the fog below and the sun above, they fail in a desperate attempt 'to recover the lost post of dominance' (171; 1.6.3). Finding the French behind them, some Russian columns attempt to escape across the ice on Satschan Lake at the same moment that 'Napoleon and his brilliant staff appear on the top of the Pratzen' (175; 1.6.4), crowned by the noonday sun on the anniversary of his coronation. We see 'a laughter that does not laugh' (Bakhtin, *Rabelais* 45) as 'The Emperor watches the scene with a vulpine smile; and directs a battery near at hand to fire down upon the ice' (175; 1.6.4). While 'two thousand fugitives are engulfed' in the shattered mirror of the lake, the whole battle is mirrored by their sounds turned inside-out: 'their groans of despair reach the ears of the watchers like ironical huzzas' (176; 1.6.4).

'War,' Napoleon tells General Mack, 'ever has its ups and downs / And you must take the better and the worse / As impish chance or destiny ordains.' His great year of 1805 begins with the worse but instead of calling himself the unfortunate (115; 1.4.5), as Mack does, he decides to 'cut the knot / Of all Pitt's coalitions' (75; 1.2.3) by land instead of sea. After 'Villeneuve has ... turned tail and run to Cadiz' (95; 1.3.1), Napoleon orders a double volte face of his own. First, in a gesture of debasement, he has the army of Boulogne '"turn its rump on Britain's tedious shore"' (96; 1.3.1) and then instead of a straight attack through the Black Forest he entraps the Austrian columns by their rear, tying his own 'knot' (108; 1.4.3) around Ulm. The outraged Mack expects a traditional invasion only to be confronted with an adversary who 'Confounds all codes of honourable war' by 'stealing up to us / Thiefwise, by our back door!' (107; 1.4.3). We begin to see that the narrator's reference to Napoleon's 'vulpine smile,' with its suggestion of the crafty fox, arises from a commonly held evaluation and point of view. Given supreme authority by the Emperor Francis, Mack overrules the Archduke Ferdinand's proposal to 'bore some hole in this engirdlement' (108; 1.4.3) on the grounds that the upstart chief and adventurer might 'of his cunning seize and hold in pawn / A royal-lineaged son, whose ancestors / Root on the primal rocks of history' (110; 1.4.3).

Like everything else in *The Dynasts*, the events at Ulm divide the Overworld and emerge with no fixed generic meaning. They could belong to a tragedy or a farce, a high genre or a low. The Spirit of the Pities solemnly insists that the 'clouds weep for [Mack]'; the Spirit Sinister enjoys his agitation: 'Ho-ho – what he'll do now!' (111; 1.4.3). A Chorus of the Years locates Napoleon's campaign in a great and famous past that will be remembered in the future:

> It will be called, in rhetoric and rhyme,
>   As son to sire succeeds,
> A model for the tactics of all time;
>   'The great Campaign of that so famed year Five,'
> By millions of mankind not yet alive.   (97; 1.3.1)

From the point of view of the defeated, a Chorus of Ironic Spirits, replete with aerial music, parodies the collective praise of the Years:

'And this day wins for Ulm a dingy fame, / Which centuries shall not bleach from her old name!' Clearly laughter has its rights even with the most serious historic subject, not as the enemy of seriousness but of all that is false about it. After all, 'The Will Itself might smile at this collapse / Of Austria's men-at-arms, so drolly done' (117; 1.4.5).

Like the Spirit of reduced laughter, Napoleon grasps the carnivalesque possibilities of war. He is the great manipulator of carnival forms, always ready, at least until the invasion of Russia, to uncrown himself in order to direct the power of the crowd. 'His projects,' comment the Ironic Spirits, 'they unknow, his grin unseen!' (165; 1.6.1). War is not some high and honourable affair to Napoleon. When it comes to his low 'trade – / That of a soldier – whereto I was bred' (115; 1.4.5), he leaves the pomp and ceremony behind at his coronation rite. We see him before the city of Ulm 'in his familiar blue-grey overcoat ... haranguing familiarly the bodies of soldiery as he passes them' (106; 1.4.3) as if they were in the marketplace. During the official surrender of the Austrian army, it is his staff who are in gorgeous uniform while he remains 'in his shabby greatcoat and plain turned-up hat' (114; 1.4.5). Napoleon attempts to do more than disarm the Austrian soldiers. He allows their 'angry gestures and words' as they file past because he wants more than moody silence and resentment from their superiors. He deliberately closes up the distance between victor and vanquished: 'Come near,' he says to Mack, 'and warm you here,' then has the Austrian officers 'stand to right and left of me' (115; 1.4.5).

The new dynast continues to appear in almost masquerade attire, the same 'grey overcoat and beaver hat turned up front and back,' to greet the head of Europe's oldest royal family after Austerlitz. The windmill of Paleny, with its continual rotation of upper and lower parts, forms an appropriate backdrop for the way Napoleon orchestrates his meeting with the Austrian emperor as a carnival misalliance: 'Here on the roofless ground do I receive you – / My only mansion for these two months past' (176, 177; 1.6.5). What both keep hidden comes out in the laughing and serious words of the spectators. A Chorus of Ironic Spirits turns the grin behind Napoleon's protest 'That rank ambitions are your own [Francis's], not mine' into a half laugh of cosmic proportions: ''Tis enough to make half / Yonder zodiac laugh / When rulers begin to allude / To their lack of ambition' (180, 181; 1.6.5). On the other hand, the real opinion of the Austrian ruling classes about Napoleon, one that not even marriage will cancel, sounds in a pair of agelasts from the officer rank. For the first, the grotesque turnover of dynasts means something entirely negative, not change and renewal:

> O strangest scene of an eventful life,
> This junction that I witness here to-day!
> An Emperor – in whose majestic veins
> Aeneas and the proud Caesarian line
> Claim yet to live; and those scarce less renowned,
> The dauntless Hawks'-Hold Counts, of gallantry
> So great in fame a thousand years ago –
> To bend with deference and manners mild
> In talk with this adventuring campaigner,
> Raised but by pikes above the common herd!   (179; 1.6.5)

Here the tones of praise and abuse are as clearly separated as past and present. There is not even a hint of the possible relativity of the past. An absolute and epic distance separates the majestic Emperor of tradition from the 'Man of Adventure' (234; 2.1.7) in modern revolutionary history. The second officer agrees by expressing his disgust in spatial terms: 'Ay! There be Satschan swamps and Pratzen heights / In royal lines, as here at Austerlitz' (179; 1.6.5). The heights are restored to the emperors who lost them but we are back on the battlefield where all emperors reveal that the superiority of royal lines depends on military lines.

Napoleon brings much more to the battlefield than great numbers of trained soldiers. Even a Paris streetwoman knows that he has 'given new tactics to the art of war / Unparalleled in Europe's history!' (186; 1.6.7). All of his victories in Parts First and Second are special instances of 'the carnival category of *eccentricity*, the violation of the usual and the generally accepted' (Bakhtin, *Problems* 126). At Jena he effects a concentration of forces overnight that makes his soldiers eager to advance by day and leaves the Prussians 'surprised at discerning in the fog such masses of the enemy close at hand' (221; 2.1.4). Relentless in his pursuit of victory, Napoleon, like carnival, turns night into day with midnight marches (284; 2.1.7) at Friedland and with words as well as fires at Austerlitz. When one of his marshals questions the proclamation he dictates on the eve of Austerlitz, Napoleon replies that 'The zest such knowledge will impart to all / Is worth the risk of leakages' (161; 1.6.1).

Napoleon again appears as a carnivalesque figure who pulls war out of its usual rut when he moves 'under the cloak of night' (321; 2.4.2) to defeat the Austrians by day on the field of Wagram (5–6 July 1809). The enormous concentration of forces in such a tight and dangerous position on Lobau is strange enough. The subsequent movements to escape from an island that itself 'stands like a knot in the gnarled grain represented by the running river' also go against the grain of traditional warfare. Instead of proclaiming his true intentions, Napoleon now hides them. While the French pretend to attack the shore by way of the one permanent bridge, their real movement is out of sight of the enemy. When they begin to cross the secretly prepared floating bridges, the narrator registers the precise time, at two o'clock in the morning, of a 'scene which, on such a scale, was never before witnessed in the history of war' (321; 2.4.2). The unusual weather – 'The night has been obscure for summer-time' – breaks in a storm amidst a great cannonade: 'The tumult of nature mingles so fantastically with the tumult of projectiles that flaming bombs and forked flashes cut the air in company.' The weird mixture of atmospheric light illuminates another extraordinary scene of mingling on the threshold of the temporary bridges where Napoleon makes history through familiar contact with the crowd. Besmirched with mud and rain, more animal than Emperor, his voice ringing out in carnival frankness, his ambition combined with self-abasement, gloomy not confident, a figure that stalks (322; 2.4.2) rather than a person who walks, the official Napoleon is almost unrecognizable.

The emphasis on Napoleon's physical presence, close to the main body of the Imperial army, continues into the next scene. The contrast between the two emperors, Napoleon and Francis, like the split between bodies moving in the world and Spirits watching from the Overworld, develops at length in terms of the difference and distance between acting and viewing. We see the battle through the words of Francis and his household officers whose dialogue, though dramatic in form, consists largely of a narrative retelling what their spyglasses reveal. In Francis's case, war becomes a third-hand experience when he gets too excited to watch and relies instead on the reports of his staff. The two-in-one image of the Emperor during the battle shares the structural characteristics of the carnival image: 'it strives to encompass and unite within itself both poles of becoming or both members of an antithesis' (Bakhtin, *Problems* 176). One opposite is reflected in another. The way Francis walks up and down the room, his face perspiring, recalls the restless energy of his rain-drenched counterpart – soon to be his son-in-law – on the bridges. Napoleon leads thousands of 'cooped soldiers' (321; 2.4.2) to the field of battle where, spying danger directly, he eliminates the distance between people normally separated in life. One opposite at least does come to know and understand the other. 'Penned useless' (324; 2.4.3) and safe in a mansion at Wolkersdorf to the rear of the Austrian position, Francis returns to his glass and notices the 'French take heart / To stand to our battalions steadfastly, / And hold their ground, having the Emperor near!' (327; 2.4.3).

To see only 'the distance the Emperor keeps between himself and ordinary people' (Dean 144) is to locate him exclusively in an epic or philosophic drama. We must remember, however, that he is also Boney, a carnivalesque figure who, to go back to Hardy's note towards a Napoleonic poem in 1875, belongs as much to the popular tradition of 'A Ballad of the Hundred Days' as to 'a grand drama' or 'an Iliad of Europe' (Life 117, 110). The Austrian glasses bring up close the power of the crowd and the new and intimate relation between the masses and their leader that is not 'a thing of show only' (Dean 146). The main French assault 'is led by Bonaparte in person, / Who shows himself with marvellous recklessness.' He remains emphatically a body in a crowd of bodies, though 'like a phantom-fiend [he] receives no hurt' (329; 2.4.3). The battle over, it is Francis who expects, like an uncrowned carnival king, 'to sleep in stall or stye / If even that be found,' while Napoleon 'may intrude beneath this very roof' (332; 2.4.3). The 'victory-gorged adventurer,' with the carnival appetite of the figure in a contemporary cartoon, begins as the subject of abuse and ends by making Francis think in terms of praise: 'Bonaparte, / By reckless riskings of his life and limb, / Has turned the steelyard of our strength to-day, / Whilst I [Francis] have idled here!' (332–3; 2.4.3).

It is only when Francis begins to see the shape of the whole battle that right and left, victory and defeat, become twin halves of not so much one august as one grotesque event:

> There is a curious feature I discern
> To have come upon the battle. On our right
> We gain ground rapidly; towards the left
> We lose it; and the unjudged consequence
> Is that the armies' whole commingling mass
> Moves like a monstrous wheel.   (327; 2.4.3)

The Spirit of the Years need not offer any comment: Francis turns the 'living spectacle' (321; 2.4.2) into a mechanism without the help of neutral monism. Nevertheless the universe of battle is more an unpredictable bodily life than a predictable moving mass. Carnivalization infiltrates the wheel of battle set in motion by Napoleon's 'wheeling moves upon our left, / And on our centre.' A turning wheel unsettles the positions of left, right, and centre that treat the battlefield as a stable map, and makes for a revolutionary event that elicits more than neutrality from Francis: 'I like it not!' The curious feature of the battle eventually 'wears a dirty look' (323, 327, 331; 2.4.3). There are no sudden shifts and reversals but slowly top and bottom switch places: the Austrians are battered off the eastern side of the plateau until the French right occupies the Wagram crest.

Wagram illustrates that battle and carnival can take the same grotesque shape of 'one single, superindividual bodily life' (Bakhtin, *Rabelais* 226). Bakhtin quotes Goethe on how the 'many-headed, many-minded, fickle, blundering monster' of Roman carnival 'suddenly sees itself united as one noble assembly, welded into one mass, a single body animated by a single spirit' (*Rabelais* 255). On the field of Ligny in *The Dynasts*, the transformation does not result in one noble assembly.[2] The French enter with festive 'bands and voices joining in songs of victory' but once they are shooting face to face with the Prussians, the Spirit of the Pities sees

> an unnatural Monster, loosely jointed,
> With an Apocalyptic Being's shape,
> And limbs and eyes a hundred thousand strong,
> And fifty thousand heads; which coils itself
> About the buildings there.

The Spirit of the Years does not challenge a revelation that gives flesh to his own abstract thoughts: 'It is,' he adds, 'the Monster Devastation' (639; 3.6.5). The One in the many, with a shape that suggests the apocalyptic end of the world's becoming, reinforces the Years' habitual way of seeing all bodies animated then destroyed by the single Spirit of the Will.

Degradation is no longer steeped in carnival's '"merry-time"' (Bakhtin, *Rabelais* 211). In the time-space of Hardy's battles, the negative moment of the grotesque prevails: 'death, sickness, disintegration, dismemberment of the body, its rending apart and swallowing up' (Bakhtin, *Rabelais* 187). Napoleon laughs in order to forget the Russian campaign, but he is troubled by more than his inability to control war's ups and downs. The 'twitch of displeasure' (492; 3.1.12) he shows at his wife's questions does not quite suggest that 'his soul is at ease' (Tolstoy 2:1267). We sense the deeper problem when he explains how he will make the citizens of Paris forget the woes of Moscow. His odd plan to cover up the past with something beautiful, 'to gild the dome of the Invalides / In best gold leaf' (493; 3.1.12), points back to the ugliness, both moral and aesthetic, that the Russian war lays bare in a shocking way. When the French pass homeward through Borodino they see a field 'Whence stare unburied horrors beyond name!' (480; 3.1.9). During the battle itself Napoleon expects 'the sun of Austerlitz!' only to experience a crowning of a very different sort: 'The ugly horror grossly regnant here / Wakes even the drowsed half-drunken Dictator / To all its vain uncouthness!' (467; 3.1.5).

What Napoleon cannot ignore at Borodino – the way the action 'takes the form of wholesale butchery by the thousand' (467; 3.1.5) – receives considerable attention elsewhere in *The Dynasts*. The most disturbing battles have a special marketplace atmosphere. The keynote for Trafalgar sounds before the fighting begins when a French officer sees the sails of the English fleet 'Bulge like blown bladders in a tripe-man's shop / The market-morning after slaughterday,' while another adds the blunt aside, 'It's morning before slaughterday with us' (125, 126; 1.5.1). The grotesque body also appears from an aerial perspective when a recording Angel uses 'the most important of all human features for the grotesque' (Bakhtin, *Rabelais* 317), the mouth, to warn of 'those teeth of treble line / In jaws of oaken wood, / Held open by the English navarchy' (123; 1.5.1). We then get close to the sights, sounds, and smells of a devouring world,[3] the point of view alternating between the two flagships in the midst of a crowd of ships, some even caught in a 'foul tangle.' Decks become worse than butcher shops, 'reeking with ... gory shows' (134, 136; 1.5.3) or slippery with blood. It is as if battle subverts 'the carnival role of butchers and cooks' (Bakhtin, *Rabelais* 193). Like Kutúzov, who refers to the 'frost-baked meat' (487; 3.1.11) of the French, Fournier begins to think in terms of food: 'Our boats are stove in, or are full of holes / As the cook's skimmer, from their cursèd balls!' (137; 1.5.3).

References to food and eating also appear throughout the last act of Waterloo. The Wellington who gives orders between mouthfuls at Salamanca takes time to sup before leaving Brussels, while his rival at Charleroi tells Ney in a warm tone, 'Now, friend, downstairs you'll find some supper ready, / Which you must tuck in sharply, and then off' (627; 3.6.3). Figurative references to food – to French arms flashing like cutlery, the road from Brussels to Charleroi running 'like a spit through both positions' (653; 3.7.1) – have numerous literal counterparts. Camp kettles are slung on the English side at Waterloo but 'the French opposite lie down like dead men in the dripping green wheat and rye, without supper and without fire' (650; 3.6.8). On the morning of the battle, 'Breakfasts are cooked over smoky fires of green wood' (653; 3.7.1), an activity that leads directly to Napoleon's comment about eating up the British. Our attention gravitates towards the human being as a body, carrying sustenance and destruction in one great knapsack. The British march with 'four days' provisions' and 'fifty-six rounds of ball-cartridge' (632; 3.6.4); the French toil 'With seventy pounds of luggage on their loins' and flee with their features masked 'by smoke and cartridge-biting' (687, 692; 3.7.8). The battle over, Napoleon's horse 'comes to a standstill, and feeds' (697; 3.7.9) in the wood of Bossu; even Hardy's note explains how John Bentley of the Fusileer Guards 'used to declare that he lay down on the ground in such weariness that when food was brought him he could not eat it.' The last stunning image of the battlefield serves up a gigantic banquet of earth, crops, and tripe in a grotesque turn on the cliché food for thought:

> The night grows clear and beautiful, and the moon shines musingly down. But instead of the sweet smell of green herbs and dewy rye as at her last beaming upon these fields, there is now the stench of gunpowder and a muddy stew of crushed crops and gore. (697; 3.7.8)

The important fact, according to Bakhtin, 'is that the fighting temperament (war, battles) and the kitchen cross each other at a certain point, and this point is the dismembered, minced flesh' (*Rabelais* 193). The repeated reference to 'Upthroated rows of threatful ordnance' (656; 3.7.1) and 'furnace-throats' (678; 3.7.7) places the main instrument of Napoleonic war on the borderline of the body and food. The open cannon-mouths at Waterloo are devouring: 'horse and foot artillery heavily bite / Into [the French] front and flank.' The cannon's range of familiar contact is so great that no one is safe. 'It nulls the power,' says Rumour, 'of a flesh-built frame / To live within that zone of missiles' (689, 690; 3.7.8). Decrowning is portrayed as a 'carnivalistic "sacrificial" dismemberment into parts' (Bakhtin, *Problems* 162). Somerset's arm is knocked to a mash, Uxbridge's leg blown off, the field strewn with 'the hot bodies of grape-torn horses and men' (684; 3.7.7). A grotesque tone begins to highlight the grimly comic aspect of this literal rending. We expect 'the damage mortal flesh must undergo' to make Sinister 'merry so' (685; 3.7.7) but the historical exchange between Uxbridge – 'I have lost my leg, by God!' – and Wellington – 'By God, and have you!' (691; 3.7.8) – introduces a sardonic humour at the very climax of the serious struggle.

After the *Achille* blows up at Trafalgar a midshipman says

> The spot is covered now with floating men,
> Some whole, the main in parts; arms, legs, trunks, heads,
> Bobbing with tons of timber on the waves,
> And splinters looped with entrails of the crew.   (143; 1.5.4)

Although not a comic device, this enumeration of parts of the body typifies carnival as well as epic anatomy. We get the carnivalized version of the 'anatomy of the Will' (Prologue 28) in the dismemberment of the human body in battle. The way the body in this 'low' spectacle is 'blended with the world, with animals, with objects' (Bakhtin, *Rabelais* 27) doubles the ghostly unity of the metaphysical transparencies. At Albuera the exchange between the dissected body and the world takes the form of a crowd symbol, the dead forming a heap with their interiors exposed and their uniforms turned into carnivalesque junk:

> Hot corpses, their mouths blackened by cartridge-biting, and surrounded by cast-away knapsacks, firelocks, hats, stocks, flint-boxes, and priming-horns, together with red and blue rags of clothing, gaiters, epaulettes, limbs, and viscera, accumulate on the slopes, increasing from twos and threes to half-dozens, and from half-dozens to heaps, which steam with their own warmth as the spring rain falls gently upon them. (409; 2.6.4)

The Dynasts abounds with similar scenes of opening up and/or mixing together. Behind the British lines at Waterloo the common speakers emphasize the lower bodily stratum. The swords of Ney's cavalry 'are streaming with blood, and their horses' hoofs squash out our poor fellows' bowels as they lie'; helping the surgeon is 'worse than opening innerds at a pig-killing' (673; 3.7.5). Sometimes the sights, sounds, and smells of battle suggest a process of interweaving more striking than the Will's. Waterloo 'continues to sway hither and thither with concussions, wounds, smoke, the fumes of gunpowder, and the steam from the hot bodies of grape-torn horses and men' (684; 3.7.7). The gloomy atmosphere of the *Victory's* cockpit is 'pervaded by a thick haze of smoke, powdered wood, and other dust, and is heavy with the fumes of gunpowder and candle-grease, the odour of drugs and cordials, and the smell from abdominal wounds' (138; 1.5.4).

The dissolving influence of battle differs in two important respects from the scene of soldiers who perish silently on Walcheren while remaining hostile towards Napoleon. First, people normally kept separate by social and spatial distance do draw close together in combat and death: 'Pale Colonels, Captains, ranksmen lie, / Facing the earth or facing sky.' Second, the boundary that creates war becomes blurred. 'Friends, foemen, mingle' (410, 411; 2.6.4) in heaps during the most murderous struggle of the war in Spain at Albuera; 'hurt and slain, / Opposed, opposers, in a common plight / Are scorched together on the dusk champaign' (338; 2.4.5) of Talavera. The waves off Trafalgar look 'Red-frothed' with 'friends and foes all mixed' (137; 1.5.3). Floating in the water or lying on the earth are always reminders of what should be the case with the living instead of the dead and wounded.

Battles also open up language, exceeding the norms of official speech. The other side of war's high argument and inflated rhetoric is 'the curses of the fighters' that 'rise into the air' (639; 3.6.5). Within the zone of familiar contact we hear 'the furious oaths ... behind the smoke' (682; 3.7.7) of Waterloo. Part of the 'barbaric trick to terrorize / The Foe' (668; 3.7.4) is to sound as well as look the part. The ominous roar of the cannons combines the loud street word spoken in the open with a monotonous amplification of church music. The other loud battles establish the pattern that culminates with Waterloo. The music of Trafalgar is 'a continuous ground-bass roar from the guns of the warring fleets' (138; 1.5.4). The 'roaring antiphons / Of cannonry' (408; 2.6.4) give Albuera the voice of a profane choir; the sound of Leipzig 'becomes a loud droning, uninterrupted and breve-like, as from the pedal of an organ kept continuously down' (519; 3.3.2). At Waterloo, the Spirit Sinister feels like an organ-stop as the cannon balls 'right tunefully through my ichor blow.' The joke about a 'holy' Spirit underscores a serious point, albeit one made with a profaning pun on host rhymed with ghost: 'One needs must be a ghost / To move here in the midst 'twixt host and host!' (685; 3.7.7).

The problem at Trafalgar is that once the ships draw close together the cry of the marketplace is the only sort of voice that can be heard, if at all. Communication of any kind becomes almost impossible and the naval engagement a semiotic nightmare. Villeneuve gives the order to 'display no admirals' flags' (126; 1.5.1) to puzzle the enemy, only to end up frustrated himself. 'We make signs,' complains Magendie, 'But in the thickened air what signal's marked?' Even shouting, as Ville-neuve discovers, serves no better: 'Amid the loud combustion of this strife / As well try holloing to the antipodes!' (134; 137; 1.5.3). Battles realize the potential chaos of the marketplace that Villeneuve fears 'may prevent my clear discernment' (125; 1.5.1). Much of the desperate action is both loud and transgressive, 'a chaos of smoke, steel, sweat, curses, and blood' (409; 2.6.4) before the British win Albuera, 'a chaos of smoke, flame, dust, shouts, and booming echoes' (499; 3.2.2) before their 'loud victory' (506; 3.2.4) at Vitoria.

Although the aim of battle is to silence the other side, the struggle itself is often conceived as a dialogue. 'Our ships,' Villeneuve predicts, 'will be in place, / And ready to speak back in iron words / When theirs cry Hail! in the same sort of voice' (126; 1.5.1). Battle means 'thrust replied to thrust, and fire to fire' (642; 3.6.6), but its reified words make dialogic agreement impossible even when 'the combatants are seen to be firing grape and canister at speaking distance' (409; 2.6.4). On the eve of Borodino the narrator hears the ideal exchange only after 'the human tongues are still': 'the sputtering ... green wood fires' on both sides 'seem to hold a conversation of their own' (466; 3.1.4). The conver-sation breaks down in the din of battle or between the extremes of shouting and silence. Almost every time the French and English fight, the dialogic contrast is between loud speech and the refusal to speak. Perceived by the British as braggarts in giant ships 'swelling up so pompously' (130; 1.5.2), the French deliver a 'bombastic blow' while the *Victory* approaches 'preserving silence with brazen sang-froid' (127, 126; 1.5.1). The French 'shout as they reach the summit' at Talavera; the English 'hold them mute, though at speaking distance' (334; 2.4.4). We hear Ney's infantry shouting defiantly as they push forward against La Haye Sainte, while the English gunners stand in comparative silence.

In both Spain and Russia irony takes the form of silence. Joseph's loud entry as new king into Madrid, a discharge of artillery and church bells announcing the arrival of the royal procession, quickly becomes an uncrowning event, a dumb show in two senses, when his subjects close their windows, walk elsewhere, or turn their backs upon the spectacle. The long process of expelling the foreigner's authoritative word begins with the refusal to repeat it. All the speaking subjects of high proclamatory genres gather at the Royal Palace – the King, nobility, clergy, generals, heralds – where they are surrounded by the silence of the Spanish people. All high sounds end in silence. The peals of the church bells 'dwindle away to a melancholy jangle, and then to silence.' Heralds read the King's Proclamation in a loud voice after trumpets are blown: 'It is received in silence' (271, 272; 2.2.4).

At the start of the Russian campaign, Napoleon reads about the further problem that the English heads decline to recognize his brother as King of Spain. An angry Napoleon threatens to 'get to Moscow / And send thence my rejoinder' (448; 3.1.1) to the English. In the dialogue of war, the invasion is both a forceful reply and an attempt to force the other to speak. When Napoleon finally captures Moscow he exclaims, '*Now* what says Alexander!' He wants to 'Hold word with the authorities forthwith' (471, 472; 3.1.7) but their word is withheld. The Russian soldiers 'mostly move in solemn silence' (470; 3.1.6), leaving behind a city where 'stagnant silence reigns' (473; 3.1.7). Inside the Kremlin, the French marshals 'stand in silent perplexity'; Napoleon himself 'remains in gloomy silence' (474, 476; 3.1.8). When we next see the French army, it is 'in retreat / From Moscow's muteness' (479; 3.1.9), as if silence alone propels it backward. The disaster in Russia confirms on a massive scale that 'there is nothing more terrible than a *lack of response*' (Bakhtin, *Speech Genres* 127). Even nature seems to embody more than quietude: 'we are struck by the mournful taciturnity that prevails. Nature is mute' (480; 3.1.9).

Hardy's emphasis on war's coercive speech, threatening silences, and wild marketplace cries intensifies the 'embattled tendencies in the life of language' (Bakhtin, *Dialogic* 272). Napoleon turns England's 'insolent and cynical reply' into a provocation for renewing his invasion plans. His rejoinder becomes a crude matter of 'piercing into England' (36; 1.1.2). The way Bakhtin imagines languages as bodies, especially in the novel and carnival, is uncomfortably close to the military leader's penetrating orders and violent means of resolving dialogue. Even when Napoleon has to attack Austria instead of England, he still thinks in dialogic terms. The alternative campaign will produce a cynical 'knock at George's door,' their conversation continuing 'With bland inquiries why his royal hand / Withheld due answer to my friendly lines, / And tossed the irksome business to his clerks' (97; 1.3.1).

In many respects, the dynasts exploit not only the bodies of soldiers but also the forces at work in language, making the other side the enemy in the constant struggle to overcome the official line. As the point where the processes of centralization and decentralization intersect, the field of battle is strikingly novelistic as well as carnivalistic. Generals are readers and 'victory belongs (but not for long) to the one who can best map the movement of hostile forces' (Holquist, Glossary to *Dialogic* 431). Hardy keeps us aware of the collision and interaction of languages in Napoleonic warfare. Battles, like the novel, most represent the multiplicity of the era's languages. At Leipzig, the narrator can only particularize the combatants 'by race, tribe, and language' (519; 3.3.2). The shape of the Battle of Nations, somewhat like the letter D, is drawn from language, just as the field of Borodino contains the letter X. More than a great road and a little stream intersect at the Russian village. On the eve of the battle, the narrator hears the different social and ideological voices blend in a carnivalesque way: 'As the night grows stiller the ballad-singing and laughter from the French mixes with a slow singing of psalms from their adversaries' (466; 3.1.4).

Scenes also intersect to convey war's Tower of Babel mixing of voices. The two scenes of Salamanca fall between the invasion of Russia and the battle of Borodino, with the French crossing the Niemen not long before the British do the River Tormes. After hearing Napoleon's centripetal verse in Russia, we listen to war's centrifugal prose in Spain. The ford may be called Santa Marta but 'Where there's war there's women' (450; 3.1.2) of a different sort. A sentinel orders two officers' wives to retreat when they cannot give the countersign. The carnivalesque mix-up that ensues revives some of the ancient ambivalence of all words and expressions: '"W" begins other female words than "wives!"' English ladies become linked to Spanish whores, then the official countersign with the lofty name, '"Melchester Steeple,"' gets sold for a few pesetas, the guard's prosaic needs – 'Government wage is poor pickings for watching here in the rain' (452; 3.1.2) – overcoming 'Lord Wellington's strict regulations' (451; 3.1.2). The concern with the password introduces the larger problem of passing words on in war. After Mrs Dalbiac and Mrs Prescott reveal that a Spanish peasant told them about the French commanding the bridge at Alba, the intelligence moves up to Wellington's staff and down in status. Something rumoured by women remains unbelieved, with the consequence that the French 'just saved themselves thereby / From capture to a man!' (459; 3.1.3). In the darkness at the close of the battle, the verse speakers in command become 'talking shapes' (460; 3.1.3) like anyone else. Instead of imposing a unitary language on events, Wellington hears about orders disobeyed and women who end up on the battle-field, Mrs Dalbiac even riding in the charge behind her husband.

Before Napoleon appears in the next scene, he too exists as a voice, here loudly and satirically responding to Marmont's letter behind the walls of a tent. Borodino becomes the field for Napoleon's Imperial voice to assert its authority and 'mend [Marmont's] faults upon the Arapeile' (463; 3.1.4). In terms of speech genres, the battle begins high and ends low. The first sound carries the Emperor's intentions and lofty style: 'the firing of a single cannon on the French side proclaims that the battle is beginning.' The last sounds blend in a roar that has nothing official about it: 'A mash of men's crazed cries entreating mates / To run them through and end their agony; / Boys calling on their mothers, veterans / Blaspheming God and man' (466, 468; 3.1.5). Throughout Part Third, the final phase of battle illustrates – to borrow Michael Bernstein's criticism of Bakhtin – 'that the resonance of multi-ple voices may be a catastrophic threat as much as a sustaining chorale' ('Poetics' 199.) On the highway from Vitoria, we hear the 'piteous shrieks and calls / From the pale mob' (500; 3.2.2). After the final cannonade at Leipzig, the 'cries from the maimed animals and the wounded men' (524; 3.3.3) spread in the distance. The difference between two armies often collapses into the cries and abuses of one marketplace crowd of wounded soldiers. 'When the tramplings and shouts of the combatants have dwindled' at Waterloo, 'the lower sounds are noticeable that come from the wounded,' including 'elabo-rate blasphemies, and impotent execrations of Heaven and earth' (697; 3.7.8). It is as if we literally return to 'the origin of most swearing' in 'the carnivalesque aspect of a body rent to pieces' (Bakhtin, *Rabelais* 193).

If our view of the battlefield continues, we watch one last transfor-mation that makes it a place of unofficial activity as well as profaning speech. At Waterloo 'black slouching shapes begin to move, the plun-derers of the dead and dying' (697; 3.7.8); at Vitoria 'Cloaked creatures of the starlight strip the slain' (500; 3.2.2). Occasionally plundering takes on a carnival licence, officially sanctioned. When one English officer warns that 'The men are plundering in all directions' on the road from Vitoria, Wellington replies, 'Let 'em. They've striven long and gallantly' (502; 3.2.3).

Laughter comes to the foreground in a series of carnivalesque pair-ings, mixups, and uncrownings. The carnival King, Joseph Bonaparte, utters 'The bare unblinking truth': 'The Englishry are a pursuing army,

/ And we a flying brothel!' He sees his men 'leave their guns to save their mistresses,' then abandons his carriage to escape on a horse. The vast procession the English army captures looks like 'a Noah's-ark of living creatures' (501; 3.2.3), except that the only people are women and these of mixed sorts: 'wives, mistresses, actresses, dancers, nuns, and prostitutes.' 'By God,' exclaims Wellington, 'I never saw so many wh—s / In all my life before!' (501, 503; 3.2.3). The exalted and the lowly, the sacred and the profane are all levelled in the marketplace atmosphere. The incongruous list of objects runs from precious 'pictures, treasure' down through 'flour, vegetables, furniture, finery, parrots, monkeys' and includes the women who 'struggle through droves of oxen, sheep, goats, horses, asses, and mules.' Almost everyone is drawn into the disorderly crowd. The English cease to be an army; their infantry 'enter irregularly, led by a sergeant ... mockingly carrying Marshal Jourdan's bâton.' Everything high and official is debased. First 'the soldiers ransack the King's carriages,' then 'cut from their frames canvases by Murillo, Velasquez, and Zurbaran, and use them as package-wrappers, throwing the papers and archives into the road' (501; 3.2.3). The English not only switch places with the French but also reverse the top and bottom of their own hierarchy. More companies of infantry enter 'out of control of their officers, who are running behind.' As the looting continues, the men begin to look more like masqueraders than soldiers: 'Some array them in the finery, and one soldier puts on a diamond necklace.' On the women's side, cross-dressing is a matter of life and death. Many are clothed in male attire, including 'One of the generals' loves' disguised as an 'elegant hussar' (503; 3.2.3). The scene ends with the misalliance of a soldier and a lady in rich costume. Their prose voices, neither knowing the other's language, replace the serious verse of Wellington and his officers, in a mock marriage for one night. The soldier abuses the power denied to him in battle but he makes one sensible point: 'There'll be no bones broke, and we'll take our lot with Christian resignation' (504; 3.2.3).

Between the initial production of force and its sometimes difficult containment at the end of a battle, the subversion of carnival has a chance to do more than just play. Although the Napoleonic battles constitute a series of licensed events to sustain or extend the power of the ruling orders, 'there is always something in excess of authority's desire' (Hitchcock 6), even for the victor. The emperors, kings, or their delegates make the wars and sign the peace treaties; they cannot, however, completely control the forces at work in a field or sea of conflict where transgression and death are no longer symbolic acts. In an unexpected and grotesque way, many of these conflicts, 'artificially brought about some hundred years ago' (Hardy, Preface to *Dynasts* 3), undermine the very distinctions between friend and enemy, high rank and low, that make them possible. As a clash of peoples rather than professional armies, the struggle for power in Europe transforms the battlefield into a marketplace that can challenge all authority. Whereas Bakhtin 'suggests that the carnival promise of the Early Renaissance eventually degenerated into the absolute monarchy of the *ancien régime*' (Gardiner 57), Hardy sees a new, if precarious, centre of unofficial life and carnivalesque acts emerging far from the public square 'on fields whose homely names / Had never swept the ear of mortal man / Beyond the haunts of neighbour peasantry' (185; 1.6.7) before the dynastic wars of the nineteenth century.

The carnivalization of war in *The Dynasts* makes possible the transfer of ultimate questions from the abstract sphere to the concrete plane of historical images and events. The very fact that the Spirits constantly interrupt the scenes of battle with their commentary about the Will makes thought itself subject to the swing of grotesque realism and the downward movement that pervades *The Dynasts*. We often begin a scene from an aerial perspective, then descend to the earth where all hierarchies, conceptual or otherwise, become unstable. Having decrowned materialism, monism has to confront the drama of bodily life with its intense conflicts and disorder. Most importantly, a system which maintains the unity of all things must account for a world divided by war. Nothing is exactly transparent when we look through 'the insistent, and often grotesque, substance at the thing signified' (Hardy, Preface to *The Dynasts* 7). The conjunction of war and the Will returns us to the Kantian foundation of monism and the premise that mind and the world do not coincide. Hardy's carnivalesque picture of carnival draws out the unresolved conflicts within monism and keeps open the question of the Will, intensifying the mystery of the One's relation to the many.

By the time Hardy wrote *The Dynasts*, the sense of life's ultimate mystery had moved from the margin to the centre of monistic thought, reasserting the importance of the many: 'Reality, life, experience, concreteness, immediacy, use what word you will, exceeds our logic, overflows and surrounds it.' Rather than using the whole to explain (or explain away) the parts as the Spirit of the Years does, William James moves from the parts towards a whole: 'Our "multiverse" still makes a universe ... through the fact that each part hangs together with its very next neighbours in inextricable interfusion' (*Pluralistic* 212, 325). A '*concatenated* union' replaces 'the "through-and-through" type of union, "each in all and all in each"' (James, *Essays* 107). The choice for James is not between the many and the One but between two forms of monism:

> Is the manyness in oneness that indubitably characterizes the world we inhabit, a property only of the absolute whole of things ... or can the finite elements have their own aboriginal forms of manyness in oneness ... yet the total 'oneness' never getting absolutely complete? (*Pluralistic* 326–7)

Never the dogmatist, James does not eliminate the possibility that the Absolute exists and takes pluralism no further than to say that 'a universe really connected loosely, after the pattern of our daily experience, is possible' (*Pluralistic* 76).

Monism occupies much the same position in *The Dynasts* that it does in the late phases of its development as a philosophical doctrine, providing Hardy with a tentative theory of the universe rather than an epic world view for distancing his subject of war. *The Dynasts* begins with a question about the Will but its double form, an inconclusive chronicle about the many framed by a dialogue about the One, prevents any final answers. For all its importance as a theme in the Overworld, the Will appears only six times and even then acquires something of the grotesque character of the world of war. The contradictions of an era necessarily push visible time into the future, not the Years' absolute past, and make the oneness of the world an incomplete and tension-filled unity.

Six

Heroism, Speech Zones, and Genres

Perhaps no aspect of *The Dynasts* better illustrates the problem of defining its generic tradition than Hardy's treatment of heroism. *The Dynasts* may be a novel without a hero, but Hardy 'cannot resist giving a certain heroic dimension to such puppets as Nelson, Pitt, and George III' (White 102). More often heroism is not a matter of inconsistency. Hardy has 'his conception of heroic character' and *The Dynasts* 'celebrates ... a kind of heroism acceptable to the self-conscious modern world' (Brooks 286, 288). The hero's position does not change with respect to the author even if 'the Immanent Will is really the hero' (Stevenson 280), or England (see Bailey 210; Duffin 272), or 'The nations themselves are the heroes' (Southerington 171). The 'new values' (Chakravarty 67) that inform the collective will, always conceived as a single consciousness, fall within the author's monologic field of vision and simply extend the qualities that distinguish the heroic individuals: compassion, foresight, and an unselfish concern for others.

The issue here is not the presence of heroism but its ambivalence and distance from the author. The narrator often praises both leaders and followers but their devotion and sacrifice do not remain on a single plane. The new heroes never get free from old concerns. Moreover, heroism is never cut off from laughter and the grotesque. The fact that a 'brave remnant' of the Imperial Guard, 'three or four heroic battalions' (694, 695; 3.7.8), refuses to surrender at Waterloo means 'the English proceed with their massacre' (695; 3.7.8) as if the battlefield were a butcher shop. Typically, Hardy combines the noble and earthy aspects of war. The famous word of Cambronne joins a shout from the marketplace with an heroic attitude expressed in blank verse, 'Life is a byword here!' British praise, the offer to 'preserve those heroes' lives,' meets French abuse, Cambronne replying 'Mer-r-r-rde!' while 'Hollow laughter ... comes approvingly from the remains of the Old Guard' (695; 3.7.8).

The laughter is far from hollow in the scene before Coruna where we hear heroism waver before standing firm. Again we begin a scene from an aerial point but our position 'over the lighthouse known as the Tower of Hercules' also reminds us of the old hero and his tasks. The point of vision then descends to the immediate rear of the English position so we can listen to the theme of heroism pass through speakers with a prosaic sense of truth. The comical pair of stragglers contemplate another pair at the front, the wounded Sir David (Baird) and Sir John (Moore), and whether courage depends on the new or the old, on modern arms or the man with 'a character to lose.' On the comic plane, the difference between firmness and straggling comes down to equipment. 'A man,' claims the first straggler in a mock serious tone, 'can't fight by the regulations without his priming-horn, and I am none of your slovenly anyhow fighters.' The second agrees, but hesitates about what they would have done with proper equipment: 'we should have been there [the front] now?' (299; 2.3.3).

In the next scene, the enclosure of San Carlos within the old upper town of Coruna emphasizes one aspect of Moore's ambivalent heroism. On the battlefield, the dying hero insists on wearing his sword, the traditional symbol of military honour, with the grotesque result that the 'pommel ... is accidentally thrust into his wound' (301; 2.3.3). In the garden with its sacred name, the dead hero ends up mixed 'with strange manures manufactured out of no one knows what!' War carnivalizes what should be a high and solemn service. Everything is incomplete from the half-dug grave, extemporized tools, coffinless body and military cloak that serves for a pall, to the meagre procession and mutilated prayers. The earthy scene is also full of reversals. It begins with a slow procession and ends as the diggers hastily fill in the grave, while the English army prepares to embark after advancing everywhere. The highest reality turns out to be the battery on the summit where the French are still ranged and not death and resurrection on the spiritual plane. The chaplain's old words are interrupted by the cannonade and revoiced by Colonel Hope who has more immediate and physical concerns 'In mercy to the living, who are thrust / Upon our care for their deliverance' (307; 2.3.4). Brought down to earth, to a scrabbled hole instead of a royal vault, Moore still emerges with the highest praise of all: he 'would be the man to bid' the ceremonies abridged for the sake of the many. Heroism is not denied but stripped of everything false. The burial is not shallow in spite of the gravedigger's wish for 'another six inches.' 'What's left unsaid' (307, 306, 308; 2.3.4) everyone deeply feels.

No hero of high contemporary reality in *The Dynasts* ever feels entirely satisfied or believes that his/her actions take place in an uncontested epic world where all meanings are shared. The leading historical figures aspire to epic or tragic stature but turn into novelistic heroes who do not completely coincide with themselves or their fate. In halting rhythms Moore can only 'hope that England – will be satisfied – / I hope my native land – will do me justice!' (302; 2.3.3). The gloomy Nelson confesses to Collingwood 'A sense of strong and deep unworded censure, / Which, compassing about my private life, / Makes all my public service lustreless / In my own eyes' (69; 1.2.1). The dying Pitt's words 'underrate his services so far / That he has doubts if his high deeds deserve / Such size of recognition by the State / As would award slim pensions to his kin' (193; 1.6.8).

The image of the heroic individual in *The Dynasts* reminds us that one of the distinguishing characteristics of the carnival tradition in literature is 'the wide use of inserted genres' (Bakhtin, *Problems* 118). Hardy does more, however, than simply put these genres on display. One of the remarkable features of *The Dynasts* is the way it anticipates much of Bakhtin's argument about the 'historical struggle of genres' (*Dialogic* 5). By explicitly representing the struggle for power in Europe as a clash between the novel and the older canonical genres, Hardy helps us to see, as Graham Pechey also points out, that 'There is every encouragement in Bakhtin' (65) for making the concept of genre a sociopolitical category.

Pitt never sees a battlefield, but the defeat of his hired armies leaves him prone and emaciated like the skeletal figure of Europe with its backbone and ribs exposed. The old dynastic system he so strenuously defends is like one of Bakhtin's 'already completed high genres' with 'a hardened and no longer flexible skeleton' (*Dialogic* 18, 3). We hear this inflexibility in George III's obstinate cry, 'Rather than Fox, why, give me civil war!,' and in his denunciation of Napoleon as the 'wicked bombardier of dynasties / That rule by right Divine' (104; 1.4.1). The new dynast occupies much the same alien position as Bakhtin's novel: 'Once it came into being, it could never be merely one genre among others, and it could not erect rules for interrelating with others in peaceful and harmonious co-existence.' When the novel reigns supreme, it reigns as a carnival king. The only developing genre dethrones its rivals but cannot become canonical any more than Napoleon legitimate. 'In the process of becoming the dominant genre, the novel sparks the renovation of all other genres' (*Dialogic* 39, 7); in the process of becoming Europe's Overking Napoleon infects the older dynasties with the spirit of nationalism that empowers him.

While Napoleon's presence necessitates great alliances to oppose him, his absence does not simply restore the old order. After his exile to Elba there is something Napoleonic about all the dynasts who have fought him. The Chorus of Ironic Spirits unmasks the Congress of Vienna as a continuation of war by other means:

> And war becomes a war of wits,
> Where every Power perpends withal
> Its dues as large, its friends' as small;
> Till Priests of Peace prepare once more
> To fight as they have fought before!   (579; 3.5.1)

Everyone, as the final rhyme suggests, wants more than before. The Priests of Peace are already turning into their opposite before Napoleon suddenly and unexpectedly returns to unite them as prophets of war against him.

The Napoleon who appears to turn man of mere traditions retains a time and value orientation different from the established order. He nevers withdraws from the present day, like Prussia's Queen Louisa, to 'pore on musty chronicles, / And muse on usurpations long forgot, / And other historied dramas of high wrong!' Why, Napoleon wonders, 'con not annals of your own rich age? / They treasure acts well fit for pondering' (244; 2.1.8). We are not surprised to learn that her country's defeat leaves the Queen slowly dying. At Tilsit she speaks as if she is already dead, 'reminded too much of my age / By having had to live in it' (244; 2.1.8). The 'heroism' that is able 'to carve new queenliness' (227; 2.1.5) out of grief turns her into a statue or memorial to the past.

As we move from one country to another in Part Second, we keep hearing verse speakers whose '*historical inversion*' makes the past 'weightier, more authentic and persuasive' (Bakhtin, *Dialogic* 147), than the Napoleonic present or future. The news from the battlefield draws a crowd in Berlin but the scene remains a patriotic spectacle with no inner contradictions. The dialogue filters everything through the inflated verse of some ladies at a window who prefer to read the official bulletins with a spyglass rather than 'hasten down, and take from [the courier] / The doom his tongue may deal us.' The ladies already occupy the heroic position that the Governor expects of all citizens. What his 'scroll proclaims' (225; 2.1.5) they quote aloud, kept at a distance from the disaster at Jena: '"The foremost duty of a citizen / Is to maintain a brave tranquillity"' (227; 2.1.5). The agitation in the street communicates itself to the room silently by the people's air and gait. From the ladies who weep silently to the Queen with her one sliding tear and the subdued emotional crowd, everyone shares the same fate and bears it in the same way.

When Napoleon enters Berlin, the spectators evaluate events along a vertical axis of upper and lower rather than along the horizontal axis of time. We hear the unspoken thoughts of the silent crowd in the verse of the anonymous ladies who see the catastrophic present – 'From earthquake shocks there is no sheltering cell!' – as cancelling the future: 'Our course, alas! is – whither?' (228, 231; 2.1.6). Everything good lies in the past. Indeed the ladies seem more upset by the way '[Napoleon] comes even now / From sacrilege' than by the fact of his arrival. They recall his flippant curiosity at Sans-Souci Palace, 'Where even great Frederick's tomb was bared to him.' The space 'where our hero's bones are urned' typifies the Prussian attitude towards time: all objects are 'cared for, kept / Even as they were when our arch-monarch died' (229; 2.1.6). It is impossible for the 'Man of Adventure' to sit 'in the seat of the Man [Frederick] of Method and rigid Rule' (234; 2.1.7) without a conflict of values. From the streets of Berlin to the Imperial Palace in St Petersburg, the old order usually responds to Napoleon as a crude and degrading voice. In Berlin's open Platz the experience of the spectators is one of carnivalesque debasement to the sounds of resonant trumpetings from the French soldiers. 'Humiliation grows acuter still' as the ladies think of how Napoleon countenances 'loud scurillity' against their Queen and 'placards rhetoric to his soldiery' (230; 2.1.6). Napoleon's effrontery also provokes Russia's Empress-mother, who feels 'a rare belittlement / And loud laconic brow-beating' in his evasive, bourgeois marriage overtures. The mother's whole conversation in verse serves to reposition Alexander in time. Although 'a Romanoff by marriage merely' (386; 2.5.7), the 'pompous old thing' (319; 2.4.1) reminds her son that

A backward answer is our country's card –
The special style and mode of Muscovy.

We have grown great upon it ...
And may such practice rule our centuries through!   (385; 2.5.7)

From the Austrian perspective, the carnival word belongs to Napoleon. The second citizen in a café in Vienna condemns 'the graceless insults to the Court / The Paris journals flaunt – not voluntarily, / But by his ordering' (310; 2.3.5). Napoleon is the 'adventurer' of present time, his 'saucy sword' (312; 2.3.5) a cutting extension of rude and familiar speech. He provokes a loud reply – 'One very animated group ... is talking loudly' – but the prophetic mood in the café has more in common with the church of St Stephen's, whose 'huge body and tower ... rise into the sky some way off' (308; 2.3.5), than with the marketplace. The terms of praise and abuse remain opposed on the high level instead of uniting in carnival fashion on the low. At first the news of military events leads to more than a novelistic concern with contemporaneity for its own sake. When the first Austrian citizen and his English counterpart discuss the gallant army under Moore, their reverential words serve the future memory of a past that is not merely transitory. They speak in the 'genre of the "memorial"' (Bakhtin, *Dialogic* 18), broadening the world of the heroic past to include the 'baffled' Moore: 'While men chide they will admire him, / And frowning, praise.' The 'unwonted crosses he has borne' (309; 2.3.5) make Moore a sacred figure in contrast to Napoleon, the 'sacrilegious slighter of our shrines' (313; 2.3.5).

As is so often the case in *The Dynasts*, we are less concerned with events than with the way characters talk about them. The Englishman recalls joining the throng, including the whole Imperial family, to witness the high service in St Stephen's where the Austrian declaration of war is sanctioned from above: 'And when the Bishop called all blessings down / Upon the Landwehr colours there displayed, / Enthusiasm touched the sky' (310; 2.3.5). The Archduke Charles, given the chief command, is the rising sun/son in this sky, his soldiers the many windows that reflect as one wall his lofty words that make 'loud victory' (314; 2.3.5) a simple continuation of loud speech. Some citizens re-enter the café and describe how in a street nearby 'the Archduke paused / And gave the soldiers speech, enkindling them / As sunrise a confronting throng of panes / That glaze a many-windowed east façade' (315; 2.3.5).

In Part Third the Austrian response to Napoleon literally becomes an image of high language when the Spirit of the Years uses the

Romantic grotesque to subdue Pity. The Years enlarges the Emperor Francis's formal declaration of war, the document 'moving like a cloud' (509; 3.2.4) from Vienna to Dresden. The object, says Pity, 'takes a letter's lineaments / Though swollen to mainsail measure, – magically, / ... and on its face / Are three vast seals, red – signifying blood' (509–10; 3.2.4). It is enough to behold the 'flat-folded, parchment-pale' letter. Pity does not need it opened to know its contents and neither do we to know its style of address. 'Sized to its big importance' (509, 510; 3.2.4), the declaration belongs to the high, proclamatory genres of emperors, kings, and their representatives. 'The beholder finds himself, as it were, caught up on high' in order to see the document as the Spirits do when they follow the Years' instruction to 'closely read / What I reveal' (509; 3.2.4). Who better than the Years to turn language into an object that moves in the distant zone of the sacred word. This is the word, like the Years' own speeches, that 'retards and freezes thought' (Bakhtin, *Speech* 133). With its indisputability and unconditionality, it floats far above the world, removed from dialogue, inert, closed, sealed, its boundaries clearly marked by 'its shape / Rectangular' (509; 3.2.4).

Hardy also represents the struggle between Pitt and Napoleon in Part First as a generic battle in which a high speaker is drawn into crude contact with the zone appropriated by the novel. The Spirit of the Years has nothing to say to Pitt on his deathbed but only because he has 'spoke too often' (195; 1.6.8) with him. Clearly the Years prefers speakers who sound like himself: serious, official, and prophetic. Never a prose speaker, Pitt addresses Parliament as a serious man on serious things. To the end of his life he concentrates on a single and deadly serious theme. His last words – 'My country! How I leave my country!' – prompt his friend Rose to observe that 'Still does his soul stay wrestling with that theme' (194, 195; 1.6.8). Although Pitt claims to have no imagination for prophecy, his Guildhall speech ends with the belief that 'England has saved herself, by her exertions: / She will, I trust, save Europe by her example!' In a prophetic mood himself, the Years treats Pitt as if he belongs to the national heroic past. His last words on a public occasion 'will spread with ageing, lodge, and crystallize, / And stand embedded in the English tongue' (153; 1.5.5). They become an object of memory for future descendants, 'projected on to their sublime and distant horizon' to stand like a statue 'molded in marble or bronze' (Bakhtin, *Dialogic* 19).

Contemporary time grotesquely inscribes a very different epitaph on

Pitt's own flesh. He experiences the open-ended present as cata-strophic, an 'evil harlequinade / Of national disasters' (195; 1.6.8). Hardy uses the tradition that the 'news of Austerlitz ... killed him' (*Letters* 3:41) to develop a series of encounters with low or everyday speech genres important to the novel: the languages of rumour, reports of the day, familiar speech and laughter. The distance between Pitt and events forces him to call on Lord Malmesbury to get a Dutch paper translated. All of the low voices in the scene conspire against him. 'There is a rumour' about Ulm that Pitt finds quite impossible. Even the 'leaves that skim the ground / With withered voices, hint that sun-shine-time / Is well-nigh past' (118; 1.4.6). When hints and rumours become the news, Pitt tries to dismiss the foreign prints as nothing more than marketplace speech, 'trustless as Cheap Jack / Dumfound-ing yokels at a country fair.' The way the Austrians 'lay down arms before the war's begun' has more than a touch of the ridiculous. What the Dutch writer unceremoniously adds to his report turns Mack's sur-render into a carnival event with things utilized in reverse: 'military wits / Cry that the Little Corporal now makes war / In a new way, using his soldiers' legs / And not their arms, to bring him victory.' Malmesbury appreciates how 'the quip must sting the Corporal's foes' (120; 1.4.6), forgetting that the joke includes Pitt. Napoleon joins the lit-tle to the great, bringing Pitt into 'the presence of a great disaster' (119; 1.4.6) that has its funny side. Caught up in the process of becoming Pitt 'alters fast ... as do events,' the 'ominous signs' of the times appearing in 'His thin, strained face, his ready irritation' (121; 1.4.6). Even when 'He looks hearty as a buck' after Trafalgar, 'It's the news – no more. His spirits are up like a rocket for the moment' (152; 1.5.5).

The talk of Pitt being ill after Ulm becomes the certainty that 'The name of his disease is – Austerlitz!' (192; 1.6.8). War closes up persons and places otherwise separated. Unheard-of names become 'familiar rhythms in remotist homes!' (185; 1.6.7). Pitt hears about Austerlitz while touring the Picture Gallery of Shockerwick House. At exactly the moment he crowns Gainsborough as sovereign of landscape and 'of portraiture / Joint monarch with Sir Joshua [Reynolds],' he hears the sounds of a messenger whose dispatch will make him think of 'monarchies in chains / To France' (182, 184; 1.6.6). The pacing of the scene suddenly changes as contemporary time loudly interrupts the polite and leisurely conversation about painting. Everything moves at the break-neck speed of Napoleon's marches. 'The gallop of the horse grows louder,' 'There is a hasty knocking,' and Pitt hurriedly opens the dispatch from a courier 'splashed with mud from hard riding' (183; 1.6.6). On the battlefield even the victors can appear debased, Napoleon and his staff 'glistening wet and plastered with mud' (114; 1.4.4) before Ulm, Wellington and his staff 'looking as worn and besmirched as the men in the ranks' (688; 3.7.8) at Waterloo. The news, like the mud, is so degrading that Pitt feels 'as though I had never been!' The unfinished present overturns 'plans through all those plodding years,' a place Pitt cannot even find on the map uncrowning his great alliance. Napoleon emerges as a colossal figure, his heel on Europe, his 'vast adventuring army ... set free.' While Pitt takes a little brandy, his grotesque rival, the Lord of Misrule, seems to be swallowing the whole of Europe: 'Realms, laws, peoples, dynasties, / Are churning to a pulp within the maw / Of empire-making Lust and personal Gain!' (184; 1.6.6).

In the final scene of Part First, the dying Pitt exists largely in the words of others, who see him as a novelistic hero with unrealized hopes and a need for the future. We hear how he spends his last days waiting for word of Lord Harrowby's mission to Berlin, so concentrated on the present that he keeps inquiring about 'the quarter of the wind, / And where that moment beaked the stable-cock' (193; 1.6.8). The contact between Pitt and everyday speech can now be read on his forehead like the headstone of a grave: 'His brow's inscription,' says Tomline, 'has been Austerlitz / From that dire morning ... / When tongues of rumour twanged the word across / From its hid nook on the Moravian plains' (192; 1.6.8).

Throughout Part First and again in Part Third, the low genres have a carnivalizing effect on the ruling classes. We can understand why Pitt has to reassure his King that 'rumours come as regularly as harvest.' By George's own bodily account, 'We'd lately news / Making us skip like crackers at our heels, / That Bonaparte had landed close hereby' (101; 1.4.1). After Napoleon escapes from Elba, we see the impact of the strange news about him on almost the whole official world of Europe gathered at the Imperial Palace in Vienna. For a moment, the carnival square glimmers through the grand saloon. Ranks and distinctions suddenly do not matter as all 'turn murmuring together' (583; 3.5.2). The difference between actors and spectators disappears as 'The Ladies of the Tableau leave their place, / And mingle with the rest, and quite forget / That they are in masquerade.' Instead of remaining an observer in the gallery behind the curtains and, as it were, off stage, Marie Louise lives in the unfinished present that disrupts the backward-looking tableaux vivants 'representing the history of the House of Austria' (584, 583; 3.5.2).

The scenes in Brussels also bring the top of society into contact with a world still in the making and its low language. The narrator emphasizes that the most famous ball in history is not for all the people. The long list of distinguished persons in bold type, most of whom never speak, foregrounds the image of a closed crowd of royalist supporters. The word about Napoleon enters their private space like a rude and uninvited guest. The news 'hurled ... in passing out' quickly spreads and 'the dance is paralysed' (614; 3.6.2). Instead of waltzing, people 'are all whispering round.' What crosses the floor in all directions moves like grotesque beetles rather than graceful dancers: 'Rumours all-shaped / Fly round like cockchafers!' (615, 621; 3.6.2). In the final transformation of Brussels, the citizens take to the streets and 'consternation reaches a crisis.' Rumours from the nearby battlefields that all is lost carnivalize the Place Royale and bring the whole of society – wounded and fugitive soldiers, ordinary citizens, foreign nobility and gentry, valets and maids – into familiar contact. As people 'quarrel and curse despairingly in sundry tongues' (644; 3.6.7), the Mayor conducts his own battle through official bulletins to control the panic. Forced to address the citizens in prose, he admits that what is whispered is true: 'the city archives and the treasure-chest have been sent to Antwerp,' though 'Only as a precaution' (645; 3.6.7).

News in *The Dynasts* seldom has an official air, especially when the Spirit of Rumour is the bearer. It is no coincidence that all three incarnations of Rumour occur in Part First when 'new aggressiveness by France's chief' is something 'daily heard' (54; 1.1.5). The 'quick-eared Shade' (391; 2.5.8), whose very name reminds us of the novel's special relation to the everyday speech genres, does more than register 'the first reverberations set off by events, before these impressions have settled in the permanent record' (Dean 30). The living present is the zone in which, as even the Years acknowledges, 'change / Hath played strange pranks' (Fore Scene 24). Every scene in which Rumour impersonates someone is a crowd event that helps disclose the contradictory meaning of the Napoleonic era. We always hear a voice made flesh that challenges the prevailing truth and the stability of the existing order, old or new. Rumour obeys the Chief Intelligences but subordinates often have a transgressive function in *The Dynasts*. The Years directs some stilted warnings against the tendency of Rumour to look ahead: 'It fits thee not to augur' (391; 2.5.8) and 'Methinks too much assurance thrills your note / On secrets in my locker' (Fore Scene 26).

If the Overworld begins to sound funny and the world as 'my locker' less distant, so does high society in London when Rumour contributes 'a new surprise' to the chatter. Each time Rumour enters, the world events lose their finished quality and fall within the category of laughter. The treaty that a cabinet minister boasts will guarantee a settled order in Europe proves 'Ha, well – / So much on paper!' (56; 1.1.5). Again uncrowning is inseparable from crowning: 'The Italy our mighty pact / Delivers from the French and Bonaparte / Makes haste to crown him!' (57; 1.1.5). Rumour's uncanny presence, like an old friend no one can identify, carnivalizes the evening party. A lady breaks into 'a sudden sweat, / That fairly makes my linen stick to me'; a gentleman feels 'Monstrous silly ... / That I don't know my friends' (58; 1.1.5). We get a comic version of the political turnabout. The notables go from feeling at the centre of the 'chequerboard of diplomatic moves' to searching the fashionable crowd for the stranger who 'put himself in masquerade' (55, 58; 1.1.5). One scene later, the other imposter, Napoleon, crowns himself in front of another crowd 'attired in every variety of rich fabric and fashion' (59; 1.1.6).

In Rumour's next incarnation, we leave behind the social elite in the drawing room for the common people on a highway near Egdon Heath. Here the flames of the signal beacon create a double crowd event, citizens retreating inland, soldiers heading towards the coast. The pairings extend to the characters at the end of the scene, two Phantoms of Rumour in the garb of countrymen matched with two pedestrians. By opening up the possibility of another truth than the official scare that Napoleon has landed, the Phantoms send all lofty and serious meanings down into the body to be reborn with carnival ambivalence. As truth becomes a story that the pedestrians only half-believe, Napoleon turns into the trickster of popular tradition. The first pedestrian calls the 'Day of Judgment' an alarm and complains about the nine times his rest has been broken 'by hues and cries of Boney upon us.' His familiar curse comes straight from the stomach: "Od rot the feller; now he's made a fool of me once more, till my inside is like a wash-tub, what wi' being so gallied, and running so leery!' No longer hearing the angel of Revelation, his companion ends with a jingle that discovers a festive possibility in the fear of invasion: 'If Boney's come, 'tis best to be away; / And if he's not, why, we've a holiday!' (90; 1.2.5).

Truth is again a tale in dispute when Rumour joins a 'vast concourse of citizens' (185; 1.6.7) in Paris. What Wright calls 'a most uneven scene' (197) has the characteristic accessories of a carnival complex: the public setting, the boisterous crowd, the spontaneous celebration at a late hour, the oxymoronic combination of a spirit in the flesh and a prostitute turned patriot. Nevertheless Hardy's point runs counter to Bakhtin, processions and festivity reinforcing rather than overturning the bonds of authority. The world turned upside down by war has a new and popular right way up. The 'eldest son' of the Revolution returns as more than a carnival King to 'surging streets' (188, 187; 1.6.7) that are no longer revolutionary. Even the street-woman becomes an ideologist, so 'caught by popular zeal' that 'I, too, chant *Jubilate* like the rest.' There is nothing puzzling about her verse. Her upward transformation suspends her true trade and makes prostitutes 'gallant dames like me' and clients 'my soldier-husbands' (186, 185, 187; 1.6.7) She accepts the official certainties to the point that her own version of the Emperor's chronicle sounds like an Imperial bulletin.

Rumour plays a Socratic role, drawing the woman into a dialogue that reveals the incompleteness of the going truth. We move from the hint of scandal about Napoleon and Stépanie Beauharnais to catastrophe. The 'groans of ... Austerlitz' are the birth pangs of a new order, solidified by Imperial marriages and crowns, but Trafalgar means 'Utter defeat, ay, France's naval death' (185, 190; 1.6.7). The scene ends with a joke, the prostitute refusing to spend the night with the 'creepy man' whom she is almost ready to call ghost, a word forbidden by the 'Goddess Reason' (191; 1.6.7) just as the true measure of Trafalgar is something the 'Emperor bade be hid' (190; 1.6.7).

We also get the popular response to victory as Pitt makes his triumphal entry to attend the Lord Mayor's banquet. Again a festive occasion serves the ruling elite but praise does not lose its ambivalence on the street as it does in the Guildhall. The second citizen cries 'Pitt for ever!,' then notices 'a blade opening and shutting his mouth' (150; 1.5.5) without a sound. The third citizen does not mind looking 'like a frog in Plaistow Marshes' when leaders feast at the people's expense and disadvantage. 'I've not,' he explains, 'too much breath to carry me through my day's work, so I can't afford to waste it in such luxuries as crying Hurrah to aristocrats.' Work does not culminate in food for the ordinary citizen, nor does life triumph over death. The banquet's traditional emphasis on abundance and excess gives way to economy as 'a very necessary instinct in these days of ghastly taxations to pay half the armies in Europe!' (151; 1.5.5).

On the street the people do have a second life, organized on the basis of laughter instead of 'patriotic spectacle.' The prose speakers transfer all that is high, spiritual, or ideal to the material, bodily level. Before

Pitt arrives, they uncrown and renew the hero 'to be tombed in marble, at Paul's or Westminster' (149; 1.5.5). It is Nelson's 'poor splintered body' that makes him 'the man who ought to have been banqueted to-night' (148; 1.5.5). The way the first citizen's son sees the dead man has nothing to do with praise of fame. The moment the father links Nelson to the 'great Egyptian admirals,' the son mentions the scandalous affair with Lady Hamilton: 'His Lady will be handy for [embalming], won't she?' (149; 1.5.5). The boy keeps asking awkward questions about the body and its appetites. Before Pitt is toasted as the saviour of England, the boy wonders about his drinking habits – 'Is it because Trafalgar is near Portingal that he loves Port wine?' – and treats him with comic familiarity: 'I don't like Billy. He killed Uncle John's parrot' (152, 149; 1.5.5). In the compressed explanation that follows, the boy's carni-valesque logic mimes the effect of war, drawing together distant and disunited things. A parrot that 'talked itself to death' has a great deal to do with the way 'Mr. Pitt made the war' (150; 1.5.5). Talk is death in *The Dynasts* when it takes the form of the 'slashing old sentences' in Parliament. In war the word is often made someone's flesh and 'Scarlet the scroll that the years ... unwind' (41; 1.1.3). The hand that signs the paper both taxes the breath and doubles the globe of dead. We do not see Pitt on his deathbed, just 'A thin white hand [that] emerges from behind the curtain and signs the paper' (194; 1.6.8). The hand looks fee-ble enough but with his dying breath Pitt continues to think about war, waiting to hear if Prussia will enter the struggle against Napoleon.

Whether the hero dies slowly or suddenly, in battle or not, death always has its grotesque side facing the carnival square. During the battle of Trafalgar, Hardy use the grotesque incident of the French cap-tain's woman who 'stripped herself stark, / And swam for the Pickle's boat' to foreground the whole problem of heroism. Burke's serious and official response, 'Such unbid sights obtrude / On death's dyed stage' (142; 1.5.4), assumes that laughter has no place in a tragic drama. The hero who dies also sees the battle as a high affair for a glorious cause. 'We must,' exclaims Nelson, 'henceforth / Trust to the Great Disposer of events, / And justice of our cause!' (128; 1.5.2). In contrast, the woman 'Desperate for life' (142; 1.5.4) swims from high to low, from the epic *Achille* to the 'Pickle's boat.' That the solemn and monumental tone on board the *Victory* should be combined with a joke is entirely in keeping with Hardy's carnivalesque picture of war. The carnivalizd mermaid with 'her great breasts bulging on the brine' does not obtrude on the rest of the scene. The heroic truth is that 'the "Achille" fought on, / Even while the ship was blazing, knowing well / The fire must reach their powder' (142, 143; 1.5.4). The naked truth is the result, a levelling spectacle of dismembered dead linked by the grotesque to the one fantastic survivor.

The way the woman switches sides, leaving her clothes behind, makes her the hero's uncrowning double. It is only a matter of dignity that finally separates her from the French Admiral who, after striking his flag and surrendering his sword, also lives to be picked up by a British boat. Unable to escape to the aptly named *Hero*, Villeneuve transfers the hero's role to Nelson: 'The bliss of Nelson's end / Will not be mine; his full refulgent eve / Becomes my midnight' (137; 1.5.3). Bliss for Nelson actually means hours of suffering before death. As he lies 'undressed in a midshipman's berth' (138; 1.5.4) he hears about the woman who undresses to live. People who are disunified and distant are brought into dialogic contact. Much of the conversation in the second Trafalgar scene focuses on the problem of the hero's clothes. It is characteristic of Hardy to develop within a scene, and from one scene to another, a dialogue of conflicting truths. Depending on the point of view, Nelson could, in Carlylean terms, belong to either the Drudge Sect or the Dandaical Body. He sees himself as serving 'all interests best by chancing it / Here with the commonest.' When he joins the crowd of dead and wounded, he claims 'I am but one / Among the many darkened here to-day!' (132, 133; 1.5.2). The French see matters differently: 'With dandyism raised to godlike pitch / He stalked the deck in all his jewellery, / And so was hit' (135; 1.5.3). The deck of a ship, like the carnival square, is a place where anyone can be uncrowned, Nelson falling, then his assailant in the mizzen-top. Unlike the gunners 'naked to the waist and reeking with sweat' (131, 130; 1.5.2), Nelson dresses to die, refusing to remove his stars and orders or cover them with his old greatcoat.

Hardy gives the last word about Nelson to some burghers and boatmen in the public space of the Old Rooms Inn. Everyone speaks in prose as we hear the story, based on William Beatty's eye-witness account instead of an academic history, of how Nelson's crew 'broached the Adm'l!' (157; 1.5.7). Here we have a true 'banquet for all the world' (Bakhtin, *Rabelais* 278) in which laughter triumphs over fear and death sustains life:

So he was their salvation after death as he had been in the fight. If he could have knowed it, 'twould have pleased him down to the ground!

How 'a would have laughed through the spigot-hole: 'Draw on, my
hearties! Better I shrivel than you famish.' Ha-ha!   (157; 1.5.7)

The new ballad – yet another inserted genre – sold about town on mar-
ket-day transfers the epic battle of Trafalgar to popular tradition and
completes the image of Nelson as a collective rather than an individual
body. The aftermath of Trafalgar unites all the living and the dead:
'Dead Nelson and his half-dead crew, his foes from near and far, /
Were rolled together on the deep that night at Trafalgár!' (159; 1.5.7).
   Many of the military leaders in *The Dynasts* view death as something
higher than life, as an heroic end to be sought, especially in battle, or as
a destiny that cannot be evaded. At its most extreme, the elevation of
death crosses the generations, uniting the dukes of Brunswick, father
and son. After hearing about the aged Duke's death in the battle of
Auërstadt, Prince Hohenlohe comments that 'Many a time of late /
Has he, by some strange gift of foreknowing, / Declared his fate was
hovering in such wise!' (223; 2.1.4). The son also experiences 'That Pre-
lude to our death my lineage know!' (620; 3.6.2) when the Spirit of the
Years addresses him. Lacking the flesh of life, the Spirits are able, in
Bakhtin's terms, 'to "penetrate" through the life-flesh of other people
and reach their deepest "I"' (*Problems* 173). Brunswick hears the Years'
prophecy of death as 'inner words, / As 'twere my father's angel calling me' (620; 3.6.2). We are concerned with more than some kind of
telepathic inheritance here. What stirs and binds the son is the sacred
word of the father connected with a past that is felt to be hierarchically
higher. The present serves only as a means of fulfilling the past. Brunswick hates the French as 'did his father before him' (646; 3.6.7) and is
bound by duty to fight them: 'I sheath not my sword till I have
avenged / My father's death. I have sworn it!' (619; 3.6.2).
   As in a novel, actions remain tied to the character's discourse. The
'Duke of Deathwounds' (619; 3.6.2) combines a romantic striving after
death with an outlook as gloomy and serious as the word he obeys. At
the battle of Quatre-Bras we see how destructive and ineffective the
authoritarian word can be. The 'expected bullet' finds the living son
and death becomes a 'told time' (641; 3.6.6) as Brunswick recklessly
gallops at the head of his hussars. All the Brunswickers appear cut
from the same family cloth, the Duke in his black 'filial weedery' (619;
3.6.2), his followers 'Full-clothed in black, with nodding hearsy
plumes,' the only bright part of their uniform an emblem of death, 'A
shining silver skull and cross of bones.' They choose this 'solemn and

appalling guise,' both frightening and funereal, 'to byspeak [the Duke's] slain sire,' but the moment the son falls so does the authority of his word: 'His troops, disheartened, lose their courage and give way' (641; 3.6.6).

We have to wait until the next scene to hear about the Duke's death wound: 'A musket-ball passed through his bridle-hand and entered his belly' (646; 3.6.7). Fatal wounds are often like 'quaint red doors set ope in sweating fells' (409; 2.6.4). Brunswick's father 'received in the face / A grape-shot that gouged out half of it' (223; 2.1.4). In Sir John Moore's case, 'The rent's too gross. / A dozen lives could pass that thorough-fare!' (301; 2.3.3). No one is exempt from the slaughter on the battle-field. Even the hero's death demands a marketplace tone instead of the morose seriousness of Brunswick or the official piety of the Mayor who tells the citizens of Brussels to 'Carry yourselves gravely' (646; 3.6.7) for the Duke's extemporized funeral procession. It is the 'roughish-mouthed' Picton, not the solemn Brunswick, who speaks as one with the crowd: '"When you shall hear of *my* death, mark my words, / You'll hear of a bloody day!"' (664; 3.7.4).

All of Napoleon's crisis dreams take the 'fantastic moulds' (624; 3.6.2) of death. He wants to believe that he is 'Ruled by the pitiless Planet of Destiny' (630; 3.6.3), but in his last campaign his dreams take him beyond the bounds of his fate, revealing the possibilities of another person and another life in him. A letter signed the Duke of Enghien so discomposes him that he cannot dismiss it as a treacherous trick. The signature takes him back to 1804, just before *The Dynasts* begins, and the controversial decision he made to execute the Bourbon prince as a warning to the real conspirators in an assassination plot. A sense of responsibility already haunts Napoleon enough to prevent him from sleeping when the Spirit Ironic intervenes:

> Thereupon a vision passes before Napoleon as he lies, comprising hun-dreds of thousands of skeletons and corpses in divers stages of decay. They rise from his various battlefields, the flesh dropping from them, and gaze reproachfully at him. His intimate officers who have been slain he recognizes among the crowd. In front is the Duke of Enghien as showman.

This panorama still takes the form of grotesque realism and contains the essentials of Napoleon's carnivalesque career. Even in his interior life he still confronts the crowd, the dead resurrected in a popular uprising of reproach against the Emperor. The Duke of Enghien is no revolutionary but he displaces the Years as the crowd's showman and reminds Napoleon of the decisive turning point that 'gained him an imperial crown' – to secure the safety of the Republic – 'and flecked the purple with innocent blood' (Rose 1:457). Death and renewal remain inseparable. Having executed the Duke to prevent the restoration of the Bourbons, Napoleon goes on shedding blood to keep his own crown. In the midst of the carnage at Waterloo, he has another dream, this time without the provocation of any of the Spirits. Again the body appears in its grotesque aspect, as the 'mutilated, bleeding' figure of Lannes openly rebukes him with the question implicit in the earlier silent vision: '"What – blood again?" he said to me. "Still blood?"' (675; 3.7.6).

It takes total military defeat and the prospect of exile to make Napoleon view death in a heroic light, and even then he feels ambivalent. In the abdication scene, Roustan's plan of dying by the sword is not 'quite expedient' (557; 3.4.4) to his master. Here death is removed from the distanced plane and made part of the carnivalesque plot. When Napoleon thinks about 'Plutarchian heroes [who] outstayed not their fame,' he asks questions in an effort to convince himself to follow their example. 'Age has impaired' (559, 560; 3.4.4) both the heroic ideal of death and the poison that Napoleon finally takes for fame, not honour. The scene is structured in terms of the sardonic laugh he vents in response to the haughty Roustan. The Mameluke may twice declare in verse that he can stay no longer under such disgrace, but he lingers to talk in prose with the expedient Constant for whom fourteen years of honourably serving Napoleon justify a monetary reward.

Napoleon 'loses his last chance of dying well' (695; 3.7.8) in battle at Waterloo and decides that 'Self-sought death would smoke but damply' in the 'lurid loneliness' (699, 698; 3.7.9) of the wood of Bossu. We know that his potential is finally spent when his only wish is 'To wander as a greatened ghost.' He ends up looking back to the future of vast repute that could have been 'If but a Kremlin cannon-shot had met me' or the 'death-drops' had worked at Fontainebleau. The time for a good death has also passed in another sense. Napoleon's regret broadens into the awareness that he came too late in history to be the great man, 'A part past playing now' (699; 3.7.9).

Villeneuve also seeks death's valorized support in a scene paired with Napoleon's attempted suicide, the hero's sword diminished to a dagger instead of poison from a little bag. Except at Trafalgar, we encounter Villeneuve in the interior spaces of his life where he embodies 'the fear to step over the threshold' (Bakhtin, *Dialogic* 248). In the scene off Ferrol, he remains seated in the cabin of his flag-ship, anxiously looking out his window at the seabirds watching him. Their piercing eyes remind him that he lacks the 'eyeless bravery' (94; 1.3.1) that can 'beard contingencies and buffet all' (72; 1.2.2). Indecisiveness haunts even his final moments of consciousness. We see him pacing up and down his bed-chamber in an inn, partly undressed and not quite ready to kill himself in spite of 'Those callings which so long have circled me' (155; 1.5.6). When 'An Emperor's chide is a command to die,' the call to death 'From skies above' (154, 155; 1.5.6) no longer sounds exclusively in lofty spheres. Instead of crowning Villeneuve's life, death ends a carnivalesque career that sees the admiral accursed by the Emperor and forsaken by his friend Decrès, taken prisoner then set free 'Like some poor dolt unworth captivity' (154; 1.5.6). His last words become the final reversal, praise and blame changing sides in a bitter farewell to an 'Ungrateful master; generous foes' (155; 1.5.6).

Villeneuve's struggle to find his own voice is as much a 'combat of despair' (154; 1.5.6) as Trafalgar. Hardy uses the exchange of letters leading up to the battle to show how the French admirals are ordained to move without the wide discretionary power Wellington leaves to his generals at Vitoria. From Boulogne Napoleon tries to be everywhere through the external authority of his discourse that performs as a set of 'rules' demanding the gravest application. Writing to Decrès, and through him to Villeneuve, he expects '"That steadfastly you stand by word and word, / Making no question of one jot therein"' (36; 1.1.2). Officially there can be no conversing with this unconditional language. Villeneuve tells Lauriston that 'I sign to every word' assuring the Emperor that 'our intent is modelled on his will' (71; 1.2.2). Inner speech does not turn freely into outer speech. The most Villeneuve can do is pen ambiguous lines to Napoleon about the rotten state of the marine, while inwardly the 'pale secret chills' (72; 1.2.2) and makes him disobey orders.

What finally proves decisive is never put in writing. Villeneuve 'Leaps to meet war, storm, Nelson – even the grave' (124; 1.5.1) after Napoleon accuses him to Decrès of being a moral coward and traitor. The din of Trafalgar does not prevent Villeneuve from continuing to hear an Emperor who sneers at his lack of 'cool audacity' (136; 1.5.3), the very 'clenched audacity' (127; 1.5.1) he sees in Nelson's ships. The way the '"Bucentaure" heroically continues ... to keep up a reply' to the English also answers Napoleon: 'To-day shall leave him nothing to desire!' (136; 1.5.3).

Ney also 'grows rash' and 'darkly brave' (124; 1.5.1) in response to
the Emperor's abusive voice. The accusatory tone Ney hears after fail-
ing to secure Quatre-Bras – 'I fear you are not the man that once you
were; / Of yore so daring, such a faint-heart now!' – makes him ask for
'one rich last opportunity' (626; 3.6.3). Ney gets his chance at Waterloo,
but his actions cease to mean only one thing in the tangle of praise and
blame. Napoleon admits 'Ney does win me!' only after condemning
his charges as a blunder (679; 3.7.6). Wellington calls him the finest cavalry commander though his attack looks like 'a madman's cruel enterprise' (667; 3.7.4). The 'Hero of heroes' is not quite the 'Simple and
single-souled lieutenant' (670; 3.7.4) the Spirit of the Pities makes him
out to be. When the Spirit Ironic looks ahead to the second restoration
to criticize Wellington for not trying to save the 'matchless chief' (668;
3.7.4) from execution as a traitor, we remember that the two-sided Ney
has a lot to answer for after being 'incline[d] to Bourbonry' (555; 3.4.4)
himself in the changing world of dynastic ambition. The carnage and
tumult of Waterloo change him from the epic leader of a grand assault
into a strange uncrowned figure the Spirit of Rumour has to identify:

> That hatless, smoke-smirched shape
> There in the vale, is still the living Ney,
> His sabre broken in his hand, his clothes
> Slitten with ploughing ball and bayonet,
> One epaulette shorn away.   (693; 3.7.8)

His cry to D'Erlon is now full of caustic wit: 'If we don't perish here at
English hands, / Nothing is left us but the halter-noose / The Bourbons will provide!' (694; 3.7.8).

Authority alone does not make Napoleon's words compelling. He
speaks from a variety of zones, often closing the distance between himself and others to unite in a single discourse the authoritative and the
persuasive word. At the height of his military and political power,
Napoleon finds a way to address the host of nearly half a million soldiers from twenty nations prepared to follow him into Russia:

> the huge array of columns is standing quite still, in circles of companies,
> the captain of each in the middle with a paper in his hand. He reads from
> it a proclamation. They quiver emotionally, like leaves stirred by a wind.
> Napoleon and his staff reascend the hillock, and his own words as
> repeated to the ranks reach his ears, while he himself delivers the same
> address to those about him. (446; 3.1.1)

The meaning of the scene lies entirely in its surface correspondences. Napoleon proclaims from above in elevated speech; his captains like heralds recite from below. He occupies two positions at once, the One and the many, simultaneously speaking and hearing the same centripetal discourse that centres each circle of soldiers. The proclamation enters the ranks as something that cannot be represented, only transmitted, as something read and fully complete, the letter sufficient to the sense. Yet it is no dead quotation. The next day soldiers enthusiastically repeat words from the proclamation by heart. The rhetorical wind that stirs them like leaves blows even higher from Russia as a 'call to the Most High' instead of 'glory' (447, 446; 3.1.1). Literally located in a distanced zone, the counter-proclamation sounds as an impersonal 'distant voice in the wind' (447; 3.1.1) that only the Spirits can hear.

The importance of authoritative discourse is also apparent when Napoleon abdicates and can shape the future only as a speaking person. What he wants and gets is a kind of religious devotion, a 'fast faithfulness' that closes down dialogue within the speech genre of the sacred oath. Filled with emotion, the officers of the National Guard respond, 'We proudly swear to justify the trust!' (540; 3.4.2) One oath is not enough; the authoritative word demands reverent repetition. After Napoleon personally presents 'my son and my successor' he asks, 'you stand by him and her? You swear as much?':

OFFICERS
We swear!

NAPOLEON
This you repeat – you promise it?

OFFICERS
We promise. May the dynasty live forever!   (541; 3.4.2)

The scene closes much the way the Russian war opens, with repetition rather than dialogic agreement swelling through the hierarchical ranks into repeated protestations: 'Their shouts, which spread to the Carrousel without, are echoed by the soldiers of the Guard assembled there' (542; 3.4.2).

Occasionally war permits a responsive understanding and frankness instead of mere repetition. When Napoleon proposes marching on St Petersburg, his marshals 'murmur and shake their heads' (476; 3.1.8).

A year later in Leipzig we hear how his 'scheme of marching on Berlin / Is now abandoned,' though 'Not without high words' (512; 3.3.1). No one even pretends to share the official line of optimism about the upcoming battle. Deprived of their old authority, Napoleon's words no longer set the tone for action. He begins to sound strident and defensive. His coldness and reserve break into open accusations – 'Except me, all are slack!' (515; 3.3.1) – that leave his marshals silent and looking at each other with troubled countenances. The way Napoleon still manages to make disciples of his followers has nothing to do with the 'Secrecy [that] lies at the very core of power' (Canetti 290) in Elias Canetti's analysis of the ruler. Though shrunk in power, Hardy's Napoleon never loses his grasp of the carnivalesque nature of war. With characteristic suddenness, 'The Emperor rises abruptly, sighs, and comes forward' to try one final appeal to familiar comrades made equal in the face of battle:

> All must prepare to grip with gory death
> In the now voidless battle. It will be
> A great one and a critical; one, in brief,
> That will seal France's fate, and yours, and mine!

The effect is the one Hardy shows so often. All promise fervidly to 'do our utmost, by the Holy Heaven!' (517; 3.3.1).

The 'last Great Man' (*Heroes* 319) to Carlyle, Napoleon is the only representative of official history whose thoughts habitually 'lie low' at the same time he is trying to 'carve a triumph large in history' (296; 2.3.2). Having reached his 'burnt-out hour' at Waterloo, he decides that 'Great men are meteors that consume themselves / To light the earth' (700; 3.7.9). The metaphor recalls Carlyle's apocalyptic belief that 'the Great Man was always as lightning out of Heaven; the rest of men waited for him like fuel, and then they too would flame' (*Heroes* 101). 'It is ever the way with the Thinker, the spiritual Hero' that 'What he says, all men were not far from saying, were longing to say' (*Heroes* 28). Hardy's Napoleon 'has words in him which are like Austerlitz Battles'; his 'shaped spoken Thought' often 'awakes the slumbering capability' (Carlyle, *Heroes* 103, 27–8) of others into thought and action. In the afterglow of the treaty of Tilsit his relationship with Tsar Alexander unfolds in the Carlylean terms of Hero and Hero-worshipper. After hearing from Napoleon how they 'As comrades can conjunctly rule the world,' the 'stirred and flushed' Alexander says:

I see vast prospects opened! – yet, in truth,
Ere you, sire, broached these themes, their outlines loomed
Not seldom in my own imaginings;
But with less clear a vision than endows
So clear a captain, statesman, philosoph,
As centre in yourself.   (240; 2.1.8)

At any moment in his speech Napoleon can show his other side, lending his ambitions a bodily substance. When Alexander asks if they should include Austria, he suddenly drops into a cynical frankness. 'It is as if the ancient marketplace comes to life in closed chamber conversation' (Bakhtin, *Rabelais* 421): 'Two in a bed I have slept, but never three.' The political theme of the great alliance leads down to the bedroom and through bodily images back to England who 'Still works to get us skewered by the ears' (240, 239; 2.1.8).

In Spain Napoleon orders pursuit – 'Bear hard on them [the British], the bayonet at their loins' – at the same level that the first straggler imagines retreat: 'Yes – he'll make 'em rub their poor rears before he [Soult] has done with 'em!' (296, 295; 2.3.2). Debasement and laughter both evoke the lower bodily stratum, turning the rearguard into an anatomical front or rear. The distribution of voices in the roadside scene has a pronounced up-and-down swing of its own. Those we hear opposed to Napoleon are more intense versions of the different sides of his own shifting and divided voice. His long soliloquy over the dispatches unfolds as a war of words, quoted threats provoking counter threats, but these dialogic oppositions do not remain on the same high plane. Napoleon encounters his own proclamatory, epic style contemptuously turned against him in the official replies to his peace negotiations. 'The ominous contents,' he tells Soult, 'are like the threats / The ancient prophets dealt rebellious Judah!' (295; 2.3.2). The effect of these impersonal voices from the old and distant zone of sacred truth is to break up his own formal style of address. A second voice emerges with comments such as, 'what is Georgy made to say besides?' and 'The devil take their lecture!' (293; 2.3.2).

These mocking and abusive words in the form of a diatribe against an absent interlocuter have more in common with the deserters from the British army whose prosaic folk humour and profaning speech Hardy intersperses with the blank verse of dynasts and Spirits. While the practitioners of war turn reversals into a serious and official affair, carnival in the true sense hides in the wine cellar with the fugitives. At the non-official level, the distinctions that apply above ground no longer matter. Napoleon's concern with the distant voice whose 'flight's too high' becomes the wish, 'Good Lord deliver us from all great men, and take me back again to humble life!' Uncrowning loses its narrow legal and military definition that treats Napoleon as '"one [who] dethrones and keeps as prisoners / The most legitimate Kings"' (294, 295, 293; 2.3.2). The nearby voices from below turn all that is above inside out or upside down: the Duke of Dalmatia into the Duke of Damnation, a bullet meant to kill into 'this bullet I chaw to squench [not quench] my hunger,' spirit or true doxology into the flesh of 'foreign doxies,' betrayals of alliances into desertions from war itself, fear into laughter ('Mate, can ye squeeze another shardful from the cask there, for I feel my time is come!'), military courage into the 'courage to do nothing.' The idea that slowly and solemnly takes shape in Pierre Bezuhof's aristocratic mind in *War and Peace* suddenly and comically occurs to the second deserter only after he has thrown away his firelock and wasted his powder: 'Yes, I could pick him [Napoleon] off now!' The first deserter does not risk even the fantasy of such heroics: 'You lie low with your picking off, or he may pick off you!' (291; 2.3.2).

Even after his most stunning success, at Ulm, Napoleon's thoughts go down to the grotesque body. 'A glowing fire,' he tells Mack,

Is life on these depressing, mired, moist days
Of smitten leaves down-dropping clammily,
And toadstools like the putrid lungs of men.   (115; 1.4.5)

These seemingly casual remarks about the weather remind Mack that he is at least more fortunate than the soldiers struck down on the battlefield. At the same time, whenever Napoleon incorporates the grotesque into his speech we can be sure that England is on his mind. His last, thought-interrupted speech at Ulm, spoken 'in a murmur, after a while' and directed more to himself than Mack, makes his victory far from complete:

Well, what cares England! She has won her game;
I have unlearnt to threaten her from Boulogne ...
    Her gold it is that forms the weft of this
Fair tapestry of armies marshalled here!   (116; 1.4.5)

By the time Napoleon reaches Austerlitz he needs more than the glow of a single fire to offset his own depressing thoughts. The news of France's crushing naval defeat at Trafalgar makes him exaggerate the negative to incredible and monstrous dimensions. The weaving of Pitt's diplomacy begins to sound like the Immanent Will or an invisible crowd:

> And, more than Russia's host, and Austria's flower,
> I everywhere to-night around me feel
> As from an unseen monster haunting nigh
> His country's hostile breath!

Hardy makes everything Napoleon says and does on the eve of Austerlitz a reply to England's 'water-rats' who 'paddle in their slush.' Victory means that 'ships can be wrecked by land!' What will become the high discourse of the Berlin Decree originates in his grotesque and sardonic explanation of what he means:

> I'll bid all states of Europe shut their ports
> To England's arrogant bottoms, slowly starve
> Her bloated revenues and monstrous trade.   (163; 1.6.1)

Such diversity of speech and voice makes Napoleon a much more complex figure than the crude monster of the ego that commentators usually find. In the huge cast of historical characters, he most embodies the web of literary and speech genres that shape the dialogue of *The Dynasts*. Once appropriated by Napoleon, carnival forms and the novelistic spirit do not remain opposed to the official way of life. Instead of representing the 'extrapolitical aspect of the world' (Bakhtin, *Rabelais* 6), they become accomplices in his attempt to unify Europe under his own Imperial rule. Even his official speeches become 'autism for the masses' (Holquist, *Dialogism* 52), playing upon the oneness of the crowd to serve his own political ends. The fulfilment of his carnival promise to lead the people out of the established order never materializes, any more than his assault upon the distanced genres destroys them. The elevated genres are not quite as moribund as Bakhtin claims. What he refers to as the process of novelization shows the tenacity of the old as much as the influence of the new.

SEVEN

The Crowds of War

The power of words, official and unofficial, to sway the masses leads directly to our next subject – the crowds of war. One moment a voice dictating orders to thousands of troops, the next a figure riding in the ranks, Napoleon would be nothing without the crowd. Before we even hear him speak in *The Dynasts*, we see the harbour of Boulogne crowded with his vessels and soldiers, the French invasion force in turn drawing a squadron of English ships. The theme of war fills the benches and packs the gallery of the English Parliament, while dividing its members into sides that oppose each other like armies with their 'riddling fire' (48; 1.1.3). As we shall see, Hardy represents war as the eruption of two crowds whose struggle brings the problem of the one in the many down from the clouds to the earth.

Not surprisingly, the little that Bakhtin has to say about the crowd is entirely positive. Carnival transforms the unruly many into the noble one: 'The carnivalesque crowd in the marketplace or in the streets is not merely a crowd. It is the people as a whole' (*Rabelais* 255). What *The Dynasts* brings out is the danger implicit in Bakhtin's idealization of the folk and their joyful relativity. The people's awareness of their immortality can in the context of war become a useful indifference towards death; the subordination of the individual to the collective can serve the purposes of a military leader; and the realization that established authority and truth are relative can be redirected at the enemy.

Since war becomes the way the people enter history in *The Dynasts*, we need a theory of the crowd that takes into account its violent tendencies. Elias Canetti, the chief modern theorist of the crowd, makes violence central to his analysis of collective action and thus it is with his ideas that we may begin.

According to Canetti, an army can be called a crowd only in a very limited sense: it is 'an artificial gathering of men,' a closed instead of an open or natural crowd. Someone must command an army; 'everyone gives commands to everyone' in a crowd and these spread horizontally rather than vertically. Nevertheless an army remains susceptible to what Canetti designates as an eruption: the sudden transition from a closed into an open crowd. 'Since the French Revolution,' he argues, 'these eruptions have taken on a form which we feel to be modern [and] have engulfed even wars, for all wars are now mass wars' (310, 324, 22).

In Part First of *The Dynasts* only Napoleon sees that the eruption of the crowd has changed the nature of warfare. The man carried to power by the 'reversal' (Canetti 48) crowd justifies his plan for invading England in revolutionary terms that presuppose a stratified society to be overthrown: invasion means 'setting free / From bondage to a cold manorial caste / A people who await it' (75; 1.2.3). He makes war sound like a struggle between two fundamentally different crowds. The French army retains something of the spontaneous character of the true crowd: 'Two hundred thousand volunteers, right fit, / Will join my standards at a single nod.' The coalition recruits 'Scarce weld to warriors after toilsome years' (116; 1.4.5). When Napoleon broods about 'England's hirelings' and 'paid slaves' (162; 1.6.1), money becomes a substitute for the closed crowds who oppose him. At Austerlitz he feels that 'Pitt's guineas are the foes' (163; 1.6.1) and at Borodino he defines the enemy with a contemptuous pun as 'this Russian horde' – and hoard – '/ Which English gold has brought together here / From the four corners of the universe' (463; 3.1.4).

Canetti gives the name crowd symbols to 'collective units which do not consist of men, but which are still felt to be crowds' (75). Money is a variation of the heap; the rest of his crowd symbols are natural: corn, forest, rain, rivers, wind, sand, fire, and the sea (see 75–90). These common units appear, some prominently, in Hardy's scenes of battle or mass movement. For example, the crowds of war have both a metaphoric and metonymic relation to rivers in *The Dynasts*. The Spirits foresee 'The eastward streaming of Napoleon's host' (99; 1.3.2); the narrator sees 'three reddish-grey streams of marching men' (396; 2.6.1) at Torrès Védras. We also watch columns following, crossing, or joining at rivers. During the Austrian march towards Ulm, the picture of 'the Inn discharging its waters' into the Danube forms the background, with the Austrian columns 'converging from the east upon the banks of the Inn' (98; 1.3.3) in the foreground. We initially locate the French army on Lobau from a bird's-eye prospect that yields a natural crowd symbol in the form of the river Danube crossing the foreground. If 'rivers are especially a symbol for the time when the crowd is forming,' for the '*slow*' (Canetti 83, 84) crowd, we are reminded of the feat of gathering 170,000 soldiers on the island, so closely packed that they have the density of Canetti's crowd. On the night before the battle of Austerlitz, 'the invisible presence of the countless thousands of massed humanity that compose the two armies makes itself felt indefinably.' What can be seen takes the shape of collective units: 'a white fog stretching like a sea' below, the wooded hills on the left, the 'innumerable and varying lights' (160; 1.6.1) mid-distance on the Pratzen plateau, and the fires of the French burning in the foreground. 'Fire,' says Canetti, '... is the strongest and oldest symbol of the crowd' (26). As the first Austerlitz scene closes, the dying fires of the French suddenly come alive in a multiple but cohesive way. Hearing his marshals proclaim that 'Nought lags but day, to light our victory,' Napoleon proceeds to turn the many torches of his soldiers into 'one wide illumination' (164, 165; 1.6.1). The light that 'grows and strengthens' (168; 1.6.2) stands for both Napoleon's popularity and the 'irresistible increase' (Canetti 82) of the crowd, including the 'most enthusiastic of the soldiers' who 'follow the Emperor in a throng as he progresses' (165; 1.6.1).

The careful timing of this eruption indicates that Napoleon has a sharp eye to the attributes of Canetti's crowd and how they can work to his advantage. When most successful, he satisfies the crowd's need for density by establishing a 'massed and menacing' position, its urge for growth by pointing to the vast new armies forming in France, its desire for direction by providing the goal of victory, and its drive for equality by 'Taking his risk with every ranksman here' (161; 1.6.1).

Most importantly, the crowd feeling of equality shares much in common with the carnival spirit of communal performance. Bakhtin and Canetti agree that 'only together can men free themselves from their burdens of distance' (Canetti 18). In carnival 'what is suspended first of all is hierarchical structure' (Bakhtin, *Problems* 123). Similarly, the 'crowd does not actually exist' until the moment of discharge when people 'get rid of their differences and feel equal.' 'Suddenly,' says Canetti, 'it is as though everything were happening in one and the same body' (17, 16).

Hardy's Napoleon is particularly adept at making the collective other indistinguishable from his own will. Paradoxically, his eminence depends on the way his immanence creates an atmosphere of equality, freedom, and familiarity. 'I can't be everywhere' (163; 1.6.1), he admits about Trafalgar, but by land he is like the Immanent Will. It is the feeling that 'He's here! The Emperor's here!' in the midst of the gathering crowd that inspires his soldiers on the eve of Austerlitz. The sequence of events is typical: first the Emperor's approach, then an old Grenadier 'approaching Napoleon familiarly' without regard for distinctions of rank. What he most wants to hear then becomes a promise on behalf of the whole army: 'We'll bring thee Russian guns and flags galore / To celebrate thy coronation-day!' (165; 1.6.1). It is as if the army and its head are two parts of the same body. ''Tis mine,' Napoleon tells his troops at Jena, 'to time your deeds / By light of long experience: yours to do them' (221; 2.1.4).

It is not until Part Second that the Napoleonic wars truly become a clash of peoples. Each scene of national upheaval shows that war is no longer simply a matter of official alliances, like Pitt's grand coalition of Part First. The outbreak of war depends increasingly on the eruption of the patriotic crowd whose shouts in the public square or its adjoining streets are the first sounds of 'war's loud trade' (216; 2.1.3). If carnival's logic of crowning and uncrowning helps illuminate these eruptions and the double crowd of war, they in turn show that 'laughter means abuse, and abuse could lead to blows' (Bakhtin, *Dialogic* 23). Each scene preliminary to battle registers 'the unique and violent feeling of the open crowd' (Canetti 25) and its tendency to find a scapegoat – someone, whether Godoy or Napoleon – to stand as 'author of our ills' (313; 2.3.5). There is no simple opposition between unofficial protest and established authority. The old dynasts usually benefit from the popular opposition to Napoleon and the crowds themselves exemplify 'false consciousness' in varying degrees. Yet as the crowd evolves in Part Second its orientation changes from past glory to present news and future freedom, if only from Napoleon's domination.

Prussia's decision to fight Napoleon alone in 1806 begins as a distant affair with the breakdown of diplomacy and ends on the battlefield where 'The King himself / Fought like the commonest' (224; 2.1.4). If war – to paraphrase the famous definition of Clausewitz who served in the Jena campaign – is the continuation of politics by other means, politics are now subject to popular pressures that broaden and intensify the King's Erfurt manifesto with its narrow emphasis on 'the safety and honour of his crown' (215; 2.1.2). Before the Prussian regiments 'crash like trees at felling-time' (224; 2.1.4), the nation erupts like fire into an open crowd. At first, 'The smouldering dudgeon of the Prussian King ... / Bursts into running flame' (215; 2.1.2). The fire spreads through the Queen to the citizens and leads the Chorus of the Pities to conclude that 'The soul of a nation distrest / Is aflame.' How the many can be one remains the problem of both the crowd and the Will. To the third citizen, unity means 'we awake, though we have slumbered long' (219, 217; 2.1.3); to the Spirits the 'blind, reckless, dynamic movement ... always present in the gathering crowd' (Canetti 197) suggests that there is little difference between the heaving Will and the thronging citizens of Berlin. 'So doth the Will,' says the Years, 'objectify Itself / In likeness of a sturdy people's wrath.' So intense is the spontaneous behaviour of the many that even the Years begins to stress the importance of the vigilance that is absent. The Pities characteristically add that the eager unrest has an aim but agree that the national soul is 'Unconscious well-nigh as the Will / Of its part.' 'It boils in a boisterous thrill / Through the mart' (219; 2.1.3) and onto the battlefield where, according to one straggler, 'patriotic rage,' uniting high and low, 'Brimmed marshals' breasts and men's' (224; 2.1.4). The loud threats and symbolic violence in the streets of Berlin make military blows the extension of carnivalesque abuse. The narrator notices how some young officers, in an unofficial 'frolic of defiance' when they are off duty, 'draw their swords, and whet them on the steps of the French Ambassador's residence as they pass.' Like the sounds of the boisterous crowd, 'The noise of whetting is audible through the streets' (219; 2.1.3).

Here and elsewhere in *The Dynasts*, the patriotic spirit coincides with one side of the marketplace, its negative pole, without offering more than a narrow and official version of carnival's chance to have a new outlook on life. 'Trusting ebbed glory in a present need' (219; 2.1.3), the Prussians seem from the Overworld to transfer to contemporary events and persons the time-and-value contour of the past. To defeat the 'rank adventurer' of low time is 'To assert [the nation's] old prowess, and stouten its chronicled fame!' (217, 219; 2.1.3). The Spirits hear no voice of reflection, no laughter, and no difference between the Prussian people and their leaders. No one takes 'count of the new trends of time' and 'modern methods counterposed,' presumably Napoleonic. Everyone speaks without reservations about the future: 'Victory is visioned, and seemings as facts are averred' (219, 220; 2.1.3).

The Spirits' own seemings make possible the facts as they understand them. The extreme evaluative contrasts that organize the response of the Pities and the Years put the old and the new, wrath and circumspection, blindness and foresight on opposite sides at the outbreak of war. In the crowd itself, some of the citizens do more than look back to a Germany united by 'one tradition, interest, hope.' The third citizen at least distinguishes between leader and followers on the French side. He starts out condemning 'This France' then corrects himself: 'or rather say, indeed, this Man – / (People are honest dealers in the mass).' Even when he invokes the epic past of fathers, a note of comic familiarity enters: 'Surely Great Frederick sweats in his tomb!' (217; 2.1.3). Official diplomacy is not a matter of high ideals to the fifth citizen: it comes down to provisions. His frank realism makes the affairs of state reappear in a zone of crude contact where the selfish and trivial interests of the dynasts appear for what they are:

> Our ambassador Lucchesini is already leaving Paris. He could stand the Emperor no longer, so the Emperor said he could not stand Lucchesini. Knobelsdorf, who takes his place, has decided to order his snuff by the ounce and his candles by the pound, lest he should not be there long enough to use more.

There may be no chorus of the laughing people in the streets but another consciousness that places the body and its needs at the centre of social reality crosses the dominant mood of high seriousness. 'Heaven,' the first citizen concludes, 'I must to beer and 'bacco, to soften my rage!' (218, 219; 2.1.3).

For Hardy, the authentic meaning of the Napoleonic era and its events is disclosed as much in the crowd scenes at the beginning of the century as by the thought at the end of the century. Whatever its forms of unity, popular and/or dynastic, the world of the many, like the Will itself, exceeds the understanding of the Spirits. Whereas Hardy usually lets us hear some individual voices in the crowd, the Spirits tend to reduce difference to a single consciousness. In the very first crowd scene in *The Dynasts*, the narrative voice mentions boisterous singing in a street near the office of the minister of marine in Paris. The Spirit of the Pities, perhaps with the Napoleonic emblem of the bee in mind, hears only 'confused and simmering sounds without, / Like those which thrill the hives at evenfall / When swarming pends' (37; 1.1.2).

Before the Spirit of the Years converts these natural sounds into quoted words, he presets them in a scornful way:

> They but proclaim the crowd,
> Which sings and shouts its hot enthusiasms
> For this dead-ripe design on England's shore,
> Till the persuasion of its own plump words,
> Acting upon mercurial temperaments,
> Makes hope as prophecy.

In Pity's transformation downward, the crowd sounds less than human; in the Year's transformation upward, festive hope becomes prophetic confidence. What they say in the crowd remains in the Years' blank verse and doubles his own belief in the One above the many and his own habit of proclaiming rather than speaking. The crowd apparently feels much the same about their 'Unwavering' and 'irresistible' (38; 1.1.2) Emperor as the Years does about the Will's 'High Influence.' Napoleon is literally absent yet present in the crowd's thoughts; the Will is 'something hidden' yet urges matter into motion. Whether the 'goverance of ... massed mortalities' is by Napoleon, nature, or the Will, the crowd makes only one confused sound and has only one deluded voice. Viewed negatively as patriotic crowds, all of the 'panting peoples' (39, 38; 1.1.2) of Europe participate blindly in a mock pastoral, gathering emotionally in the streets only to fight desperately in the fields.

The danger of judging the crowds of war by what the Spirits say can be seen in the few commentaries that recognize how *The Dynasts* addresses the modern, mass phenomena of war as well as the monistic theory of the universe. Like the Spirit of the Years, Amiya Chakravarty obliterates the man in the mass: all crowds have lapsed into the 'Nature-"Will"' (36). F.R. Southerington does not so much contest the terms of Chakravarty's argument as reverse the relative positions of 'the hope for collectivist action' versus 'the disease of the Will.' To subscribe to this view, however, we must, like the Spirit of the Pities, look beyond the individual and beyond the various specific crowds to the nations 'seen collectively as a character' (Southerington 232, 170, 188).

In its entirety, including the voices in the streets, and as one of numerous crowd scenes, the Berlin spectacle contributes to the ongoing and relative relation between old and new. The high and serious voices in the Overworld, often forming into choruses or crowds of their own, and often taking the supreme crowd of the Will as their new way of understanding old doings, overlook the world's carnivalesque ambivalence that joins the old and the new. Napoleon is the first to modernize or novelize war, but he does so in the name of the old, for Empire and, eventually, a dynasty. The Prussian nationalism that he inadvertently awakens is not simply old-fashioned: it is a concrete sign that the struggle against French imperialism now moves in the direction of total war. Hardy never tries to get around the popularity of the Napoleonic wars on both sides, though this is unstable and can waver or even reverse itself in France or be contested in the English parliament. Patriotism is not without its transformative effects. To fight Napoleon successfully the old dynasts must mobilize the patriotic crowd, and though the birth of a new political system is forestalled, the nation begins to emerge as something higher than King or Emperor.

In Spain the invasion of one crowd, the 'multitudes of Napoleon's soldiery' (251; 2.2.1), provokes the spontaneous gathering of another in the square at Aranjuez near Madrid. In one respect carnival's logic works in reverse: the people want to prevent the King from abdicating, not to mock and uncrown him. The narrator hears 'the peaceful purl of the Tagus,' signalling the time when the crowd is still 'Pouring in / By thousands from Madrid' (254, 257; 2.2.2) and its movement is still under control, 'before the eruption and discharge' (Canetti 84). People 'shout and address each other vehemently' to encourage their growth beyond the public space already filled. From the aristocratic point of view, the clamour is mistaken for that of a reversal crowd. The Queen fears 'The Paris terror will repeat it here' (254; 2.2.2), while the King, 'thinking [the crowd] wanted his head' (259; 2.2.2), is reluctant to show himself. This 'night of comic horror' (Wright 175) is also a night in carnivalized time when the Queen in cloak and veil has to bribe her way back into the Palace and the King, bowing and trembling before the crowd below from the balcony above, is forced to speak in humble prose as he reads the decree that grants 'the wish of the people' to have Godoy dismissed. The topsy-turvy scene registers many of the new trends of time as they affect the old Bourbon regime. The threat of Napoleon closes up the distance between the King and his subjects, the soldier and the citizen, the high leader and the low crowd. The traditional centre of unofficial life, the square, now appears right in front of the Royal Palace and serves as a place for the people to communicate their grievances. Far from homogeneous, they consist of 'a mixed multitude of soldiery and populace' (259, 254; 2.2.2) led by 'Uncle Peter,' in reality the Count of Montijo.

Throughout the scene names take on a carnivalesque ambivalence or, as Montijo observes, 'Our titles are put to comical uses in these days.' His reference is to Godoy's mistress, the self-styled Countess of Castil-lofiel, uncrowned in public as 'only that pretty wench of his, Pepa Tudo' (258; 2.2.2). The Favourite and the Prince of the Peace, Godoy, turns into his opposite. The other side of 'Long life to the King' becomes 'death to Godoy!' (260; 2.2.2) when the populace becomes a baiting crowd. It is not just Godoy's love, spread comically over three jealous women, that 'burns not in singleness!' (253; 2.2.2). The single phenomenon of the crowd also has many names. From a palace window, Godoy and the Queen look down in both senses on the unruly mob. Hardy uses only the term 'crowd' to indicate their collective voice. The citizens defend themselves as an injured people and the narrator, as if unable to decide, refers to the multitude, mob, crowd, populace, people, and throng who are never quite predictable, one moment yelling, the next silent, or changing directions in sudden rushes and surges.

One scene earlier, the slow crowds of French serpentine into Spain in three river-like processions that also carry the threat of snakes. On the night at Aranjuez, with Murat close to Madrid, the question of Napoleon's intentions divides the Spanish court from its people. We hear that Prince Fernando 'lauds the French / As true deliverers' but the last word belongs to the crowd's favourite, Montijo, who subverts the official interpretation of Bonaparte by linking him to Godoy: 'We have saved our nation from the Favourite, / But who is going to save us from our Friend?' (253, 264; 2.2.2). The repeated emphasis on the crowd swelling, still increasing in numbers, until they are now a great throng (257, 260, 262; 2.2.2), with no mention of their dispersal, suggests that the eruption will soon spread to the nation as a whole. One scene later, the French and the Spanish emerge from the crisis of ambivalence prepared for war. The Rumours chant how the high motive of patriotism unites the Spanish people who look to England rather than their court to 'crown a cause which ... bond and free / Must advocate enthusiastically' (265; 2.2.3).

As one of Hardy's historical ordinates, the crowd at Aranjuez embodies the start of the Spanish insurrection. Even listening to Napier's serious and caustic account, we can sense the carnivalesque possibilities of a popular uprising more tangled and contradictory than Godoy's personal affairs:

The Spanish insurrection presented indeed a strange spectacle. Patriotism was seen supporting a vile system of government; a popular assembly working for the restoration of a despotic monarch; the higher classes seeking a foreign master; the lower armed in the cause of bigotry and misrule. The upstart leaders, secretly abhorring freedom, though governing in her name, trembled at the democratic activity they had themselves excited; they called forth all the bad passions of the multitude, and repressed the patriotism that would regenerate as well as save. (1:v)

It is not finally the bad passions of the multitude that Hardy stresses. Their climax of destruction occurs within a carnivalesque atmosphere of familiar contact, misalliances, scandal, disguise, and a serio-comical mixture of prose and verse. After the crowd literally moves up, everything comes down. We hear with Godoy's wife their rude 'trampling up the stairs' (261; 2.2.2) of the mansion, then watch how

They begin knocking the furniture to pieces, tearing down the hangings, trampling on the musical instruments, and kicking holes through the paintings they have unhung from the wall. These, with clocks, vases, carvings, and other movables, they throw out of the window. (263; 2.2.2)

Although the crowd's behaviour 'shows but useless spite' to the aristocratic Montijo and leaves a scene of desolation to the narrator, we need not conclude that 'there is no sense in it.' The deeper logic suggests the destruction of a hierarchy which is no longer recognized. 'Smash [Godoy's] nicknacks,' exclaim several citizens, 'since we can't smash him' (263; 2.2.2). By lowering what the narrator initially describes as objects of rare workmanship to trivial nicknacks, the crowds thinks in a carnival way. When Godoy's richly furnished room turns into the equivalent of the public square, high art goes out the window or onto the floor as something only the selfish rich can collect.

The Spanish crowd acts on the borderline between carnival and war, laughter and terror, symbolic gestures and real destruction. On the one hand, they twice have altercations with Godoy's guards of honour and a shot is fired. The way they break the line of his hussars, invade his mansion, and rout his furniture suggests a military action. On the other hand, no one is actually killed and rather than being out of control the crowd stops and listens to Montijo's warning at the end of the scene. The people who force dynasts to get 'wrapped up for flight' (257; 2.2.2) resemble a crowd of masqueraders, their leaders armed with 'various improvised weapons,' the life-guards who join them in a state of undress, and the citizens uncovering when they realize that the woman sitting alone in the room is Godoy's wife. The misalliance of a Bourbon princess calmly confronting the passionate people helps keep the violence in a laughing perspective and allows individual voices to disrupt the cohesiveness of the crowd. At first the 'citizens,' not crowd, switch into respectful verse to address 'an injured wife' (261, 262; 2.2.2) and offer her safe conduct, but when some of them place too much trust in her word – 'She said [Godoy] was not here, and she's a woman of honour' – the first citizen drily offers the reminder, 'She's his wife' (263; 2.2.2).

The historical nature of displacement is such that the tense time in Vienna repeats with difference the excited and anxious mood in Berlin in 1806 and the critical night near Madrid in 1808. The year is 1809 in the city of the waltz where dancing and patriotism illuminate each other. Like Napoleon himself and during the same dynastic period, the waltz conquered Europe without the sanction of royal courts. It began as a dance of the people and became the first of the non-aristocratic ballroom dances, a madly whirling intruder from the lower classes into polite society.

Hardy introduces the waltz at the close of a scene of patriotism built on a public square intensity of sound, specifically a café in the Stephans-Platz where we hear 'a clinking of glasses,' 'thumping on the tables' (312, 313; 2.3.5), and 'a band ... in a distant street, with shouting.' Austria's 'upping to the war in suddenness' (311; 2.3.5) is mimicked in the movements of the citizens. The sounds and reports of 'swiftly swelling zeal' outside the café intensify the general enthusiasm for the war inside. 'The young sitters jump up with animation and go out'; the rest look up from their newspapers and stand up to drink to the war. The upping to the war has the abruptness of a carnival reversal. The image of people rising from seats gives way to the view of dancers not just turning but whirling round and round:

> The figures are seen gracefully moving round to the throbbing strains of a string-band, which plays a new waltzing movement with a war-like name, soon to spread over Europe. The dancers sing patriotic words as they whirl.

There is something new about the war as well as the dance with which it is linked. The struggle against Napoleon is now as popular as the waltz: 'Hot volunteers vamp in from vill and plain – / More than we need in furthest sacrifice!' (315; 2.3.5).

To Walter F. Wright, 'the eagerness of "hot volunteers" and the joy of the dance suggest the hypnotic yielding of the individual will to the Will that impels the multitude' (206). This kind of hierarchical reading, from the Overworld and the Spirit of the Years' metaphysics down, effects a double erasure of the individual by confusing the crowd with the multitude and by subordinating this 'sign for the unknowable' to the invisible Will. The 'crowd in its metaphysical aspect' (Carey 53, 21) yields up the idea of undifferentiated power; the crowds that can be seen or heard – citizens, church attendants, soldiers, volunteers, dancers – suggest a complicity of forces. The anonymity of the common speakers does not mean that they lack individuality. In the café conversation, the second citizen consistently leads the argument to fight again. No one disagrees with his idea of war's fierce necessity. It is a matter of popular consent, not a condition imposed by the ruling elite. 'If war,' says the second citizen, 'had not so patly been declared, / Our howitzers and firelocks of themselves / Would have gone off to shame us!' He also predicts that 'The Russian cabinet can not for long / Resist the ardour of the Russian ranks / To march with us' (312, 314; 2.3.5). Patriotism conquers Austria at the same time the waltz does the dancing-rooms of Vienna, but both are imperial in another way, strengthening the cause of old empires at the expense of the new one. In the streets the abusive word threatens Napoleon, not dynastic power as such; in the ballroom, the subversive waltz gets recycled as a patriotic dance.

Germany, Spain, Austria: it is not the case that 'before turning to the battles themselves Hardy interposed scenes of a quite different nature' (Wright 175). In the streets, cafés, and squares of Europe we still watch crowd events that deepen the carnivalesque picture of war. The peoples 'distressed by events which they did not cause' (Fore Scene 27) in Part First become a cause themselves in Part Second. By 1809 Napoleon can no longer scoff at the enemy's soldiers as 'compulsion's scavengings' (116; 1.4.5) or count in most countries and states on marshalling the popular impulse on his side. He cannot finally control the conditions that he helps bring into existence. We often see him after Wagram watching the crowd, only to be caught up in their irresistible movements, until at Waterloo he 'is involved none knows where in the crowd of fugitives' (696; 3.7.8).

More than any of Napoleon's other military adventures, the Russian campaign lends itself to a carnivalesque conception of the historic process and all the more so when compressed, from Borodino on, into an uninterrupted series of crises, one surprise following another so that always the 'near-seeming happens not' (481; 3.1.9). In spite of the sombre tone, carnivalization functions with enormous external visibility, carried into the open, as it were, with the long columns that stretch out carnival's special time in the vast spaces of Russia. Everyone is drawn into the same mass movements; everything is seen as a double crowd event. If 'carnival images closely resemble certain artistic forms, namely the spectacle' (Bakhtin, *Rabelais* 7), Hardy represents history as a massive spectacle without footlights and for all the people. The Russian army follows almost an entire city's populace out of Moscow; the French army also abandons the city, leaving with a 'train of followers – / Men, matrons, babes, in babbling multitudes' (479; 3.1.9). The epic distance that separates the Emperor from the crowd on the way to Moscow disappears during the retreat. Going forward, he views events from a hillock above the Niemen River, from the Shevardino redoubt, the Hill of Salutation, and from the summit of the Ivan tower, 'a small lone figure gazing / Upon his hard-gained goal' (473; 3.1.7); going back, he 'can be discerned amid the rest, marching on foot through the snowflakes, in a fur coat and with a stout staff in his hand' (481; 3.1.9) like an ironic pilgrim. The shape of the entire action is a stunning reversal in which the pursuer and the pursued switch places and the role of the trickster passes from Napoleon to the fox Kutúzov with his foul tricks (476; 3.1.8), such as wheeling round Moscow to cut off the French. One turnabout forces another, the French army treading 'the trail by which it came.' The carnival categories that permeate the scenes of mass upheaval, slaughter, and catastrophe come down to earth in a literal and frightening way. Carnival logic is a matter of life and death. A bringing down to earth means just that when 'marching figures drop rapidly, and almost immediately become white gravemounds' (480; 3.1.9). Hunger and cold, not carnival play, force objects to be utilized in reverse. The French soldiers shoot horses for meat and use gunpowder for salt; some wear 'rugs for warmth, some quilts and curtains, some even petticoats and other women's clothing' (481; 3.1.9). From the perspective of the clouds or the earth, uncrowning and debasement share the same road as the dream of winning for 'Imperial splendor ... a crown / Unmatched in long-scrolled Time!' (492; 3.1.12).

Although the Years responds to the question 'Why doth [Napoleon] go?' (448; 3.1.1), he is not concerned with the lonely traveller. All of his transparencies are attempts to explain the behaviour of various peoples, armies, crowds, and processions by seeking unity in diversity. Yet the Will's 'inexplicable artistries' only deepen a mystery already present. The invasion at the beginning of Part Third seems strange enough as a phenonemal movement. The grand army emerges as 'a shadowy amorphous thing in motion,' then returns to 'blackness' (445, 450; 3.1.1) on the other side of the stream. When the scene shifts to Borodino and the army becomes a crowd, there is something magical as well as mechanical about their motions. Now the crowd 'sway and show' the Years their Will rather than his Will anatomizing the human spectacle. The huge massacre at the great redoubt makes the Years think of the combatants as mindless minions of the spell cast by a Will that is indistinguishable from the web of rage that forms when 'the action almost ceases to be a battle' (467; 3.1.5) and the two sides become one emotional crowd intent on slaughter.

The field of Borodino, 'which is mostly wild, uncultivated land' (461; 3.1.4), is in keeping with the carnivalesque nature of war. When 'wild war is on the board again' (446; 3.1.1) and the unenclosed land of Russia replaces the open spaces of the public square, almost anything can happen – and does. The huge size and strange shape of subsequent events make the war a weird phantasma without any reference to the Will. The soldiers sway in 'mechanized enchantment' (467; 3.1.5) at Borodino; Enchantment itself 'seems to sway from quay to keep' (473; 3.1.7) in Moscow.

The 'persistence of the unforeseen' (Hardy, *Mayor of Casterbridge* 411) allows no impression or evaluation to become stabilized. The natural shades into the fantastic, the fantastic into the grotesque, and the grotesque into something so monstrous as to seem deprived, like nature's 'skinny growths' (478; 3.1.9), of any sustaining role. The Russians retreat 'like autumnal birds of passage' and a 'migrant multitude' (470; 3.1.6) in an ordinary seasonal occurrence but what they leave behind shocks Napoleon: 'Moscow deserted? What a monstrous thing!' (473; 3.1.7). When the invaders retreat, the viewpoint shifts to high amongst the clouds and history seems as spectral and monstrous as the Years' Will. The French appear to be 'An object like a dun-piled caterpillar' that moves 'as a single monster might' (479; 3.1.9) across a landscape where 'all is phantasmal grey and white.' Even as a series of optical effects, the clouds opening and closing like the shutter of a camera or the lid of an eye, the scene has the peculiar oneness of the grotesque world. The falling snow and the crawling caterpillar seem linked in a soft and ambivalent way. Feet shuffle slowly in painful heaves through the snow, while bodies drop off quickly and painlessly into it. The first 'white morsel' from the sky appals the living with the threat of starvation; the flakes that follow leave the dead 'enghosted' with a pall of 'caressing snow.' Natural proportions as well as features are confounded. The objects of war come into focus on the confused expanse of earth like tiny things magnified under a microscope. Endowed with the Spirits' enlarged powers of vision, the narrator sees Cossacks with lances 'like huge needles a dozen feet long' and watches the enormous caterpillar change shape in a surprising way: 'instead of increasing in size by the rules of perspective, it gets more attenuated, and there are left upon the ground behind it minute parts of itself' (480; 3.1.9).

The panoramic view of the caterpillar reminds us that the unusual point of view in *The Dynasts* is always from on high. Critics agree that the great aerial perspectives, though justly famous (Stewart 211), serve a negative purpose: 'to emphasize Hardy's theme of the inconsequence of man and his designs' (Carpenter 197). The physical elevation of the Spirits or narrator makes for a continual gazing down in the pejorative sense and has lofty implications that turn likeness into fundamental identity, figurations into literal truth. The levelling and equalizing metaphors 'suggest man's unimportance to the Will' (Bailey 113).

We also reach a negative conclusion by a different route, that of the crowd. Critics do not forget that the interweavings of the distance perspective 'always refer to men in the mass' (Dean 210). Hardy 'needed no literary prompting in order to perceive something monstrous, even horrific, about crowds' (White 115), including the collectives of war with their dehumanizing effect on the individual. He grew up in the aftermath of the fear and horror of the revolutionary mob and spent time in London, a city he saw as a collective personality, as both a wheel or mechanism and a beast, 'two of his most powerful metaphors' for the Will. His observations of the unconscious behaviour of London crowds developed 'the technique of the panoramatist' (Sherman 1024, 1018) and deeply influenced the somnambulistic traits of history and the cosmic mind in *The Dynasts*.

What appears to be a 'novel way of treating European vistas' (Orel, Introduction xix), so new that it 'anticipates the cinema' and the 'conventions of an art that had not yet been invented' (Wain x, ix), has some very old roots. One aspect of the 'special type of *experimental fantasticality*' that Bakhtin claims first made its appearance in the menippea becomes fully realized in *The Dynasts*: the bird's-eye view that 'results in a radical change in the scale of the observed phenomena of life' (*Problems* 116). Hardy's technique of defamiliarization points back to the carnivalistic genres, to the line of the menippea 'that estranges earthly reality' (Bakhtin, *Problems* 148) and to the tradition of grotesque realism. We scarcely hear the term grotesque mentioned in discussions of Hardy's panoramic imagination, yet the object viewed always 'transgresses its limits, ceases to be itself. The limits between the body and the world are erased.' The combination, for example, of human and animal traits in *The Dynasts* has more than a modern and negative aspect: it is also 'one of the most ancient of grotesque forms' (Bakhtin, *Rabelais* 310, 316). The old contradictory unity of grotesque becoming finds a new basis in the monistic theory of the universe. The crowd and the Will turn out to be two versions of the same problem of the One and the many. When 'the Will heaves through Space, and moulds the times, / With mortals for Its fingers' (265; 2.2.3), It becomes embodied in crowds and made strange by the conjunctions that 'Time's weird threads so weave!' (99; 1.3.3), the 'firmament / Of causal coils' (407; 2.6.4) displacing the 'Twining and serpentining' (Fore Scene 28) Will-webs.

In the Years' transparencies, the Will seems to unite and control 'all humanity and vitalized matter included in the display'; in the high phenomenal perspectives the crowd and processions of 'bodies substantive' (Fore Scene 28) seem to contain all that exists in the universe, from atoms and insects, to rivers and clouds. So massive is the contest at Leipzig 'that we soon fail to individualize the combatants as beings, and can only observe them as amorphous drifts, clouds, and waves of conscious atoms, surging and rolling together' (519; 3.3.2). Distance gives the mass movements in *The Dynasts* a disturbing ambivalence. The 'sinister black files' of 1815 crawl as softly as 'slowworms through grass' (612, 613; 3.6.2). 'The silent insect-creep' (99; 1.3.2) of the Austrian army in Part First seems harmless enough; the equivalent movement in Part Third carries the threat of inundation, 'like water from a burst reservoir' (539; 3.4.1). The silence of the Dumb Shows is both reassuring and ominous. On the high metaphoric plane, the crowds of war always look strange, but the way they merge with natural phenomena makes them very real as well. The exchange between their collective bodies and the world does not so much overturn the distinction between nature and art as reverse the terms of difference. Rivers appear as a silver thread or a crinkled satin riband; people in uniforms move together like rivers. The French soldiers on the island of Lobau 'are like a thicket of reeds in which every reed should be a man' (321; 2.4.2); the compact plateau of Wagram looks 'so regularly shaped as to seem as if constructed by art' (322; 2.4.3).

The aerial perspectives have the same 'tendency toward duality' (Bakhtin, *Rabelais* 323; see also *Problems* 126) characteristic of carnival and grotesque images. From high aloft the English ships bound for Portugal appear in light, almost playful contrast to their weight of arms and men. After thousands of soldiers get packed like sheep, the 'moth-like' ships undergo their own metamorphosis on the 'liquid plain' (272, 2.2.5). They could belong to earth, sky, or water: each has an 'aëry fin' and all float on before the wind 'like preened duck-feathers' (273, 274; 2.2.5). In Part Third the armies invading France seem to move on the borderline of a series of shifting oppositions. The narrator's reference to beetling castles on the Rhine is as hard to pin down as the Dumb Show that follows. Beetling could mean overhanging, scurrying, or hammering. The beetle or heavy wooden hammer recalls the pounding the castles both received and returned in past wars. The castle might look like the insect with its hard shell or Hardy might be alluding to Wordsworth's sonnet about the 'dance of objects' in space and time, 'Each beetling rampart, and each tower sublime' sweeping past his carriage on the banks of the Rhine and moving backward in 'The venerable pagentry of Time' (266). In *The Dynasts* the stillness of the opening panorama allows the narrator to appreciate the beautiful country but the moving shapes do not obey the aesthetics of the beautiful and the sublime. The 'strange dark patches in the landscape' keep changing shape in a grotesque way. The 'riband-shaped' Russian columns begin to 'twinkle as if they were scaly serpents.' Man and the snake switch places. The town of Mannheim – even the name foregrounds the problem – has 'the look of a human head in a cleft stick' (538; 3.4.1), while the serpents advance without opposition. One reptile is not enough to define the armies: they are 'mostly snake-shaped, but occasionally with batrachian and saurian outlines.' They are also like water and 'glide on as if by gravitation, in fluid figures, dictated by the conformation of the country.' We might be looking at a machine as well, an immense human mechanism or 'train of war-geared humanity' that can be fashioned into a variety of new shapes. In the case of the Austrian army, 'the ductile mass of greyness and glitter is beheld parting into six columns, that march on in flexuous courses of varying distinction' (539; 3.4.1).

The grotesque comparisons convey a variety of tones, depending on the speaker and the type of crowd. The narrator watches the languid motion of the allied armies with both fascination and foreboding. Even when people are reduced to insects, the grotesque is never just satiric. Pity does not believe that the painful heaves of the retreating French army make it 'nothing but a wounded caterpillar' (Carpenter 197), any more than the narrator finds 'the comparative insignificance of man' (Hopkins 436) when the motion of the English columns at Torrès Védras 'seems peristaltic and vermicular, like that of three caterpillars' (396; 2.6.1). *The Dynasts* is not 'a storehouse of images belittling mankind' (Southworth 152). The Years feels contempt for 'great' men, not the crowd, and from the perspective of time, not space. Men such as Napoleon 'Are in the elemental ages' chart/Like meanest insects on obscurest leaves' (701; 3.1.9).

The sinister context of war prevents the grotesque transformations from becoming ludicrous, but the way most of them develop as Dumb Shows provides a link with popular comic genres and festive forms. The military movements unfold in the style of an unconscious mime or mimic fray, a silent *Commedia del Arte* with the soldier as Harlequin. Everyone participates in the low spectacle, its transgressive acts and appearance ironically continuing the mime's ancient tradition of freedom and mockery. Laughter begins to emerge when we follow the mass movements made for peace rather than war. Except for one sentence registering the beautiful forest scenery, the scene of Maria Louisa's procession out of Vienna is a Dumb Show. In *The Dynasts* laughter does not necessarily bring an object up close. We see the sadness of the ladies from the ground, then the 'point of sight is withdrawn high into the air.' Instead of the sublime we get the ridiculous, instead of the beautiful, the grotesque. The 'multitude of Court officials, ladies of the Court, and other Austrian nobility' shrinks to a 'puny concatenation of specks,' 'the huge procession ... looks no more than a file of ants,' speed turns into a crawl, and the great road across Europe into 'a strip of garden-matting.' The comic grotesque is interwoven with the historic theme of the renewal of dynasties, the women 'conscious that upon their sex had been laid the burden of paying for the peace with France' (379; 2.5.5). The 'animated dots pause for formalities' on the frontier of France where Maria Louisa undergoes an abrupt carnivalistic change in fate, becoming 'Marie Louise and a Frenchwoman' (380; 2.5.5).

Whether a distant view introduces the events of war or peace, military turnabouts or 'An old wife doffed for a new' (383; 2.5.6), its grotesque images always reflect an historical world in carnivalesque transformation. In Part First England declares war on Spain; in Part Second their alliance results in the liberation and arming of Spanish prisoners so they can fight for their independence. The official reversals quickly take on a grotesque meaning. For the common soldier, England's entry into the Peninsular War is downward through the gaping mouth into the bodily underworld of the ships. A Semichorus of Years invokes the ancient link between death and swallowing at the very start of the campaign: 'And transports in the docks gulp down their freight / Of buckled fighting-flesh' (271; 2.2.3). Conversely, the last phase of a war can be associated with new beginnings. 'It is the morning of New Year's Day' when the narrator sees the serpents invading France, an uncrowning movement that brings peace but only for a year. The old devouring world of war keeps renewing itself; it has a history of changing shapes and disputed borders. Modern armies cross the Rhine with its old castles because 'At this date in Europe's history the stream forms the frontier between France and Germany' (538; 3.4.1). Much more recent is the boundary formed by the northernmost line of Torrès Védras, still in the process of being built. The two-bodied image of 'innumerable human figures ... busying themselves like cheese-mites' blends feeding with decay and makes construction a matter of destruction, while linking one foreign body with another. The narrator admires the collective energy and work, then notices a harsh reason for the discipline: 'two or three of the soldiers are dangling from a tree by the neck, probably for plundering' (396; 2.6.1). Before the Dumb Show, we are told that the tract which the line crosses looks 'like a late-Gothic shield' (395; 2.6.1). Soldiers continue to need a shield of some sort; now it coincides with a whole peninsula. Masséna arrives knowing that the English lines have 'outer horns and tusks' but has no inkling of their size and position. The shock of the unexpected makes him speak of the prim ponderosities seen through his glass as a grotesque shield of 'burly, bossed disfigurements' (397; 2.6.2). Instead of being driven to the sea, the British entrench themselves in the peninsula. The completion of their lines means that nothing conclusive has yet taken place and the war will enter a new phase.

In every grotesque view we have no difficulty in identifying the human purpose as well as natural process at work. Outside the British lines in Portugal, Loison calls them 'Lord Wellington's select device, / And, like him, heavy, slow, laborious, sure' (398; 2.6.2). From their bird's-eye perspective, the narrator and Spirits repeatedly explain the strange movements below as planned. The French armies that make a creeping progress or serpentine into Spain all form 'part of the same systematic advance' (251; 2.2.1). The Imperial columns gliding and creeping towards Belgium form 'one great movement, co-ordinated by one mind' (611–12; 3.6.1). The Spirit of Rumour sees the way the Austrian army glides into France of 'one intention' (539; 3.4.1) with the other invading forces. A Recording Angel compares the Austrian army nearing Bavaria to molluscs on a leaf, then explains that the movement is one 'manoeuvred by the famous Mack' (98; 1.3.2).

In all these scenes, we are concerned with the movement of peoples from all parts of Europe across great distances. We are often located above frontiers or borders that, while they may coincide with natural features, are man-made and unstable. As the crowd makes history by crossing or transgressing these boundaries, political life assumes the deep ambivalence of the grotesque. Mack's army creeps towards Ulm and the King of Bavaria 'Wavers from this to that,' 'torn between his fair wife's hate of France / And his own itch to gird at Austria's bluff / For riding roughshod through his territory' (99, 98; 1.3.2). The French enter Spain as both guests and intruders, the Spanish royalty seeking their protection, the people treating them as unwelcome comers. One year (1805) Austria sends a vast army to fight against Napoleon, another (1810) a huge procession to pacify him. Neither death nor birth brings anything to an end. Marie Louise brings Napoleon a baby but 'Europe's madding movement' (264; 2.2.3) begins again. Tying one knot begins another severance. Near the end of Part Second we hear how Napoleon and Alexander, 'late such bosom-friends – / Are closing to a mutual murder-bout / At which the lips of Europe will wax wan' (434; 2.6.7).

In Bakhtin's words, 'everything is taken to the extreme, to its outermost limit' where it 'is prepared ... to pass over into its opposite' (*Problems* 167). When the Russians abandon Moscow, Kutúzov is already 'a strange scarred old man with a foxy look, a swollen neck and head, and a hunched figure' (470; 3.1.6); by winter he 'presents a terrible appearance ..., his one eye staring out' (487; 3.1.11). Again the unexpected happens: so close to death himself, he does not prevent Bonaparte, so nearly 'a captive or a corpse,' from escaping. The Russians move parallel to the French columns and when they attack the front and the rear become reflected in one another, Kutúzov and Ney forming 'A pair as stout as thou, Earth, ever hast twinned!' With growing nearness the army, once called the grand, also looks strangely double. The body of regular columns has a tail that 'shows itself to be a disorderly rabble of followers of both sexes.' Nevertheless both order and disorder wear the same 'motley raiment' (481; 3.1.9). For the 'tattered men like skeletons' who reach the open country between Smorgoni and Wilna, everything grand becomes a memory. After sharing a meal, 'officers and privates press together' (484, 486; 3.1.11) in familiar contact around a fire that now means only warmth. The next morning they form another curious picture of carnival in war. What appear to be sleeping men are literally two-sided and ambivalent: 'They all sit / As they were living still, but stiff as horns,' with 'Their clothes ... cindered by the fire in front, / While at their back the frost has caked them hard.' The last marvel of the campaign, that 'they were not consumed' (487; 3.1.11), is also the final twist: after escaping from the flames of Moscow, the French cannot get close enough to the fire in Lithuania.

Laughter does not die with the bivouackers but grows increasingly hollow as the grotesque turns monstrous. At first, the French leaders understand the grotesque from the distance appropriate to irony and humour as something distinctly Russian, though fascinating or alluring. Napoleon finds his attention attracted to the 'slow, weird ambulation' of ecclesiastics at Borodino. Watching through his glass, he laughs at how 'men can be so grossly logicless' (465; 3.1.4). At first sight, Moscow also looks curiously grotesque, 'the peacock of cities to Western eyes.' Davout shares a joke with Napoleon about the 'scores of bulbous church-tops': 'Souls must be rotten in this region, sire, / To need so much repairing!' (471; 3.1.7).

After Moscow, Hardy gives no direct words to the French command. The Dumb Show continues until something as soft as the first snowflake sends a shudder of a different sort through the bivouackers. The news that a straggler whispers has the same effect on the common soldiers in their 'deserted expanse' of land as the spectacle of a city left open has on Napoleon. The initial denials are tinged with a monstrous fear: 'No, surely! He could not desert us so!' (484, 485; 3.1.11). The Emperor's 'great need' comes down to the hard truth that another army 'shall replace our bones' (486; 3.1.11). The feeling of betrayal drives some soldiers insane and sends them dancing round as if the turn of events were a cause for celebration. The 'theme of madness,' as Bakhtin explains, 'is inherent to all grotesque forms, because madness makes men look at the world with different eyes' (*Rabelais* 39). One mad soldier sings for all his grinning cronies, bidding a frank farewell to an ingrate leader while remembering bitterly how 'we loved you true!' The grotesque is no longer foreign, nor laughter one-sided and official. The graveside humour of the song – 'Yet – he-he-he! and ho-ho-ho! – / We'll never return to you' (486; 3.1.11) – seems to reach all the way back to Paris where Napoleon adds his own 'ha-ha!' to an enterprise that 'is quite ridiculous, / Whichever way you look at it' (492; 3.1.12). His laughter allows him cynically to invoke 'the very process of replaceability' (Bakhtin, *Problems* 125) that carnival celebrates. The 'layers of bleaching bones' in Russia only remind him that 'Fishes as good / Swim in the sea as have come out of it' (492, 493; 3.1.12).

In spite of the reduced laughter, the scenes from the hell of Moscow to the limbo of gloom in Lithuania do not belong to any vertical, Dantesque conception of the world. The march back from Moscow is in one respect forward into the future where the crowd assumes the leading role. Seeking to establish an eternal hierarchy – 'The Emperor and the King of Rome for ever!' (464; 3.1.4) – the French find themselves stretched out along the horizontal line of real space and historic time. Everything high or transcendental, including the Will, turns into physical realities and bodily needs. The hope of salvation becomes a bridge over the Beresina, the promised land the homeward bank, the 'Sacred Squadron' a few thousand 'half-naked, badly armed wretches, emaciated with hunger' (483; 3.1.10), the 'souls' of the dead 'Pale cysts' (484; 3.1.10). What Pity sees after Smolensko is emphatically a 'Thing' and 'yet not one but many.' The Years indentifies the object as an army while referring vaguely to how it is 'urged by That within It.' When Pity asks 'And why such flight?' the answer is very different than for the invasion. The Years tells the Recording Angels to rise and sing but their 'minor plain-song' describes the 'master-sway' of the 'Israel-like' (479; 3.1.9) host in terms of fear and hunger.

Canetti himself cites the fate of Napoleon's grand army as a striking example of 'a retreat which was bound to degenerate into a mass flight' (55). Though a picture of diversity, the flight crowd has a coherence that makes this picture misleading. The 'most comprehensive of all crowds' is also the one with the 'greatest tenacity' (53, 54). 'Its motley colours,' Canetti believes, 'are only incidental and, measured against the overpowering force of direction, utterly insignificant.' Until this direction is repeatedly blocked, the mass flight 'remains one powerful and undivided river' (53, 54).

In Hardy, the point of vision descends to earth at exactly the moment when the motley appearance of the French can be seen and their flight becomes checked by a large river. The Beresina is both the obstacle that forces the French to gather as a diverse crowd and, with the Russians closing in, another threat that unites everyone trying to escape. The Dumb Show here is very different than the one at Lobau, though both are threshold scenes set in crisis time on temporary bridges. The narrator mentions how Napoleon passes to safety, then focuses on the real interest of the scene, 'the confused crowd ... pressing to cross.' On this 'stage which is to be such a tragic one' (482; 3.1.10), we see tragedy from the point of view of the marketplace. When the artillery bridge gives way, the Pities hear a loud, marketplace frankness from the fugitives who roll into the stream: 'So loudly swell their shrieks as to be heard above the roar of guns and the wailful wind, / Giving ... their last wild word' – as unrestrained as carnival or war – 'on that mock life through which they have harlequined!' (483; 3.1.10).

By Canetti's standards, what happens on the second bridge, 'the weak pushed over by the strong' (483; 3.1.10), ceases to be a crowd event. The Pities respond to the moment when the 'character of mass flight ... turns into its exact opposite' and becomes a panic. Surprisingly, not 'everyone is intent only on saving himself' (Canetti 53, 54). A counter movement upwards suddenly reverses the image of people clutching like snakes while they are submerged and borne along in the river. The heroic emerges from the grotesque as the Chorus of Pities commemorates the actions of anonymous women in lines so long as to be almost indistinguishable from prose:

> Then women are seen in the waterflow – limply bearing their
>   infants between wizened white arms stretching above;
> Yea, motherhood, sheerly sublime in her last despairing, and
>   lighting her darkest declension with limitless love.   (483; 3.1.10)

To the very end the scene consists of contrasting paired images like the fire on the bridge and the ice in the water. The next morning, as Death itself appears in a thousand motley forms, the 'carnivalization of passion is evidenced first and foremost in its ambivalence' (Bakhtin, *Problems* 159). It is impossible to tell whether the 'Charred corpses hooking each other's arms' are 'bent to embraces of love or rage' (484; 3.1.10).

Hardy shares with Tolstoy the belief that though 'The ancients have passed down to us examples of epic poems in which the heroes furnish the whole interest of the story ... history of that kind is meaningless for our epoch' (Tolstoy 2:897). Both see the Napoleonic period as a mass experience in which life is taken out of life: 'The first fifteen years of the nineteenth century in Europe present an extraordinary movement of millions of people. Men leave their customary pursuits' (2:975). Tolstoy conceives events outside their traditional and official interpretation; history becomes 'the unconscious, universal, swarm-life of mankind' that 'uses every moment of the life of kings for its own purposes.' There is something carnivalesque about his narrator's insistence that 'a king is the slave of history' (2:718), indeed the least of slaves, 'the most enslaved and involuntary' even though every 'unit in the human swarm ... must inevitably obey the laws laid down for him' (2:896, 718). The debasement of the so-called great man, especially Napoleon, is so extreme that he has little or no carnival ambivalence. The crowd fares little better. To 'select for study the homogeneous, infinitesimal elements which influence the masses' (2:977) creates an insurmountable problem for purely historical analysis: 'It is beyond the power of the human intellect to encompass all the causes of any phenomenon.' The very reason monists posit a One in the many leads Tolstoy to assert that 'There is, and can be, no cause of an historical event save the one cause of all causes' (2:1168). When Pierre Bezuhof finally learns to see the 'eternally great, unfathomable and infinite life around him,' the question 'Why?' about life has a clear answer: 'Because God is' (2:1309). The uncrowning of the great man ultimately means the elevation of 'Him who governs men and worlds.' In Tolstoy, the belief that 'the course of earthly happenings is predetermined from on high' (2:972, 932) is a monologic certainty; in Hardy the Will's 'High Influence' (39; 1.1.2) remains a dialogic possibility.

Although Hardy has the Years provide a high explanation for Napoleon's invasion of Russia, the relation between the leader and the crowd continues to be an important version of the One and the many. If Napoleon sways the multitudes to cross the Niemen, they in turn exert a powerful influence on the campaign that follows. Hardy does not lose interest in the crowd as Tolstoy does after Borodino; he gives relatively more weight to the retreat, including the scene of the Beresina that is only mentioned in War and Peace. There are times when the Overworld sounds as abstract and ironical as Tolstoy's narrator, but the theme of historic death and renewal never loses its grotesque bodily character.

The common criticism that The Dynasts suffers from the 'lack of development of a majority of the characters' (Carpenter 187) misses the point of Hardy's grotesque realism. Hardy may not go to the Rabelaisian extreme of showing that 'life has absolutely no *individual* aspect' (Bakhtin, *Dialogic* 234) but his carnivalesque art limits the 'development of character and motive' (Preface to *The Dynasts* 6). The individual body does 'cease to a certain extent to be itself' (Bakhtin, *Rabelais* 255) as carnival and monism converge to reveal the one in the many.

In responding to the Napoleonic era as a series of crowd events, Hardy offers more than the grim monotony of war and conquest with the grotesque emphasizing only the dynasts' craving for power (see Armstrong 486). The remarkable variety of crowd scenes makes war a drama without footlights played out on the grotesque body of Europe where the people as well as their leaders create history. The nationalism that eventually defeats Napoleon is very much a popular affair that embodies the growing historic consciousness of the people. For all the bloodshed, Hardy does not have the same fear of the crowd that David Lodge argues powerfully affected the early Victorian novel or the contempt for the masses that John Carey finds in much high modernist art. There can be no deep carnivalistic faith in the future when violence and death are grimly real, but the crowds of war at least ensure, to apply one of Bakhtin's signature remarks, that *'nothing conclusive has yet taken place in the world'* (*Problems* 166).

EIGHT

Chronotopes and the Death-Birth
of a World

That 'time and space are one' (Freeman 167) in Hardy's fictional world has become an axiom of recent criticism, yet the job of 'Discovering the Chronotope,'[1] to cite the title of one article, still remains to be done. Surprisingly, critics have not drawn on Bakhtin's account of time-space in the novel and have ignored the one work of Hardy's that, like Goethe's Rome, is a "great chronotope of human history" (Bakhtin, *Speech Genres* 40) – *The Dynasts*.

In the context of neo-Kantian thought, both Hardy and Bakhtin see time and space as the basic categories for organizing and representing the world. Time dominates Bakhtin's definition of the novel, space Hardy's thinking about *The Dynasts*. Indeed his choice of a Napoleonic subject depends on history becoming localized. Hardy may have been distant in time from past events but lived close enough to be familiar with three places where the past ceased to be estranged: George III's favourite summer residence during the war with Napoleon, the coast once rumoured to be the site of invasion, and the birthplace of Captain Hardy, a distant relative and Nelson's flag captain at Trafalgar. Hardy's chronotopic imagination makes the plan of *The Dynasts* the map of an era. When the Spirits look into "Space" and "traverse" Europe, they "close up Time," bringing "cradles into touch with biers" (Fore Scene 28). Such compression means that Hardy makes little use of relatively uninterrupted historical or biographical time. As he explains in the Preface, borrowing a term from geometry to express time in spatial terms, his panoramic show has the apparently loose shape of a series of historical ordinates.

What binds the scenes together goes much deeper than the reader's foreknowledge of historical events. Hardy chooses his ordinates to deal with the turning points of the era when history seems to take on some of the logic of carnival with its crownings and decrownings. Napoleon's strange career, so full of stunning reversals, lends itself to a carnivalized conception of the historical process. We keep seeing him at extreme moments of triumph, ultimate decision, or catastrophe. It is the course of his life in its critical moments that makes the plot not so much a straight line as 'a line with "knots" in it' (Bakhtin, *Dialogic* 113). There are so many crucial moments that the turning point becomes the norm. Everything Napoleon says and does remains linked to the chronotope of crisis and break in life, or to such related chronotopes as the street, the square, and the battlefield where his falls, renewals, and decisive moments occur.

Each time Napoleon reverses the hierarchic levels of old and new on the battlefield in Part First, there follows a scene next to a fire. We recall that he invites the humiliated Mack to warm himself by a fire; he also has the two Emperors 'left by themselves before the fire' (177; 1.6.5) so that he can personally dictate the terms of the armistice to Francis II. Fires of one size or another burn in Napoleon's career at times of crisis or change. From the torch and bivouac fire to Moscow burning, they retain some of the ambivalence of the carnival flame 'that simultaneously destroys and renews the world.' 'Sparks of carnival fire' (Bakhtin, *Problems* 126, 284) appear, for example, on the road to Astorga in Spain. It is not for warmth but light that Napoleon orders, 'Let there be a fire lit ... / The lines within these letters brook no pause / In mastering their purport.' The flames that 'throw a glare all round' (291; 2.3.2) allow him to glare at the 'veerings of ... new developments' (295; 2.3.2) all across Europe. The ups and downs of war (and carnival) are now concentrated in Napoleon's movements and thoughts, and mimicked by the sputtering flames that rise as a mixed rain and snow falls. He 'settles to reading by the firelight' and 'sinks into the rigidity of profound thought, till his features lour.' Then 'he jumps up, furious, and walks to and fro beside the fire. By and by cooling he sits down again' (293; 2.3.2), only to rise and make the decision to turn back that the Spirit of the Years finds so ominous.

Napoleon's career in *The Dynasts*, like his restless movements on the road in Spain, develops with a continual rising and falling and turning. When the Imperial stakes carry the risk of losing all, he talks like the gambler or condemned prisoner, living the moment equal to years. Although he lives to cross the threshold that determines his whole life, his decisive moments remain subordinate to carnival and mystery time. The chronotopic Napoleon has a folkloric basis that makes his own development inseparable from the life of the people. All the events in his life acquire a public significance and "are liable to public reckoning on the open square or its equivalent" (Bakhtin, *Dialogic* 122). His fate remains bound up with the transformation of an era. In the palace or on the battlefield, we are always watching, to borrow Carlyle's words about the French Revolution, the "Death-Birth of a World" (1:171).[2]

We hear this theme in both the dialogue and narration as 'death throes are combined with birth' (Bakhtin, *Rabelais* 435) in a misalliance that threatens carnival's regenerating ambivalence. For the defeated, the grotesque is deprived of its renewing role. Prince Hohenlohe fears that 'this too pregnant, hoarsely-groaning day / Shall, ere its loud delivery be done, / Have twinned disasters to the fatherland / That fifty years will fail to sepulchre!' (222; 2.1.4). Amidst the 'mad current of close-filed confusion' of the Russian withdrawal from Moscow, the Spirit of the Pities sees "emissaries knock at every door / In rhythmal rote, and groan the great events / The hour is pregnant with' (469, 470; 3.1.6). Battle-time gives birth to events of frightening proportions. Dawn on the second day of fighting at Leipzig seems to one citizen to be 'outheaving this huge day, / Pallidly – as if scared by its own child' (521; 3.3.3), while to the narrator a 'huge event of some kind is awaiting birth' (321; 2.4.2) at Wagram.

The kind of birth that takes place at Wagram is not the one Francis expects. Victory to the official Austrian mind is conceived on the high plane of 'Austria's grand salvation!' When the French appear to retreat, 'Then is the land delivered. God be praised!' (326, 327; 2.4.3). As the narrator keeps reminding us, time passes, and eventually brings a delivery of another and lower sort in the tradition of grotesque realism. The groan of Davout's guns from the Wagram heights turn out to be the pangs of a birth whose 'advance is laboured, and but slow.' Time itself seems to participate in the reversals that give the battle its distinctive shape: 'Time passes, till the sun has rounded far to the West' (331; 2.4.3). In Bakhtin's words, 'this is not, of course, the day of tragedy ("from the rising to the setting of the sun") ... This is a day in special carnival time' (*Problems* 175). Tragic time is close in type to carnivalized time but cannot have "too many calamities" without producing "an unintended farcical effect" (Moses 241). "The menippea," on the other hand, "loves to play with abrupt transitions and shifts, ups and downs, rises and falls, unexpected comings together of distant and disunited things, mésalliances of all sorts" (Bakhtin, *Problems* 118).

On the field of Wagram Napoleon experiences the time of gambling when 'it is neck or nothing.' In the words of one Austrian officer, 'striking with a river in his rear / Is not the safest tactic to be played.' Distant from the action, Francis still walks from crisis to crisis in the mansion until its 'walls no longer yield safe shade' (330, 323, 332; 2.4.3). The final outcome of the battle lives on the very border of its opposite. Just when 'The turn has passed,' the columns of the Archduke John 'glimmer in the Frenchmen's rear' (331; 2.4.3). For Francis the battlefield becomes haunted by one of the many 'ghost plots' (Beer 239) of Hardy's fiction: 'This might have been another-coloured day / If but the Archduke John had joined up promptly; / Yet still he lags!' (331; 2.4.3). Bakhtin points out that the carnival sense of the world 'knows no period, and is, in fact, hostile to any sort of *conclusive conclusion*: all endings are merely new beginnings' (*Problems* 165). The ending for Francis means 'We are worsted, but not whelmed,' allowing him to add, with a new sense of the unforeseen, 'Who knows to-morrow may not see regained / What we have lost to-day?' (331, 332; 2.4.3).

More than a military victory is born for Napoleon. Wagram leads to peace with Austria, marriage to Francis's daughter, Maria Louisa, and a son who 'took some coaxing, but he's here at last' (404; 2.6.3). As Felix Markham notes of the historical Napoleon, Wagram 'had shaken his confidence in battle as the trump card' (183). At least in August 1809 he realized that no one could control the cartwheels of battle: '"Battle should only be offered when there is no other turn of fortune to be hoped for, as from its very nature the fate of a battle is always dubious"' (quoted in Markham 183).

We next see Hardy's Napoleon as a sombre figure sitting alone and 'apparently watching the moving masquerade' (347; 2.5.1) in the house of Cambacérès, while brooding on the 'trustless, timorous lease of human life.' The Spirit of the Pities' questions catch him at a moment of crisis and reinforce one of the rejoinders in his own internal dialogue that weighs battle against diplomacy. The way he answers, as in soliloquy, is structured in the form of an argument with himself. His decision to take immediate diplomatic 'steps to rid / My morrows of ... weird contingencies' (348; 2.5.1) leads to an unexpected pause and a review of the disturbing aspects of the late campaign. He has already witnessed the staunchness of the Austrian resistance and the panic of his raw recruits, 'Thousands of merest boys' (312; 2.3.5); now he remembers 'The unexpected, lurid death of Lannes' and the 'quick pants of expectation round / Among the cowering Kings, that too well told / What would have fared had I been overthrown!' By looking back he tries to convince himself to go forward. A way opens but it leads through the world of diplomacy that is as trustless as the fortunes of war. Instead of confronting the enemy directly on the battlefield, Napoleon must now look behind him. The violence and uncertainty of battle follow him in the hidden form of 'Tiptoed Assassination haunting round / In unthought thoroughfares.' The 'near success / Of Staps the madman' during the peace conference at Schönbrunn suggests that 'Perhaps within this very house and hour, / Under an innocent mask of Love or Hope, / Some enemy queues my ways to coffin me' (348; 2.5.1). Again he pauses as the interior vision that leaves him hollow-eyed coincides with the external spectacle. He speaks as if making an ultimate decision and though far from the battlefield he continues to live on the threshold – literally a withdrawing room that opens out into the main saloon – where 'one is renewed or perishes' (Bakhtin, *Problems* 169).

His need to act 'this eve, / This very night' (348; 2.5.1) makes him cross the boundary into the chamber of official carnival where the stab in the back he fears goes beyond his personal safety. The 'revels that might win the King of Spleen / To toe a measure' (347; 2.5.1) belong to the 'chamber masquerade line' of carnival's development after the Renaissance and preserve 'a bit of the license and some faint reflections of the carnival sense of the world' (Bakhtin, *Problems* 131, 130). 'What scandals of me,' Napoleon asks Berthier, 'do they bandy here?' (348; 2.5.1). After taking Madame Metternich unceremoniously by the arm, Napoleon confides, in an uncrowning moment, that 'It's hard I cannot prosper in a game / That every coxcomb plays successfully.' If he feels like less than a fool, Madame Metternich sees him contemptuously as the would-be customer who 'turns toe / To our shop in Vienna' (349, 353; 2.5.1). Yet given the chance to thrust a thorn in Russia's side, Austria provides him with a marriage that is a carnivalesque misalliance of the aristocratic girl who hates the French with the bourgeois Corsican whom she regards as the Apocalyptic Beast. At the same time, the uncrowning of Joséphine is as much a reversal as the crowning of Marie Louise. As one member of a club in St James's Street reports – in laughing prose not serious poetry – the divorce is both oxymoronic, 'short and sweet, like a donkey's gallop,' and 'a turning of the tables,

considering how madly jealous she used to make him by her flirta-
tions!' (373, 374; 2.5.4).

Reversals look like the peripeteia of tragedy but are never allowed to
stay within the boundaries of a high genre. The structure of so many of
the dynastic scenes is based on the idea of the reversal that goes back
to the very beginnings of carnivalized literature in the Socratic dialogue and ancient menippea. The sheer number of unexpected shifts
and changes of power gives official history the appearance of a series
of carnival events. Metternich remains undisturbed by the suddenness
of Napoleon's attempt to 'hedge in my diplomacy' (348; 2.5.1) as if it
were a bet. He sees Napoleon as throwing the dice, his proposal to
Russia a 'first crude cast-about' (365; 2.5.3), his second to Austria something that can be turned against him.

Even at the height of Napoleon's power, the shape of things to come
appears in the ballroom at Cambacérès during carnival time in Paris.
At the very moment Napoleon decides to attach himself to the dynastic
version of one of life's normal plots, to the security of marriage and
family as well as the uncertainties of war, he is watching a crowd of
masked dancers whose revolving movements suggest that his future
will remain filled with sudden turns and changes. At the beginning of
the scene Napoleon occupies the front; at the end the maskers surge
into the foreground. As their waltzing motions become more and more
fantastic, the gloom that he initially feels becomes the impression the
crowd makes, while the grin he supposedly hides from his loyal soldiers can be seen on the masks of the trustless dancers. Like the
'bizarre lights and shadows' (275; 2.2.6) in Joséphine's boudoir when
Napoleon speaks of divorce, 'A strange gloom begins and intensifies,
until only the high lights of their grinning figures are visible' (354;
2.5.1).

More passing strange than any of the destinies in *Tess of the d'Urbervilles*, Napoleon's loud career continues to unfold in a fantastic atmosphere that intrudes upon the innermost space of his life. Even in his
dressing-gown awaiting the commonplace event of the birth of a child,
Napoleon confronts the extraordinary in carnivalized 'tight time.' As
the Emperor walks up and down the unenclosed space of an antechamber to Marie Louise's bedchamber, Hardy accentuates the rises
and falls, the abrupt transitions and shifts in the historical situation.
Dubois, with his 'long years of many-featured practice,' cannot
remember 'An instance in a thousand fall out so' (400, 399; 2.6.3). As on
the battlefield, birth is a matter of death. Wanting an heir but loving

the Empress, the divided Napoleon, half shuts the door to her bed-chamber and on his dynastic plans by choosing to save the mother's life instead of the child's. Like the victory at Wagram that helps bring him a new wife, the birth itself is a turnabout: Dubois announces through the threshold of the doorway that the child is dead; Madame Blaise suddenly corrects him with the unexpected news that the child's alive.

Although indoors, the setting is not far from the equivalent of the carnival square. To look out the window at one end of the antechamber is to see the Tuileries' gardens thronged with an immense crowd, kept only 'a little distance off the Palace by a cord' (402; 2.6.3). At the spatial border of the window a radiant Napoleon draws the curtains to watch his suspense and joy made public in the crowd whose own excitement is doubled when the twenty-second cannon shot announcing a boy follows a deliberate pause. On the other threshold of the door, a pale and nervous Napoleon listens to the terrible moments of labour experienced by his frightened wife.

As the carnival plot proceeds, the birth of the son in 1811 seems strangely connected in retrospect with the deadly war of 1812. The matter goes deeper than the political severance from Russia that begins with Napoleon's choice of a Hapsburg instead of a Romanoff princess to found his dynastic line. It is as if the future is already present in an unexpected way during the birth scene, the 'live star / Upon the horizon of our history!' (403; 2.6.3) reappearing in 'what at first sight seems a lurid, malignant star' (473; 3.1.7) when fire breaks out in Moscow. Napoleon again appears walking up and down the interior space of a palace in agitation, torn between staying – literally sitting down on the bed – and leaving, the decision that he finally makes. All his choices are again ultimate decisions. At stake is the survival of a whole army of 'soldier-sons' (464; 3.1.4). Instead of cheering citizens outside the Tuileries, 'explosions and hissings are constantly audible' outside the Kremlin and amid these destructive sounds 'can be fancied cries and yells of people caught in the combustion' (473, 474; 3.1.7). With 'Incendiarism afoot,' the fire assumes the character of a hostile crowd, the many uniting into one: 'All the conflagrations increase, and become, as those at first detached group themselves together, one huge furnace' (476, 473; 3.1.7). Moscow proves no more a refuge from the haps of war than the birth of a dynasty. Instead of good news floating up in balloons, 'large pieces of canvas aflare sail away on the gale like balloons' (474; 3.1.7).

Although Napoleon's son never sees a battlefield, the portrait of the young King of Rome playing at cup-and-ball with no less than the world serves as an Imperial icon that draws a great crowd of French soldiers before the fighting begins at Borodino. The brandy and hot napkins that bring the son to life become the spirits and hot water that turn the father, resting on a campstool like the picture, into a 'drowsed half-drunken Dictator' (467; 3.1.5) separated from his marshals by the haze of battle. A spectator during the birth, Napoleon remains one throughout the advance to Moscow, 'watching through his glass the committal of his army to the enterprise' (447; 3.1.1.) and later its futile attacks on the great redoubt, or talking about distant affairs in Spain just before the portrait of his son arrives as he does soon after his son is born.

'Nobody knows,' observes Canetti, 'what Napoleon's real feelings were during the retreat from Moscow' (231). Hardy waits until Paris to have him comment privately on the 'Disasters many and swift' in Russia. In particular he remembers that 'Since crossing – ugh! – the Beresina River / I have been compelled to come incognito; Ay – as a fugitive and outlaw quite' (490; 3.1.12). Napoleon now sees the campaign in carnivalesque terms, full of sudden reversals, including his own uncrowning. In spite of the enormous spaces of the retreat, the only time that matters is a single step: 'From the sublime to the ridiculous / There's but a step!' Whereas Tolstoy contemptuously dismisses this grand saying, Hardy has Marie Louise simply question its justice, forcing Napoleon to answer, 'I meant the enterprise, and not its stuff.' To have stepped over the threshold – 'that step has been passed in this affair!' (442; 3.1.12) – means the death of an army.

Hardy's crisis portrayal of Napoleon and his carnivalesque career emerges with great clarity in Part Third of *The Dynasts*, a part crowded, as Hardy wrote in a letter, with big events (*Letters* 3:197), where we find a pattern of flights and descents, returns and rises. Almost a prisoner in Russia, Napoleon escapes to fight again at Leipzig; sent into exile on Elba, he 'snatches the moment ... / To reconquer Europe / With seven hundred sabres' (580; 3.5.1). Until the last critical moment at Waterloo, time always has a loophole that makes it inconstant, like the name of the brig that takes him from Elba.

In both the Leipzig and Waterloo campaigns, Napoleon plays 'the dynasts' death-game' (335; 2.4.4) for the highest of stakes. On both occasions, he is no ordinary gambler; all his energy goes into battle, leaving him so exhausted that he falls asleep in the midst of the action. In 1813 he wonders which card to play, repeating the same question, 'To Leipzig, or Berlin?' (512; 3.3.1), without deciding which means ruin and which success. In 1815 the language of betting permeates his military speeches until he runs out of cards to play. The good chances he refers to at Charleroi become clearly defined on the morning of Waterloo: 'our odds are ninety to their ten!' Wellington 'plays our game!' and 'All prospers marvellously!' (657, 658, 660; 3.7.2) until the Prussians appear. Napoleon reassures Soult, 'We have threescore [chances] still'; in an aside he has 'one battle-chance' while 'The allies have many such!' (662; 3.7.2). 'The crisis [that] shapes and nears / For Wellington as for his counter-chief' joins them like gamblers. The one comments on how 'The game just now / Goes all against us' (679, 684; 3.7.7); the other sees Ney come 'within an ace' (679; 3.7.6) of breaking the English lines.

Battle shares with gambling a carnivalistic atmosphere 'of sudden and quick changes of fate, of instantaneous rises and falls, that is, of crownings/decrownings' (Bakhtin, *Problems* 171). Some English officers, 'honestly concluding the battle to be lost' (685; 3.7.7) at Waterloo, ride off to Brussels. One moment 'it's victory!' for the Old Guard, the next, 'we are beaten!' (690, 691; 3.7.8). Similarly, the bells of Leipzig ring when the French cavalry break the Allied centre but 'simultaneously Marmont is beaten at Möckern' (520; 3.3.2). Everyone at Leipzig lives in carnivalized time. The citizens, siding as they do with the French, look 'saucer-eyed from anxiety and sleeplessness' (521; 3.3.3). From the first 'weird wan day,' when Bavaria 'Swerves on the very pivot of desertion' (511, 515; 3.3.1), to the last, nothing can become stabilized. The battle 'which is to decide the fate of Europe, and perhaps the world' (519; 3.3.2), takes everything to the extreme. When 'the urgency of victory / Is absolute,' anything less 'will be worse than Moscow' (513; 3.3.1) for the French. 'Half-won is losing!' (520; 3.3.2) on the first day of fighting; Saxony's desertion on the second 'magnifies / A failure into a catastrophe.' Napoleon addresses this unexpected turnabout at exactly the moment we see a 'newly lighted fire' in conjunction with the Thonberg wind-wheel. He no longer walks complacently as at the windmill of Paleny but 'up and down, much agitated and worn.' The new trends of time shock him. The 'troth-swearing sober Saxonry' not only fight against Napoleon but also abandon their own king in a double decrowning. Even treacherous mists appear, making a lurid cloud of the firelights as the French 'recede precipitately, / And not as hope had dreamed!' (525; 3.3.4).

The risk of losing all that Napoleon brings to Leipzig sharply intensifies as the feeling of a condemned prisoner. In another of war's strange reversals, he finds himself in a position similar to Mack 'enjailed in Ulm' (120; 1.4.6). In Part First, the Great Alliance fails to put 'a muffler round [the] Cock's steel spurs' (103; 1.4.1); in Part Third the Allies 'have welded close the coop / Wherein our luckless Frenchmen are enjailed' (521; 3.3.3). For Bakhtin, the prisoner and the gambler both live 'an identical *type of time*, similar to the "final moments of consciousness" before execution or suicide, similar in general to the time of crisis' (*Problems* 172). Napoleon's experience at Leipzig is like the 'dream of one sick to death.' Time takes the form of a 'narrowing room / That pens him, body and limbs and breath, / To wait a hideous doom.' He feels so taken out of ordinary life that he wonders, 'Am I awake, / Or is this all a dream?' Yet he knows that 'I have seen ere now a time like this' (526; 3.3.4).

From Wagram on, battle ceases to be a festive occasion for Napoleon and the carnival that is war turns increasingly bitter. When 'the combat dies resultlessly away' at Borodino, 'no notes of joy / Throb as at Austerlitz!' (468; 3.1.5). Jena is the last of Napoleon's stunning and one-sided victories. The closer the battle, the more crisis-ridden it becomes; the greater the risks, the more each minute is equal to years. In Spain, where Napoleon is absent, the equilibrium of forces in Part Second makes the climax of each battle the last in a series of turns. When 'there ticks / The moment of the crisis' that brings the final 'turning stroke' (337; 2.4.5) at Talavera, the English are too reduced and exhausted to pursue the retreating French. Soldiers 'spin / Like leaves' in one turnabout after another at Albuera. The French 'fail, and win, and win, and fail.' Even the climax of the strife has two crises. 'The critical instant has come, and the English break'; reinforcements 'make one last strain to save the day,' startling the enemy 'on a spot deemed won' (410; 2.6.4).

The time from which Napoleon never fully escapes tightens and compresses to the point at Leipzig that days can no longer measure its importance. The Allies 'wax denser every hour' (519; 3.3.2) before the battle; 'Each minute is of price' (527; 3.3.5) during the retreat. Nothing ever loses touch with the threshold; everything Napoleon says and does remains linked to the chronotope of crisis and break in life. Only at Waterloo, where 'if staunchness fail / But for one moment ... / Defeat succeeds!' (684; 3.7.7), is time so charged with emotion and value.

In the first Leipzig scene, the theme of the threshold intrudes into one of the interior spaces of life, transforming the sitting room of a private mansion into quarters where the outside shapes everyone's thoughts. 'An atmosphere of scopeless apathy' (515; 3.3.1) surrounds Napoleon inside; 'three hosts close round' (519; 3.3.2) outside. Inside the room world conflagration is reduced to a stove-fire and funereal candles; outside the enemy's fires, in a reversal of Austerlitz, 'bespot / The horizon round with raging eyes of flame' (514; 3.3.1). The wind strikes the old windows mournfully; Napoleon's staff look as overcast as the weather. Their faces make visible his hidden thoughts. The 'combat of Napoleon's hope' is 'not of his assurance' when he 'broods beneath October's clammy cope' (519; 3.3.2).

Moving to a spatial border, Napoleon draws a window curtain and watches his enemies signalling with rockets. For the first time they manage to co-ordinate their efforts to fight a triple battle. Even the army of Bohemia 'marches concentrically' in 'three great columns' (522; 3.3.3) against Napoleon's lines. The dialogue in the air, 'three coloured rockets ... sent up, in evident answer to the three white ones,' has the same structure. The tense pause between rockets, 'during which Napoleon and the rest wait motionless' (517; 3.3.1), does not quite seem frozen in time as in Bakhtin's paradigm of the crucial instant (see Eckstrom 107). The narrator keeps track of the passing minutes. When the flashes of light continue they bring insight, showing the enemy are ready, but there is nothing more for Napoleon to do than muse and let the curtain drop. The time has long passed since he could say 'No hurry, Lannes! Enjoy the sun' (170; 1.6.3) of Austerlitz; his experience on the threshold of Leipzig is of 'Time's disordered deaf sands' (511; 3.3.1) running out.

The battle itself also develops concentrically on the threshold of the inside/outside. The two sides face each other in identical shapes, the inner horseshoe of French defending the city, the outer horseshoe of Allies attacking it. Together they form one 'huge elastic ring / Of fighting flesh' that contracts 'as those within go down, / Or spreads, as those without show faltering' (519; 3.3.2). The shape of things, the new dynastic structure struggling against the old dynastic routine, the one inside the other, suggests that they are more than opposites. Though 'All is lost to One, to many gained' (531; 3.3.5), the Ironic Spirits do not forget that 'Poland's three despoilers primed by Bull's gross pay / ... stem Napoleon's might' (511; 3.3.1). The shift of world orders becomes ambivalent, raising the question, 'The which is seemlier? – so-called ancient order, / Or that the hot-breath'd war horse ramp unreined?' (531; 3.3.5).

The Battle of the Nations completes the transformation of war into a mass experience: 'Nationalities from the uttermost parts of Asia here meet those from the Atlantic edge of Europe for the first and last time' (519; 3.3.2). That they meet at a city strengthens the connection between the battlefield and the carnival square. As the fighting contracts to the city streets, we are reminded that modern war reawakens and transforms the ancient spirit of communal performance. In the final scene at Leipzig, the chronotopes of the street, the gate, and the bridge extend the threshold to a space where all draw close together 'in hurried exit.' The cityscape is both animated and illuminated by the dangerous possibilities of carnival life, by its debasement, disorder, and confusion. Forced to say his long goodbye to the Saxon royalty in an inn, Napoleon now has to go by foot through an alley to reach the Ranstädt Gate where 'the throng / Thrusts him about, none recognizing him.' Hardy filters almost the whole view of Napoleon through the verse of ordinary citizens who still regard him with sympathy or awe as a means of contrasting the carnival King of a world turned inside out. The third citizen who 'stood i' the crowd / So close I could have touched him!' is one of the few who 'discerned / In one so soiled the erst Arch-Emperor!' (529; 3.3.5).

The principle of degradation continues to organize events after we lose sight of Napoleon among the troops that choke the road on the far side of the bridge of Lindenau and swing back to the corps that block its entrance. When the bridge explodes, the Pities transform the terrifying into a scene of grotesque realism reminiscent of the disaster on the threshold of the Beresina. Their logic of debasement has an absolute and strictly topographical meaning. Upward is to heaven, downward to a gulf that swallows and gives birth. The top and bottom merge in the grave, 'as though / Some rebel churchyard crew updrave / Their sepulchres from below.' Limits are transgressed as 'There leaps to the sky an earthen wave, / And stones, and men.' Ranks and distinctions disappear as 'every current ripples red / With marshals' blood and men's' (530; 3.3.5). In spite of the serious tone, the scene has some of the contradictory unity of grotesque becoming where 'To degrade is to bury, to sow, and to kill simultaneously' (Bakhtin, *Rabelais* 21). The river with its abundance of dead is also a field ready for planting: 'rank and file in masses plough / The sullen Elster-Strom' (530; 3.3.5). The bodily grave keeps its indispensable link with time and historic change. The new bridge breaks down; the old is destroyed. On the threshold, the destructive folly of the French – 'Feeble foresight! They should have had a dozen [bridges]' (529; 3.3.5) – is creative for the Allies. Again we watch, the Death-Birth of a World though without the assurance that something more and better is emerging. The joy of change does not belong to everyone. 'The cheers of the approaching enemy grow louder'; 'A hoarse chorus of cries becomes audible' (527, 530; 3.3.5) from the French. The new world is retreating and dying, the old striving for renewal.

The Russian war, Leipzig, and Waterloo all end in catastrophe for Napoleon but catastrophe, as Bakhtin astutely observes, 'is not finalization' (*Problems* 298). Battles lost and won decisively do not resolve the collision and struggle of different points of view. Nothing is ever quite finished in *The Dynasts*, whether the focus is the Will or Europe. The tension between the One and the many continues even when all is lost to One. The restoration of the Bourbons still means discontent in Paris: 'Medals are wrought that represent / One now unnamed. Men whisper, "He / Who once has been, again will be!"' (579; 3.5.1).

During the Hundred Days, Napoleon is like the short-lived King of a carnival event. We begin at the port of Ferrajo where everyone participates in his departure. 'The crowd exclaims "The Emperor!"' and sailors sing the Marseillaise and shout '"Paris or death!"' (580, 581; 3.5.1). Again Hardy concentrates the action at a point of crisis and radical change. It is a tense moment as Napoleon prepares to cross the forbidden line. The deck of his ship takes on a carnival square significance while he stands motionless, not just in the here and now, but for four aching hours on the threshold of 'salvation' and 'Retention eternal.' The time is so pivotal that the Chorus of Rumours invokes the ambivalence of carnival's basic act to describe the weather. Though far apart in meaning, what 'will save him' and 'would enslave him' draw close together in sound. 'The calm plays the tyrant,' Napoleon the slave; the south wind returns his crown, 'Restoring the Empire / That Fortune once gave him!' (581; 3.5.1).

As we leap again over space and time to the scene near Grenoble, Napoleon moves in adventure time along a lonely road that becomes a crucial meeting-place between royalist troops and his little army shipped from Elba. We may be several miles from a village square but Napoleon turns the road into a threshold where he will perish or be renewed, inviting anyone who would to slay him. Power depends on his creating one festive crowd from two opposing sides, with himself elected king. He chooses a friendly tone of address in keeping with his dress, 'the old familiar "redingote grise," cocked hat, and tricolor cockade, his well-known profile keen against the hills.' Although 'people from the village gather round with tragic expectations' (588, 589; 3.5.3), they end up witnessing a bloodless carnival turnover. Hardy also lets us see with perfect clarity the unresolved conflicts that Napoleon exploits as the bottom replaces the top in a debasement and crowning of colours: 'The soldiers tear out their white cockades and trample on them, and disinter from the bottom of their knapsacks tricolors, which they set up' (590; 3.5.3). The dynastic world again appears to be passing through the phase of death on the way to birth, Imperial power disinterred, Royalist turned 'death-white at [Napoleon's] words!' (589; 3.5.3).

Napoleon forms the whole body into a square, literally a public square, to further his political aims. The victims of his address become the Bourbons with their 'treasons, tricks, / Ancient abuses, feudal tyranny.' The scapegoat also crosses the scene in the form of a 'howling dog ... with a white cockade tied to its tail' (590; 3.5.3), provoking the soldiers of both sides to laugh loudly. From an historical perspective, 'Carnival may not be the source of such violence, but its forms certainly accompanied it' (Dentith 75). The laughing soldiers who will 'march with [Napoleon] to death or victory' participate in a very carnivalesque conclusion to the day's unexpected turnabout. The feasting traditionally associated with popular merriment appears in the form of drinking: 'Peasantry run up with buckets of sour wine and a single glass; Napoleon takes his turn with the rank and file in drinking from it.' Throughout the scene, Napoleon carefully appears to be one soldier talking and drinking with others, 'throwing open his great-coat and revealing his uniform and the ribbon of the Legion of Honour' (590, 589; 3.5.3), or mixing the hierarchical levels, a single glass for everyone in the same rank and file. The wine may be sour, just as 'the singing has a melancholy cadence' (581; 3.5.1) when he leaves Elba, but even in a different key carnival is still the "feast of time, the feast of becoming, change, and renewal' (Bakhtin, *Rabelais* 10).

The 'Angel of the Lord' to his grenadiers presents himself as a timely saviour: 'Soldiers, I come with these few faithful ones / To save you from the Bourbons.' The words he utters privately, 'All is accomplished, Bertrand!' (590; 3.5.3), identify his own rebirth with Christ's death. In the gospel according to St John, the Jesus who knows 'that all things were now accomplished ... saith I thirst' (19:28). The vinegar he receives becomes the sour wine Napoleon drinks. It is, after all, Napoleon's carnivalesque aim, both crowning and uncrowning, 'To shoulder Christ from out the topmost niche / In human fame' (699; 3.7.9) and like his predecessor he has a remarkable talent for turning wine into blood.

The image of the Christ of war drinking wine with his soldiers leads on to the final act and the grotesque feast of Waterloo. Hardy accentuates two historical aspects of the war in Belgium, its proximity to sacred place names and to the very bread of life, to create the special atmosphere of degradation and violation in the last Napoleonic battles. Nowhere in *The Dynasts* does war take on a more profaning role or more strikingly set in opposition the creative and destructive poles of carnival's regenerating ambivalence. In Spain we get brief reminders that the field of battle has other purposes. A warm rain brings out 'fragrant scents from the fields, vineyards, and gardens, now in the full leafage of June' (498; 3.2.2) at Vitoria; 'Wrecked are the ancient bridge, the green spring plot / The blooming fruit-tree, the fair flower-knot' (408; 2.6.4) at Albuera. At Trafalgar battle time gets mixed in Captain Hardy's mind 'with flashes of old things afar' from the cyclical time of Wessex, 'the grey dial there, / Marking unconsciously this bloody hour, / And the red apples on my father's trees / Just now full ripe' (144; 1.5.4). In Belgium the emphasis falls heavily on the way the ordinary agricultural world is drawn into the battles. The French advance down the slopes of green corn towards the village of Ligny with its thatched cottages, gardens, and farmhouses. There are farmsteads near Quatre-Bras and covering rye for Picton's infantry. On the eve of Waterloo, the French take up their positions amid the cornfields around La Belle Alliance. The next morning the whole field of Waterloo appears as a green expanse, almost unbroken, of rye, wheat, and clover. Napoleon watches the battle from a hillock near the farm of Rossomme, Wellington from behind the key point of dispute, the farm of La Haye Sainte. The beautiful alliance of man and nature in peace appears turned into a misalliance in war. The forms so foreign to field and tree remind the Pities of 'the carnivalesque figure of Harlequin' (Bakhtin, *Rabelais* 267). The soldiers from various nations seem impersonators in a 'harlequinade' that crosses the footlights onto the 'artless champaign' (650; 3.6.8). Harlequin's wooden sword becomes flashing steel ones and his parti-coloured patches the 'oblong and irregular patches' (653; 3.7.1) of the battlefield itself. Though foreign, war seems to merge as though native with country life, the French arms 'glittering like a display of cutlery at a hill-side fair' (653; 3.7.1) where 'the amusements ... usually bore a carnivalesque character' (Bakhtin, *Rabelais* 220).

Two chronotopes, both related to carnival space and time, intersect when war becomes the link between history and the earth. Napoleon stalks into the fields of Belgium 'swiftly and unexpectedly as in carnival' (Bakhtin, *Problems* 175), drawing everyone onto the threshold. At the ball in Brussels, Wellington 'Affects a cheerfulness in outward port, / But cannot rout his real anxiety!' Lost time is critical. 'Napoleon,' he tells his staff, 'has befooled me, / By God he has, – gained four-and-twenty hours' / Good march upon me!' (615, 618; 3.6.2). The dialogue keeps recording the rush of events: news hurled into the ballroom, the French vanguard burst on Quatre-Bras, the call to instant war, orders sped to the front, generals eager to start at once, a wife ready to haste to Antwerp, Blücher threatened by the French at Ligny at this moment. Time speeds up to the point that the Allied plan uncovers of itself as 'Signs notify / Napoleon's plans are changed!' (637; 3.6.5). Wellington and Blücher look like opposites when they meet at the windmill of Bussy, the one 'deliberate, judicial, almost indifferent,' the other 'eager and impetuous' (636; 3.6.5). Battle-time reverses their roles after Ligny and brings the moment 'when the steadiest pulse / Thuds pit-a-pat.' While Wellington waits desperately for Blücher to arrive, 'The hour is shaking him, unshakeable / As he may seem!' (679; 3.7.7).

Another sense of time is already in place and attached to specific places at Waterloo. In Bakhtinian terms, the folkloric chronotope pervades the whole scene of cultivated nature. This is the collective time of agricultural labour and productive growth that forms the basis of the Rabelaisian chronotope and the carnival view of the world. When the Spirits see the idyllic field of Waterloo everything is 'maximally tensed toward the future' (Bakhtin, *Dialogic* 207) but no longer simply as a seasonal process of ripening and blossoming. Crisis time sends 'thrills of misgiving' through the earth itself: 'The green seems opprest, and the Plain afraid / Of a Something to come.' War interrupts the 'calm' (650; 3.6.8) that should be with a tense watching and waiting in the very spaces of peaceful and productive labour:

A dense array of watching Guardsmen hides
Amid the peaceful produce of the grange,
Whose new-kerned apples, hairy gooseberries green,
And mint, and thyme, the ranks intrude between.   (655; 3.7.1)

The ancient nexus of death with new life changes in the context of modern war. A time measured by destruction supplants a time measured by growth. History itself, as the Spirits foresee, will be 'sunk deeply in the earth' (Bakhtin, *Dialogic* 208), its 'foul red rain' soaking the worm that 'wriggles deep from a scene so grim.' Death will make life one, from 'ears that have greened but will never be gold, / And flowers in the bud that will never bloom' to 'a youth of promise struck stark and cold!' (651; 3.6.8).

The contrast between war and peace, the one intruding upon the other, seems all the more jarring given the religious names or associations of many places. The worst moment at Ligny takes place around the church where soldiers 'fight without quarter, shooting face to face, stabbing with unfixed bayonets, and braining with the butts of muskets' (639; 3.6.5). The narrator also carefully observes that the battle of Waterloo begins shortly after 'the clock of Nivelles convent church strikes eleven in the distance' (656; 3.7.1). When Napoleon turns his glass to St Lambert's Chapel Hill, he sees something earthy and grotesque, 'a darkly crawling, slug-like shape / Embodying far out there' (658; 3.7.2). For the Arch-Emperor, 'hell's own legions' (677; 3.7.6) have their very real equivalent in the form of the Prussians. Whether the locale is Mont Saint Jean or La Haye Sainte, everything spiritual gets immersed and uncrowned in the atmosphere of the body. The Farm of the Holy Hedge becomes a 'bath of blood' (680; 3.7.7), prompting Pity to ask 'Whence lit so sanct a name on thy now violate grange?' (666; 3.7.4). The profaning attitude extends to the cemetery as well where Pity hears 'uplift and move / The bones of those who placidly have lain / Within the sacred garths of yon grey fanes.' While the living die the dead awaken to ask, since it is Sunday, 'What Sabaoth is this?' (693; 3.7.8).

The fact that the historical Waterloo was fought on rain-soaked ground allows Hardy to turn carnival's playful gestures into a real besmirching. As the two armies take up their positions, we see 'Cannon upon the foul and flooded road, / Cavalry in the cornfields mire-bestrowed.' Soldiers huddle together 'on the ploughed mud' (650; 3.6.8) to sleep and 'scrape the mud from themselves' (653; 3.7.1) to fight. The battle itself becomes a deadly mud-slinging and the ground a miry tomb. An earth that impedes makes time more critical, delaying the start of the battle and slowing the arrival of the Prussians who have to drag their heavy cannon through a muddy valley where wheels get stuck.

From the moment Napoleon crosses the Sambre, war becomes a kind of farming and eating, 'The occasion favouring [Death's] husbandry' (621; 3.6.2). The battlefields provide the grim reaper with a harvest of dead where the crops are not quite ready for the scythe. When we get to Waterloo, the figurative expression of Death the reaper literally returns to the earth from which it grew: cavalry and corn both 'Lie stretched in swathes' (678; 3.7.6).

The theme of war does not simply run counter to the idyll of agricultural life. We see that battle is as much a communal effort as the struggle to make nature productive. Both labour processes are aimed forward in the unified time of collective human life. In both, life and death are a common affair, not merely aspects of personal life. Victory at Waterloo depends on the joining of forces. 'If Grouchy but retrieve / His fault of absence,' says Napoleon, 'conquest comes with eve!' (662; 3.7.2). Wellington swears to Müffling that we will 'hold our present place at any cost, / Until your force cooperate with our lines!' (666; 3.7.4). 'It matters not one damn' that he personally takes 'Endless risks' (682, 683; 3.7.7). The same command applies equally to all: 'to hold out unto the last, / As long as one man stands on one lame leg / With one ball in his pouch!' (682; 3.7.7). It is little wonder that Auguste Comte, in a book Hardy read, could refer to the best feature of Military Life as 'its tendency to promote *collective* action' (*System* 3:47).

Napoleon enters the collective time of his second reign in the name of the people and succeeds in joining them to his ambiguous body. For critics, his changing appearance acquires only a single meaning, moral or philosophical. In the usual view, the bodily references form a pattern of epic degradation in which Napoleon's 'physical deterioration, like that of Milton's Satan, symbolizes spiritual decay,' his character becoming 'steadily more cynical and egoistic until his monstrous lie to his men at Waterloo' (Garrison 100; Carpenter 200). In desperation, Napoleon announces that the Prussians are Grouchy's men, a feint that Ney rejects as 'not war-worthy' (687; 3.7.8). The temptation is to hear something unique in the French cry 'We are betrayed!' (692; 3.7.8) and to turn Napoleon into a 'Satanic Emperor' (Giordano 123). Yet at Charleroi he is the one who has to bear 'the much-disquieting news / That Bourmont has deserted to our foes / With his whole staff,' and the rumours about another grotesque turnover involving Count Neipperg, who 'Interred his wife last spring' (626, 629; 3.6.3), and Marie Louise. From start to finish, the world of the dynasts is filled with betrayals, ranging from marital infidelity (we think of the Prince Regent) and assassination plots, to shifting national allegiances and treachery in the midst of battle.

Instead of remaining an individual life, Napoleon's body merges with the crowd and the unfinished world of death and renewal. The imagery constructs a 'double body' (Bakhtin, *Rabelais* 318) in which the basic contrast is between his 'unhealthy face and stoutening figure' (293; 2.3.2). The upper region carries the taint of decay. We see the sun yellowing his face when he invades Russia. He is yellow-faced on the way to Elba and has a sallow face at Waterloo. The lower body is all growth. He is growing fat at Tilsit and shifts his weight from one puffed calf to the other as he watches his army cross the Niemen. Escaping Elba, he looks much fatter than when he left France and during his last battle his stumpy figure accentuates his stoutness. We do not need to connect Napoleon's physical condition 'with the difficulty of the Will in manipulating him' (Bailey 145). The Emperor who gets drowsy or falls asleep is 'Worn with war's labours' (580; 3.5.1). Only his ambition remains undiminished, a carnivalesque need to devour that has an egotistical and alienating character in him. The unofficial and popular view of Napoleon, voiced early by a Wessex woman in undertones, connects the beginning and end of life in his giant eating habits:

> I can tell you a word or two on't. It is about His victuals. They say that He lives upon human flesh, and has rashers o'baby every morning for breakfast – for all the world like the Cernel Giant in old ancient times! (85; 1.2.5)

The grotesque imagery that prevails with the people informs Hardy's representation of Napoleon as a body that combines the symptoms of life and death, that 'swallows the world and is itself swallowed by the world' (Bakhtin, *Rabelais* 317). The thirst for a new beginning at La Mure becomes the appetite for conquest at Waterloo. Speaking roughly to Soult, Napoleon boasts that 'This clash to-day / Is not more serious for our seasoned files / Than breakfasting.' The mounting bill of blood at Hougomont disturbs him; his long-brewed plot pours to waste. As in some grotesque carnival, he wants to turn a battle into a meal but his 'gloomy resentful countenance' is far from the merriment of the true feast of time. Instead of eating, he 'takes rapid pinches of snuff in excitement' (657, 658; 3.7.2) until his face is stained.

The question remains whether death, when life becomes its food, is also constructive. By the last act of Waterloo, the uncertainty of birth goes beyond 'the momentous event impending' (494; 3.2.1) or the turmoil in which 'no man could speak / On what the issue was' (223; 2.1.4). The very possibility of the world's unfinished becoming seems at stake.

Hardy gives us life and death on both sides of the English centre at Mont Saint Jean. Behind the hill and the English lines, a woman who has just given birth lies near the wounded, and a camp-follower is playing a fiddle in spite of the thundering of the cannon. On the battle side of the heights, Waterloo ends like a demonic carnival, the only movement downward. With the balance of forces upset, the two-crowd structure changes drastically. In terms of Canetti's typology of emotional crowds, the two oldest, the 'baiting' and the 'flight' (49, 53) crowds, now appear, the one in pursuit of the other. The coherent character of the mass flight quickly disintegrates when the retreat of the French grows into a panic. The event becomes 'senseless-shaped,' with 'all wide sight and self-command' (695; 3.7.8) deserting both the strong and the weak: 'The streams of French fugitives ... are cut down and shot by their pursuers ... Some French blow out their brains as they fly' (692; 3.7.8). As the sun sets the action of the battle degenerates to a hunt, leaving only primitive packs of the kind from which all crowds originated.

'Is this,' Pity asks, 'the last Esdraelon of a moil / For mortal man's effacement?' (693; 3.7.8). Esdraelon, the fertile valley of so many decisive battles in the Old Testament, and where Napoleon himself defeated an army of Arabs in 1799, is also referred to by the Apocalyptic writer as Armageddon. While Pity thinks in terms of old things and last things to the sounds of the dead awakening, the Spirit Ironic sees another kind of effacement:

> Warfare mere,
> Plied by the Managed for the Managers;
> To Wit: by frenzied folks who profit nought
> For those who profit all!   (693; 3.7.8)

No ultimate question can hide war's more immediate and persistent problem that no matter which side wins, the dynastic system in one form or another continues. If carnival celebrates the destruction of the old and the birth of the new world, the Napoleonic wars allow everything old to be perpetuated and renewed.

The very way the battle is fought, Napoleon pounding away '"in the ancient style, / Till he is beaten back in the ancient style' (680; 3.7.7), prepares us for its political consequences. The Spirit of the Years takes a certain grim satisfaction from knowing that a world which consciousness does not change for the better confirms the unchanging rule of the unconscious Will:

> So hath the Urging Immanence used to-day
> Its inadvertant might to field this fray;
> And Europe's wormy dynasties rerobe
> Themselves in their old gilt, to dazzle anew the globe!   (697; 3.7.9)

Certainly the uncrowning of Napoleon does not mean that old clothes give way to new in Carlylean fashion, but the grotesque world of historic conflict may be a new world still in the making. Although no battle results in a victory for the future and all the people, the Napoleonic wars help make history 'for the first time ... a *mass experience*' (Lukacs 20). The Spirit Ironic's last words to Napoleon make his defeat an exception to war's asymetrical power relations between Managed and Managers:

> Yea, the dull peoples and the Dynasts both,
> Those counter-castes not oft adjustable,
> Interests antagonistic, proud and poor,
> Have for the nonce been bonded by a wish
> To overthrow thee.   (700; 3.7.9)

The convergence of wishes here is very different from the divergence Pity sees at Albuera where the mixed nationalities seem to act 'In moves dissociate from their souls' demand, /For dynasts' ends that few even understand' (407; 2.6.4). Waterloo can be seen as the victory of the many – peoples and dynasts – over the one, of the Allies over the man who would be Overking with 'every monarch throned in Europe / Bent at [his] footstool' (700; 3.7.9).

The historical plot of *The Dynasts* ends with a feast of battle that marks a crisis in the development of Europe. When 'mighty things are native born' (643; 3.6.6) they assume some of the cyclical shape of folkloric time and impart a forward impulse to the ploughed mud of native things. Victory renews the old dynasties but war links villages to cities and the rest of the world. The clocks of the world strike when the last movement downward of the French at Waterloo is towards literal disaster. The defeat of Napoleon is only possible in the spirit of grotesque feasting that makes history one great communal performance of bodies in real space and time. The subject of the Napoleonic wars does not make Hardy address 'catastrophe and terror in a highly benevolent and unrealistic way' (Morson and Emerson, *Mikhail* 470). He faces the implications of carnival at its least reduced and the result, though far from the symbolic forms that inspire Bakhtin, does not competely undo the positive negation of carnival proper. Its guiding image of fertility, growth, and abundance still survives as the trace left by death and destruction.

The grotesque spectacle of death and renewal returns us to the time/space of the folk[3] and the popular roots of the novel. Hardy's ability to see time in space is not so eccentric as to have no literary antecedent except 'the art of the mentally ill' (Dessner 155). The carnival tradition becomes the organizing centre of his sense of time, providing a chronotope that 'has room in itself for an unlimited number of radical shifts and metamorphoses' (Bakhtin, *Problems* 176). The discontinuities that make *The Dynasts* look like a modernist work, with the reader 'assumed to fill in the junctions' (Preface 6), also move us from one crisis or turning point to another, broadening the space of carnival to include the historical development of a Europe at war.

Conclusion: Hardy and Bakhtin

If thinking in Bakhtin's categories helps to illuminate *The Dynasts*, then extending his ideas into an area he did not explore – the disturbing context of war – does more than just add another challenge to his celebration of the forces of carnival. By way of a conclusion, I want to consider how the pairing of Bakhtin and Hardy can be mutually illuminating. Reading *The Dynasts* allows us to rethink some of the problems of Bakhtinian carnival, especially its relation to history and violence, while the carnival tradition has some important implications for the study of Hardy beyond *The Dynasts*.

As many commentators have observed, Bakhtin is not a systematic or consistent thinker. From one book to another, we encounter different and, at times, contradictory accounts of the carnival chronotope. In *Rabelais and His World*, Bakhtin claims that carnival's grotesque images contain 'a mighty awareness of history and historic change' (25)[1]; in the revised (1963) version of *Problems of Dostoevsky's Poetics*, he argues that carnivalized time is 'excluded ... from historical time' (175–6). We can understand why the threshold and its variants form the main places of action in Dostoevsky: he tries, in Bakhtin's view, to see things simultaneously, 'as if they existed in space and not in time' (*Problems* 28). At the opposite extreme, Goethe emphasizes the fullness of time, striving to see everything as stages in one evolving sequence. Where, then, should we position Hardy who appears to use a synchronic time, 'essentially instantaneous' (Bakhtin, *Dialogic* 248), to organize a diachronic work, a 'chronicle-piece' (Hardy, Preface to *The Dynasts* 6)?

Here we arrive at an important difference between Hardy's practice and Bakhtin's theory. Although the threshold is the only literary chronotope in which the primary category is space,[2] Hardy fills its crisis time with historical events. The 'impossible temporality' (Stam 105) of the menippea becomes renewed in a strange carnivalesque plot bound by history. Yet the many threshold scenes in *The Dynasts* point to one of the implications of Bakhtin's own thought: carnival's time out of time can lead to an awareness of crisis, sudden change, and reversal in the plot of history.[3] Instead of being 'so utterly untypical' (Eagleton, 'Bakhtin' 183) of history, carnival emerges as strikingly typical of some periods of upheaval. The liminal view of history implicit in the carnival chronotope allows Hardy to explain the Napoleonic era as a threshold age[4] when history became a stage without footlights and ordinary people ceased to be spectators opposed to war. When the carnival of war becomes the theatre of history, popular festive forms do 'reveal the deepest meaning of the historic process' (Bakhtin, *Rabelais* 447–8). And since 'it is precisely the chronotope that defines genre and generic distinctions' (Bakhtin, *Dialogic* 85), we find another reason for calling *The Dynasts* a novel in the carnival and menippean tradition rather than a failed epic or drama. Carnivalized time envelops and dominates the other chronotopes in *The Dynasts*, forming the ground for the selection and representation of events and entering the work in scene after scene where we are invited to 'see' the time of crisis and turnabout in the spaces of extreme conflict and ultimate decision.[5]

The conjunction of carnival and war in *The Dynasts* also throws into relief the language of violence in Bakhtin's writings. Even at one remove from Bakhtin, we still encounter this language in the way critics discuss the 'arsenal' (Emerson, 'Problems' 520; Morson and Emerson, *Rethinking* 51) of his concepts. Heteroglossia means the 'ceaseless battle' (Holquist, *Dialogic* xviii) between centripetal and centrifugal forces of language. The author of a polyphonic novel, 'a genre which destroys genre,' cannot be 'above the battle' (Dentith 60, 44), 'a battle [that] takes place in discourse and among discourses to become "the language of truth"' (Carroll 77).

To say that this 'cheerful war' is 'not a negative or negating process' (Holquist, *Dialogic* 433) is a bit misleading. For someone who believes that 'in dialogue, the destruction of the opponent destroys that very dialogic sphere where the word lives' (*Speech Genres* 150), Bakhtin does not hesitate to speak of destruction himself. Uncrowning is not simply the removal of an object from the distanced plane; it is 'the destruction of epic distance, an assault on and destruction of the distanced plane in general.' Laughter 'destroys the epic' (*Dialogic* 23); Rabelaisian laughter 'destroys traditional connections.' In the prehistory of novelistic discourse, 'parodic-travestying forms ... destroyed the homogenizing power of myth over language' (*Dialogic* 170, 60). Once the novel came into being, a 'lengthy battle for the novelization of the other genres began.' The novel 'fights for the renovation of an antiquated literary language' and 'fights for its own hegemony in literature' (*Dialogic* 39, 67, 4). Bakhtin's social and ideological theory of language provides the crowds necessary for war: language 'is populated – overpopulated – with the intentions of others.' The individual's ideological becoming depends on the long struggle between authoritative discourse, with its power to 'organize around itself great masses of other types of discourses,' and the internally persuasive word that 'organizes masses of our words within' (*Dialogic* 294, 343, 345). Like a military leader ordering the rank and file, the novelist orchestrates a diversity of voices representing the languages of heteroglossia. The crowds of war are already inside a novel. There might be 'compact masses of direct authorial discourse'; in Turgenev's novels 'substantial masses of this language are drawn into the battle between points of view, value judgements and emphases that characters introduce into it' (*Dialogic* 302, 315). A 'character zone' or 'field of action for a character's voice' is both a war zone and a battlefield formed 'from those invasions into authorial speech of others' expressive indicators' (*Dialogic* 316). Such militarized language is not limited to *The Dialogic Imagination*. When Bakhtin writes about Dostoevsky's characters, he claims that 'they all do furious battle with ... definitions of their personality in the mouths of other people.' Microdialogue means that 'dialogue has penetrated inside every word, provoking in it the battle and the interruption of one voice by another.' Isolation does not help: 'the consciousness of the solitary Raskolnikov becomes a field of battle for others' voices' (*Problems* 59, 75, 88).

The extreme 'conflictual character' (Dentith 101) of Bakhtin's theories turns out to be of fundamental importance and strangely at odds with the absence of any recognition of violence in historical carnival. But if blood constitutes the political unconscious of Bakhtinian carnival, with history suppressed and an ideal future imagined, violence returns in his very choice of language to express the carnival aesthetic: we are repeatedly told that 'negation and destruction' (*Rabelais* 62) form one pole of grotesque realism. Such language strongly suggests that carnival and war are compatible, a point that Bakhtin seemed to concede during his defence of his doctoral dissertation on Rabelais:

'"Laughter is a weapon, like fists and sticks"' (Emerson, *First* 96).

By extending carnival to include the 'Great Historical Calamity' (Hardy, Preface to *The Dynasts* 3) of war, we can better understand Hardy's long fascination with Napoleonic history.[6] Hardy saw the difference between the old method of fighting and the new in terms of what amounts to the carnival category of familiar contact. 'I am doing the battle of Jena just now,' he wrote in 1904, '... in which the combatants were *close* together; so different from modern war, in which distance and cold precision destroy those features which make the old wars throb with enthusiasm and romance' (*Letters* 3:135). *The Dynasts* serves as a reminder that carnival cannot be the solution to war when it is part of the problem that the 'dominant narrative of history to date has been one of carnage.' Carnival cannot come out on 'the other side' (Eagleton, 'Bakhtin' 182) of history when the content of this narrative *is* its carnivalesque form.

The return to history in *The Dynasts* restores a true ambivalence to the grotesque world of becoming and renewal. Instead of death being subordinate to life's rejuvenation, as in Bakhtin, negation balances affirmation, with neither prevailing. The past gives birth to the future but history does not clearly point to a higher degree of human development. Without Bakhtin's faith in a utopian future – 'When life is reborn it does not repeat itself, it is perfected' (*Rabelais* 406) – carnival cannot rescue history from repetition. Commenting on Hardy's novels in general, and on *Tess of the d'Urbervilles* in particular, J. Hillis Miller identifies the alogic of their plots as a form of immanent repetition with difference (142). If *The Dynasts* is any indication, however, the deeper design has the peculiar logic of the '"inside out"' and '"turnabout"' (Bakhtin, *Rabelais* 11), the cartwheels of popular humour. We need not conclude that 'history for Hardy is deeply negative' (Terence Wright 51) but its ceaseless crownings and decrownings cannot sustain any final hope. History's very inconclusiveness, cyclical repetitivness checking time's forward impulse, turns Hardy to monism to open a loophole on the distant future. The Will that the Pities finally hear is one version of Bakhtin's superaddressee 'whose absolutely just responsive understanding' (*Speech Genres* 126) might one day fashion all things fair.

Bakhtin's theoretical insights do more than make for a new reading of *The Dynasts*: they also cast light on Hardy's relation to tradition and on the role of laughter in his work – one problem, not two, since any attempt to insert him into tradition must also account for the laughter.

The heterogeneous materials that make Hardy 'the least "recuperable" of poets for tradition' (Neill 62) and, 'as a novelist, hard to place within any tradition or tendency' (Lock 19) can be seen at their most extreme, and therefore most instructive, in *The Dynasts*. Hardy's 'monster' combines the serious and the comic in a way that invites us to reposition laughter in the rest of his work.

All but ignored by critics, laughter remains the least understood aspect of Hardy's writing. Indeed nothing illustrates better the value of a Bakhtinian approach to Hardy's laughter than one of the few attempts to recognize its importance. In trying to give Hardy's humour its due, F.B. Pinion makes precisely the points that usually block a fuller appreciation: 1) Hardy's true humour is warm and genial; 2) it provides only comic or light relief to the main tragic perspective; 3) it declines with the darkening picture of life in his later novels; and 4) it places Hardy in a suitably vague but great tradition of Shakespeare, Richardson, and George Eliot. None of these assertions holds up when measured against *The Dynasts*. Its remarkable range of humour,[7] including the satire and farce that Pinion excludes, shows that Hardy's laughter does not diminish with the sombre colours of a work. Laughter is the other side of tragedy[8] and has a cognitive value that cannot be translated into logical language. In *The Dynasts*, where even the 'masters of thought' (Bakhtin, *Problems* 118) in the Overworld are not above mockery, this laughter grasps and comprehends the historical process of change and transition, always being directed at the crises that turn the world of action or the life of ideas inside out or upside down.

Although critics agree on the main source of Hardy's laughter, tracing its roots to folk culture has not helped define the traditional basis of his fiction beyond the oral tale. 'I do not,' Donald Davidson admits, 'know how to account for him' (164) except to imagine Hardy in the company of the frontier humorists of the Old Southwest. Bakhtin takes us beyond the culture of folk humour to show how it created the carnival tradition in literature, a textual tradition flexible enough to include even a writer as contradictory as Hardy.

By reading *The Dynasts* as a menippean novel in the carnival tradition, we can account for both Hardy's 'popular' and 'educated' writing.[9] Instead of being an 'indiscriminate maw' (Emerson, *First* 105), Bakhtin's open-ended genre allows us to move beyond the usual discussions of philosophy to see the relation between thought and dramatic action, the interplay of historical scenes, and the structure of any given scene down to its smallest details. We can also understand why

Bakhtin claims that the menippea continues to be the 'primary conduit for the most concentrated and vivid forms of carnivalization' (*Problems* 137). Monism may be the official philosphy of *The Dynasts* but carnivalization is Hardy's artistic means of staging its conflicts and visualizing the spectacle of war. In this respect, Bakhtin may well be wrong about the decline of carnivalistic laughter in modern literature. Written at the beginning of the twentieth century, *The Dynasts* contributes in its own strange way to 'a kind of renaissance of folk humour within great literature' (McKenna 129). Even in reduced form, laughter makes philosophy a realm of ultimate questions, not final answers, opening up the unity of all things to difference and contradiction that make the many as important as the one.

Notes

Introduction: Relocating *The Dynasts*

1 Bakhtin claims that 'Carnival, with its complex system of images was the fullest and purest expression of the culture of folk humor' (*Rabelais* 80).

2 Ruth Firor concludes that Hardy's intimate knowledge of folklore and folk-custom 'deepened a temperament already melancholy' (304) and profoundly influenced his brooding outlook on life.

3 It is not just a coincidence that in 1907, the same year that Hardy finished *The Dynasts*, William James gave a lecture entitled 'The One and the Many' to illustrate the practical consequences of philosophical belief.

4 When quoting from *The Dynasts*, I have followed the practice of most critics in spelling Napoleon's name without an accent and in standardizing the miniature type of the stage directions and the italicization of the Spirits' speeches. My aim is to produce an uncluttered page that will not distract the reader.

5 Compare F.R. Southerington, who argues that '*The Dynasts* is, in a sense, not about Napoleon at all: Hardy could as well have illustrated his conception from the Punic or any other wars' (164).

Chapter 1: Hardy's Longest Novel and the Monistic Theory of the Universe

1 To avoid distracting the reader, I have, when quoting, standardized the abbreviations '&' and '&c' that Hardy often uses in his *Letters*, *Life*, and *Notebooks*.

2 In the 1922 'Apology' to *Late Lyrics and Earlier*, Hardy uses the discourse of

naturalism in a way never intended by its exponents, speaking of 'the modicum of free will conjecturally possessed by organic life when the mighty necessitating forces – unconscious or other – that have "the balancings of the clouds," happen to be in equilibrium, which may or may not be often' (*Personal Writings* 53). The language of equilibration does not mean that '[Hardy] needed a metaphysic and he got Herbert Spencer' (Hynes, *Pattern* 40). Spencer borrows the term equilibrium, one of his favourites, from mechanics to express the tendency of evolution towards a balance of antagonistic forces, not to speculate about free will.

3 In the British Museum manuscript of *The Dynasts*, Hardy says that his Spirits 'will, without much forcing, be found to lend themselves as readily to the Predestinarianism of the Theologian as to the Determinism of the Scientist' (Preface v).

4 Hardy's one abridged quotation is from elsewhere in 'Science and Morals.' See *Literary Notebooks* 1:177. Hardy told Helen Garwood that '"My pages show harmony of view with Darwin, Huxley, Spencer, Hume, Mill, and others, all of whom I used to read more than Schopenhauer"' (Weber 246–7).

5 Rutland says that Hardy read Stephen's essays that appeared throughout the 1870s (79). Hardy refers to Stephen in 1874 as 'the man whose philosophy was to influence his own for many years, indeed, more than that of any other contemporary' (*Life* 102).

6 Hardy quotes from another part of E. Armitage's 'The Scientists and Common Sense' (*Literary Notebooks* 2:418).

7 At the perceptual level, Dean argues that 'in the poem's presentation of the spirit views, all ... are equally valid' (33). White, following Rutland, says 'The Phantom Intelligences in *The Dynasts* are as lively and differentiated personages as any of the "real" characters' (119).

8 See *Literary Notebooks* 2:223, 224, 406, 407, 414. Hardy also cut out reviews of Höffding's *Philosophy of Religion* (*Literary Notebooks* 2:189–90, 282–6, 384–8).

9 Compare Blanche Leppington: 'But every conception of the cosmos demands a corresponding form of religious belief' ('Amiel's Journal' 349). Hardy quotes from another part of this article (*Literary* Notebooks 1:162).

10 Hardy quotes from another part of Huxley's article (*Literary Notebooks* 1:175).

11 For Hardy's abridged quotations from the *Life and Letters of Charles Darwin*, see *Literary Notebooks* 1:204–5. In a letter (22 February 1888), Hardy wrote that 'Perhaps Dr. Grosart might be helped to a provisional view of the universe by the recently published Life of Darwin, and the works of Herbert Spencer and other agnostics' (*Letters* 1:174).

12 For Hardy's series of entries from *Natural Causes and Supernatural Seemings*, see *Literary Notebooks* 1:195–7.

13 For Hardy's numerous entries from Ellis's *New Spirit*, see *Literary Notebooks* 2:14–17.

14 A *Times* review quotes Höffding's image (*Philosophy* 245) of how '"Existence is unrolled before us as a great web of interrelated and continuous elements"' (Hardy, *Literary Notebooks* 2:189).

15 In *Concepts of Monism* (1907), A. Worsley comments on how 'the boundaries of the three domains [science, philosophy, and religion] have overlapped each other in all directions' (15).

16 For Hardy's cutting of all but the last two sentences of a negative review of Haeckel's book, see *Literary Notebooks* 2:98–101. In his letter (17 May 1902) printed in *Academy and Literature*, Hardy argues that '"the original difficulty [i.e., pain] recognized by thinkers like Schopenhauer, Hartmann, Haeckel ... remains unsurmounted"' (*Life* 338) by Maurice Maeterlinck's *Apology for Nature*. Bailey argues that 'Several passages in *The Dynasts* ... seem to reflect Hardy's reading of *The Riddle of the Universe*' (19).

17 See *Literary Notebooks* 1:371 for Hardy's entry, part summary and part quotation, from Mallock's review of Clifford's *Lectures and Essays*.

18 Hardy quotes from the second volume of H.S. Chamberlain's *Foundations of the Nineteenth Century* (*Literary Notebooks* 2:204–5). As Francis Darwin also explains, 'The one act of faith in the convert to science, is the confession of the universality of order and of the absolute validity in all times and under all circumstances, of the law of causation' (1:553). 'This,' James Ward reiterates, 'is the *faith* of science; on this point all are agreed' (1:175).

19 Hardy quotes from elsewhere in Conrad Guenther's *Darwinism* (*Literary Notebooks* 2:224–5). Monists agreed that 'feeling and thought ... are not two elements which exist separately, the one from the other' (Haldane 2:11–12). 'There is no such thing,' A.T. Ormond argues, 'as thought purged of emotion, or feeling purged completely of intellectual elements' (405). In retrospect, even Kant's 'extreme rationalism seems to have been but the obverse side of a profound susceptibility to feeling' (Adler 190). It now seemed a 'fundamental fact' that 'all our knowledge *springs from*, and is *limited by*, Feeling' (Lewes, 'Course' 319). The 'truth that feeling rather than intellect guides' (Spencer, *Autobiography* 2:366) made feeling the pioneer of knowledge.

20 Hardy quotes from both William James's *A Pluralistic Universe* and *The Meaning of Truth* (*Literary Notebooks* 2:201, 241).

21 Hartmann is one of the most quoted writers in Hardy's *Literary Notebooks* (1:185 and 2:109–14).

22 'Counsels and Maxims' is one of seven books, each with separate pagination, in the one-volume *Complete Essays of Schopenhauer*. All parenthetical page references follow the titles of the 'books' rather than the volume. The full titles of the books are as follows: 'Wisdom of Life,' 'Counsels and Maxims,' 'Religion: A Dialogue,' 'The Art of Literature,' 'Studies in Pessimism,' 'On Human Nature,' and 'The Art of Controversy.'

23 On 13 May 1891 Hardy recorded a series of entries from Schopenhauer's *Studies in Pessimism*. See *Literary Notebooks* 2:28–31.

24 Hardy quotes from elsewhere in E.A. Ross's 'Turning towards Nirvana' under the heading 'The Pessimism of Europe' (*Literary Notebooks* 2:48).

25 Hardy quotes other parts of Frederic W.H. Myers's 'The Disenchantment of France' (*Literary Notebooks* 1:218, 219).

26 See also Hardy's comment on how George Meredith did not 'let himself discover the tragedy that always underlies Comedy if you only scratch it deeply enough' (*Life* 474).

27 Hardy's entry is from elsewhere in Theophile Ribot's *The Psychology of the Emotions*. See *Literary Notebooks* 2:63.

28 For Hardy's excerpts from *The French Revolution*, see *Literary Notebooks* 1:64, 78–83, 88 and 2:460–1, 464–5, 472.

29 Hardy quotes other parts of Stephen's *Studies of a Biographer* (*Literary Notebooks* 2:77).

30 A long abridged quotation from Goldwin Smith's 'Inmortality of the Soul' appears in *Literary Notebooks* 2:164–5.

31 Hardy quotes from Christlieb's discussion of Spinoza's 'one universal Substance' (163) in a section on pantheism, the second modern conception of God (*Literary Notebooks* 2:108).

32 Hardy quotes from a review of Henry Footman's *Reasonable Apprehensions and Reassuring Hints* (*Literary Notebooks* 1:152–3).

33 Hardy quotes from elsewhere in *Hume* (*Literary Notebooks* 2:95, 222).

34 Hardy summarizes and quotes from other parts of a review of Careth Read's *The Metaphysics of Nature* (*Literary Notebooks* 2:183–4).

35 Hardy quotes from a review of Walker's *Christian Theism and Spiritual Monism* (*Literary Notebooks* 2:185).

36 Hardy quotes from John M.E. McTaggart's review of Ormond's *Concepts of Philosophy* (*Literary Notebooks* 2:225).

37 Hardy's abridged quotation from this important article appears in *Literary Notebooks* 1:174. Like Hardy in the Preface to *The Dynasts*, Romanes speaks of one theory but then proceeds to consider several versions of it.

38 Hardy's long abridged quotation is from another part of Ritchie's *Philosophical Studies* (*Literary Notebooks* 2:222–3).

39 See the Hartmann-Haeckel correspondence in Darnoi (176–89).

40 Hardy quotes from positive reviews of both Ward's *Naturalism and Agnosticism* and *The Realm of Ends, or Pluralism and Theism* (*Literary Notebooks* 2:165, 205).

41 For a long abridged quotation from Felix Adler's essay on Kant, see *Literary Notebooks* 2:161.

42 A summary of one of John Fiske's ideas from *Outlines of Cosmic Philosophy* heads off the 'Notes in Philosophy' section of Hardy's 'Literary Notes II' (*Literary Notebooks* 2:108).

43 See also entry 2042, *Literary Notebooks* 2:94.

44 Hardy's one quotation is from another part of *Appearance and Reality* (*Literary Notebooks* 2:95).

45 For Hardy's cuttings from reviews of R.B. Haldane's *The Pathway to Reality*, see *Literary Notebooks* 2:145–8, 159–60.

46 Hardy quotes another sentence from Carl Du Prel's *Philosophy of Mysticism* (*Literary Notebooks* 2:95).

47 Hardy quotes from another part of G.H. Lewes's 'The Course of Modern Thought' (*Literary Notebooks* 1:92).

48 Hardy quotes another part of this review of James's *Pragmatism* (*Literary Notebooks* 2:224).

49 Norman Page speaks of 'the importance of the novelistic element' (179) in *The Dynasts*. John Bayley argues that Hardy gave himself 'the pleasure of writing a novel with all the things he enjoyed putting in, and none of the ones he supposed a novel-reading audience expected' (232).

Chapter 2: The Will's Official Spirit

1 In a recent account (1999) of 'The Influence of Religion, Science, and Philosophy on Hardy's Writings,' Robert Schweik misses the chance to advance our understanding of the development of Hardy's thought beyond such usual influences as Darwin, Mill, Stephen, Schopenhauer, and Hartmann, all considered in the most general way.

2 Hardy cut and pasted another part of 'Pluralism and Theism.' See *Literary Notebooks* 2:205.

3 Hardy took about twelve pages of notes from *Social Dynamics*, the third volume of *System of Positive Polity* (*Literary Notebooks* 1:64, 66–78).

4 Hardy's entries are from the second part of 'Evolution and Positivism' (*Literary Notebooks* 1:113–14).

5 Hardy quotes another part of 'The Apostle of Evolution' (*Literary Notebooks* 2:153).

6 For Hardy's long abridged quotation from Allen's 'Tropical Education,' see *Literary Notebooks* 2:6–7.

7 Hardy quotes from another part of Morgan's '"The Riddle of the Universe"' (*Literary Notebooks* 2:164).

8 Even Haeckel admits that monism needs faith (in the scientific sense): it 'is the imagination that fills up the gaps left by the intelligence in our knowledge of the connection of things' (*Riddle* 299). The idea that science depends on a 'symbolic concept of truth' (Höffding, *Problems* 84) no longer appeared strange.

9 Compare the 'Moving Finger' of Destiny that 'writes; and, having writ, / Moves on' in one of the most popular documents of Victorian pessimism, Edward Fitzgerald's translation of *The Rubaiyat of Omar Khayyam* (1859). Omar asserts that 'the first Morning of Creation wrote / What the Last Dawn of Reckoning shall read' (First Version LI, LIII). Hardy had a verse (LVIII) of the *Rubaiyat* read to him just before he died (*Life* 480–1).

10 For Hardy's excerpts from *Heroes*, see *Literary Notebooks* 1: 179–82.

11 See also Hardy's abridged quotation from Carlyle's 'Death of Edward Irving': 'Our phantasmagory of a world' (*Literary* Notebooks 2:463). The 'magic-lantern image which may have derived from Schopenhauer' (Pinion, *Thomas* 159) was actually quite common.

12 Hardy's abridged quotation (*Literary Notebooks* 2:107) is from another part of William Caldwell's entry on Schopenhauer in *Chamber's Encyclopedia* (1892).

13 A notable exception would be W.K. Clifford for whom the thing in itself or mind-stuff means the subjectivity of things as they appear to the things themselves.

14 Hardy recorded some of the key terms in *First Principles* (*Literary Notebooks* 2:108, 457).

15 'In truth,' Haldane argues, 'thought no more exists apart from its object, than does the object exist apart from thought' (1:301). To use Maudsley's quaint term, every thought and its object combine to form 'a *think*' (36; Hardy, *Literary* 1:195). Even Spencer, for whom 'the reality existing behind all appearances is, must ever be, unknown' (*First* 69), rejects the Kantian doctrine 'that Time and Space are nothing but subjective forms' (*Autobiography* 1:252). Hartmann finds it 'highly probable that common sense is right in believing that Space and Time are just as much objective forms of existence as subjective forms of thought' (1:333). 'Time and space ... belong,' Ward explains, 'neither to the subject alone apart from the object, nor to the object alone apart from the subject, but to experience as the duality of both' (2:149).

16 'There is ... no prospect,' Höffding reminds us, 'of freeing ourselves from the historical elements of our knowledge' (*Problems* 106). In this way 'Absolute individualism is nonsense': 'No one can think but through the general thought, refined by centuries of culture and experience' (Leppington 344). Certainly Hardy never forgets that 'words are ... shot and coloured with past emotions and accepted meaning' (Symonds 169).

17 Hardy's abridged quotation (*Literary Notebooks* 1:203) from the *Encyclopaedia Britannica* (9th ed.) article comes under the heading '"*Schopenhauer.*"'

18 For a long abridged quotation from John Tulloch's 'Morality Without Metaphysic,' see *Literary Notebooks* 1:88–9.

19 Hardy quotes another part of the *Autobiography* (*Literary Notebooks* 2:163).

20 On 27 February 1902 Hardy wrote to Clodd, 'I have finished reading every word of your "Huxley"' (*Letters* 3:5).

21 See also *Personal Writings* (49) and *Literary Notebooks* (2:163) where Hardy again quotes from the conclusion to Spencer's *Autobiography* (2:470).

22 Hardy took several pages of notes from *Service* (*Literay Notebooks* 1:189–92).

23 Hardy quotes from another place in Rashdall's review of Haldane's *The Pathway to Reality: Stage the Second* (1904) (*Literary Notebooks* 2:159).

24 Hardy quotes from other parts of the *Principles of Biology* (*Literary Notebooks*: 1:90–2).

25 Hardy quotes another part of W.H. Mallock's review of Clifford's *Lectures and Essays* (*Literary Notebooks* 1:135).

26 For a long series of entries from *The Life of Goethe*, see *Literary Notebooks* 1:14–15.

27 Rutland was the first to point out this connection (57).

28 Gary Saul Morson points out that 'parody is most readily invited by an utterance that claims transhistorical authority or implies that its source does not lie in any interests or circumstances of its speaker' ('Parody' 78).

Chapter 3: Unconscious or Superconscious?

1 Hardy quotes from Norman Smith's review of Strong's *Why Mind Has a Body* (*Literary Notebooks* 2:167).

2 Hardy paraphrases William Caldwell's description of the Will 'as blind irresistible energy or impulse' ('Schopenhauer' 221). Hardy's early notes on the 'Mode for a historical Drama' all emphasize this reasonless will. In March 1881, he thought of applying the theory of automatism to the Hundred Days: 'Action mostly automatic, reflex movement, etc. Not the result of what is called *motive*, though always ostensibly so, even to the actors' own consciousness' (*Life* 152). On 16 February 1882 he proposed writing 'a his-

tory of human automatism, or impulsion – viz., an account of human action
in spite of human knowledge, showing how very far conduct lags behind
the knowledge that should really guide it' (*Life* 158). In a Query dated
20 October 1884, he wondered: 'Is not the present quasi-scientific system of
writing history mere charlatanism? Events and tendencies are traced as if
they were rivers of voluntary activity ... But are they not in the main the
outcome of *passivity* – acted upon by unconscious propensity?' (*Life* 175).
When he again 'Considered methods for the Napoleon drama' on 26 June
1892, he imagined the 'Forces; emotions; tendencies' of characters who 'do
not act under the influence of reason' (*Life* 261).

3 Hardy read John M.E. McTaggart's *Some Dogmas of Religion* (1906). See *Life*
   317.
4 Hardy quotes another part of a review of Francis Galton's *Inquiries into
   Human Faculty and Development* (1883). See *Literary Notebooks* 1:154–5.
5 'That ... the subordinate nerve-centres must also have a consciousness, if of
   a vaguer description,' says Hartmann, 'plainly follows from the continuity
   of the animal series' (1:68). To Du Prel there remains no doubt 'that a capacity for consciousness must be attributed to every nerve-cell' (1:244), human
   or not. 'And having admitted,' asks Symonds, 'that there is no abrupt
   breakage between these cells and us in the long chain of organised existence, how can we refuse mind in its simpler form to ... simpler organiza-
   tions?' (13). 'As we cannot admit,' says Guenther, 'that the mind is formed
   in any animal out of nothing, we must ascribe psychic phenomena to the
   protist' (403).
6 Hardy quotes from elsewhere in W.K. Clifford's *Lectures and* Essays (1879).
   See *Literary Notebooks* 1:186–7 and 2:108.
7 See also James, who praises Gustav Fechner for considering a similar alternative: 'Must every higher means of unification between things be a literal
   brain-fibre, and go by that name? Cannot the earth-mind know otherwise
   the contents of our minds together?' (*Pluralistic* 162).
8 Under the heading, *'The stronghold of the spiritualist's case,'* Hardy quotes
   another part of 'Mr. Justice Fry on Materialism.' See *Literary Notebooks*
   1:147–8.
9 Hardy summarizes part of Wilson's article, 'Concerning Protoplasm.' See
   Literary Notebooks 1:122.
10 Hardy quotes from elsewhere in Maeterlinck's *The Treasure of the Humble*
   (*Literary Notebooks* 2:78). 'Let empiricism once become associated with religion,' James predicts, 'as hitherto, through some strange misunderstand-
   ing, it has been associated with irreligion, and I believe that a new era of
   religion as well as of philosophy will be ready to begin' (*Pluralistic* 314).

'Far from being hostile to Religion,' Walker argues, 'we can find in it [scientific monism] the strongest support for a religious conception of the world' (82).

11 Hardy did not substitute 'prócessive' for 'purposive' until 1919 and the Mellstock edition of *The Dynasts*. Wright cites this revision among others as evidence of Hardy's desire for 'maintaining consistency in the philosophic terminology which the Spirits should use' (296). As I have tried to show, Hardy could not represent the monistic field of thought without inconsistencies. The word 'prócessive' does not eliminate the possibility of an *'unconscious idea of purpose.'* In this sense, Hartmann sees world history as a 'purposive process' (1:88; 2:257).

12 According to Mallock, the theory of mindstuff 'which Clifford flattered himself was a new form of monism, is in reality nothing but the dualism it was intended to replace' (258–9).

13 The family metaphor seemed closer to the truth: 'mechanism and idealism are sisters' (Chamberlain 2: 109). 'Is it not ... conceivable,' asks Taylor, 'that both idealism and determinism may be the truth?' (255).

14 Some of the last entries in Hardy's 'Literary Notes II' bear on the issue of probability versus possibility. An abridged quotation from F.W. Hirst's *Early Life and Letters of John Morley* explains how J.S. Mill's 'religion displaces the idea of providential government by an omnipotent deity, and substitutes the "idea of the possibility, and in a low degree even the probability," of a universe governed by a deity with limited powers.' Hardy also summarizes the definition of the Absolute in Michael Kaye's 'The Possibility of Man's Freedom': 'The exhauster, includer, of all possibilities' (*Literary Notebooks* 2:248, 249).

15 The issue is an important one given what some critics assume about *The Dynasts*. Desmond Hawkins, for example, says that the 'simultaneity of the One with the All makes an illusion of individual will' (177).

16 'There is first,' Romanes points out, 'the antecedent improbability that the human mind should be the highest manifestation of subjectivity in this universe of infinite objectivity.' Furthermore, 'there is unquestionable evidence of some one integrating principle' so that 'wherever we tap organic nature, it seems to flow with purpose' (54, 54–5).

17 Hardy quotes another part of Spencer's 'Last Words about Agnosticism and the Religion of Humanity.' See *Literary Notebooks* 1:160.

18 Hardy quotes in abridged form from the same page: 'If the idea of a better world [could] have lain in the omniscient [clairvoyant] [Unconscious], the better one [would] have come to pass' (*Literary Notebooks* 2:112).

19 F.B. Pinion also argues that 'The "consciousness" which [Hardy] thought

might inform the Will "till It fashion all things fair" was that of mankind, the most important part of "the general Will'" (*Thomas* 102). Compare Southerington (205), Chakravarty (75), and Morrell (87).

Chapter 4: Poetry and Prose

1 Buckler notes how the dynasts sometimes act in 'parodic solemnity' ('Thomas' 221). Dean also discusses some of the parodic images (102–4).
2 According to Desmond Hawkins, 'To English ears the mighty line of Marlowe and Shakespeare at once suggests the dignity and eloquence of high tragedy' (181).
3 For a brief discussion of the relevance of Bakhtin's concept of grotesque realism to the world of the folk in *The Return of the Native*, see Wotton (61–3).
4 Critics invoke various forms of tragedy to describe *The Mayor of Casterbridge*, usually Greek or Shakespearian (Paterson, Edwards, Kramer, and Bloom), but also antitraditional (Starzyk), romantic (Stewart), Darwinian (Page, Mistichelli), Hegelian (Lothe), and bourgeois (Moses). For Henchard's epic significance, see Gregor (115) and Brooks (196).
5 Compare Thomas H. Dickinson who calls the Napoleonic era 'The last great period in human history worthy of an epic' (529). Orel claims that Hardy 'was convinced the epical qualities of the Napoleonic struggle had hitherto been minimized or ignored' (*Thomas Hardy's* 43). See also Wang (177).
6 Hayden White explains that 'The Epic plot structure would appear to be the implicit form of chronicle itself' (*Metahistory* 8). In 'Proving Nothing: History and Dramatic Strategy in The Dynasts,' Barton R. Friedman draws on White to analyse the plot of *The Dynasts* as a combination of heroic romance and dramatic irony.
7 Wotton comments that 'What the people perceive as a joke permissible under the rules of topsy-turvy, the licence of the temporary release from the world of work, Henchard means seriously and in that act which refuses the spirit of festival he places himself in a position of antagonism to the workfolk, an antagonism which grows with time' (63–4).
8 Hardy includes Napoleon's botched suicide attempt in the carnival plot of *The Dynasts*.

Chapter 5: A Carnivalesque Picture of Carnival

1 See also Bernstein ('When' 100), LaCapra (*Rethinking* 295), and Emerson (*First* 165).

2 R.J. White points out that some of the historians Hardy read describe armies as monsters and serpents (114).
3 In Barton R. Freidman's words, 'Kings devouring and devoured, their subjects consumed and consuming, epitomize the action of *The Dynasts*' (117).

Chapter 8: Chronotopes and the Death-Birth of a World

1 See Simon Trezise, 'Places in Time: Discovering the Chronotope in *Tess of the d'Urbervilles.*'
2 David Lodge comments that 'Carlyle's treament of the Revolution is, then, frankly apocalyptic' (106). I would add that the way Carlyle joins death and birth also places his history in the tradition of grotesque realism.
3 Bakhtin claims that 'Folklore is in general saturated with time; all of its images are profoundly chronotopic' (*Speech Genres* 52).

Conclusion: Hardy and Bakhtin

1 See also Bakhtin's comment that 'folklore interprets and saturates space with time, and draws it into history' (*Speech Genres* 52).
2 Bakhtin argues that 'in literature the primary category in the chronotope is time' (*Dialogic* 85).
3 Hayden White lists four types of historical plots: romance, tragedy, comedy, and satire (*Figural Realism* 11). The historical plot of *The Dynasts* suggests that carnival can also be a mode of emplotment.
4 Katerina Clark and Michael Holquist compare Rabelais and Bakhtin in terms of them living in 'threshold ages, border situations on the map of history. Each created in the inhabitants of its moment an urgent awareness of radical change. Each was a rip in the fabric of time' (*Mikhail* 296).
5 Compare Gary Saul Morson's comment that 'a genre's chronotope is not actually an element in a work' ('Prosaic' 76).
6 Kathryn R. King and William W. Morgan emphasize the contradictions in Hardy's attitude toward war: 'War always both intrigued and revolted him' (67).
7 Jacob Lothe comments that 'the notion of comedy as a generic variant in Hardy needs to be diversified' (125).
8 Compare Hardy's remark that 'All tragedy is grotesque – if you allow yourself to see it as such' (*Life* 315).
9 According to Terry Eagleton, 'The ideological effectivity of [Hardy's] fiction inheres neither in "rustic" nor "educated" writing, but in the ceaseless play and tension between the two modes' (*Walter* 129).

Works Cited

A.W. 'Dr. Maudsley on Free-Will.' *The Spectator* (4 Aug. 1883): 996.

Adler, Felix. 'A Critique of Kant's Ethics.' *Mind* 11 (1902): 162–95.

Allen, Grant. 'Tropical Education.' *Longman's Magazine* 14 (1889): 479–88.

Archer, William. 'Real Conversations: Conversation I – with Mr Thomas Hardy.' *Critic* 37 (1901): 309–18.

Armitage, E. 'The Scientists and Common Sense.' *The Contemporary Review* 87 (1905): 727–38.

Armstrong, Isobel. *Victorian Poetry: Poetry, Poetics and Politics.* London: Routledge, 1993.

Bailey, J.O. *Thomas Hardy and the Cosmic Mind: A New Reading of The Dynasts.* Chapel Hill: U of North Carolina P, 1956.

Bain, Alexander. *Mind and Body: The Theories of Their Relation.* 2nd ed. London: Henry S. King, 1873.

Bakhtin, Mikhail. *The Dialogic Imagination: Four Essays.* Ed. Michael Holquist, trans. Caryl Emerson and Michael Holquist. Austin: U of Texas P, 1981.

– *Problems of Dostoevsky's Poetics.* Ed. and trans. Caryl Emerson, intro. Wayne C. Booth. Minneapolis: U of Minnesota P, 1984.

– *Rabelais and His World.* Trans. Hélène Iswolsky. Cambridge, Mass.: MIT Press, 1968.

– *Speech Genres and Other Late Essays.* Ed. Caryl Emerson and Michael Holquist, trans. Vern W. McGee. Austin: U of Texas P, 1986.

Bayley, John. *An Essay on Hardy.* Cambridge: Cambridge UP, 1978.

Beach, Joseph Warren. *The Technique of Thomas Hardy.* Chicago: U of Chicago P, 1922.

Beer, Gillian. *Darwin's Plots.* London: Ark, 1983.

'Bergson and Balfour.' *The Review of Reviews* 44 (1911): 473–4.

Bernstein, Michael André. 'The Poetics of Ressentiment.' *Rethinking Bakhtin: Extensions and Challenges*. Ed. Gary Saul Morson and Caryl Emerson. Evanston: Northwestern UP, 1989: 197–223.

– 'When the Carnival Turns Bitter: Preliminary Reflections upon the Abject Hero.' *Bakhtin: Essays and Dialogues on His Work*. Ed. Gary Saul Morson. Chicago: U of Chicago P, 1986: 99–121.

Bloom, Harold. Introduction. *Thomas Hardy's The Mayor of Casterbridge*. New York: Chelsea House, 1988.

Bové, Carol Mastrangelo. 'The Text as Dialogue in Bakhtin and Kristeva.' *University of Ottawa Quarterly* 53 (1983): 117–31.

Bradley, F.H. *Appearance and Reality: A Metaphysical Essay*. 9th impression. Oxford: Oxford at the Clarendon Press, 1955.

Brennecke, Ernest, Jr. *Thomas Hardy's Universe: A Study of a Poet's Mind*. Boston: Small, Maynard, 1924.

Bridges, J.H. 'Evolution and Positivism.' *Fortnightly Review* 22 (1877): 89–114.

Brooks, Jean R. *Thomas Hardy: The Poetical Structure*. London: Elek, 1971.

Buckler, William E. '"In the Seventies": A Centennial Assessment of the Unlocking of Thomas Hardy's Vision.' *Dickens Studies Annual* 9 (1981): 233–63.

– 'Thomas Hardy's "chronicle-piece" in "play-shape": An Essay in Literary Conceptualization.' *Victorian Poetry* 18 (1980): 209–27.

Buckley, Jerome Hamilton. *The Victorian Temper: A Study in Literary Culture*. New York: Vintage, 1951.

Caldwell, William. 'The Epistemology of Ed. W. Hartman.' *Mind* 2 (1893): 185–207.

– 'Schopenhauer.' *Chamber's Encyclopedia* 9 (1888–92): 221–2.

– 'Schopenhauer's Criticism of Kant.' *Mind* 16 (1891): 355–74.

Canetti, Elias. *Crowds and Power*. Trans. Carol Stewart. New York: The Noonday Press, 1993.

Carey, John. *The Intellectuals and the Masses: Pride and Prejudice among the Literary Intelligentsia, 1880–1939*. London: Faber and Faber, 1992.

Carlyle, Thomas. *The French Revolution: A History*. New York: Modern Library, 1934.

– *On Heroes and Hero-Worship*. London: Oxford UP, 1968.

– *Sartor Resartus*. Ed. Charles Frederick Harrold. New York: The Odyssey Press, 1937.

Carpenter, Richard C. *Thomas Hardy*. New York: Twayne, 1964.

Carroll, David. 'The Alterity of Discourse: Form, History, and the Question of the Political in M.M. Bakhtin.' *Diacritics* 13 (1983): 65–83.

Chakravarty, Amiya. *The Dynasts and the Post-War Age in Poetry.* 1938. New York: Octagon Books, 1970.

Chamberlain, Houston Stewart. *The Foundations of the Nineteenth Century.* Trans. John Lees. 2 vols. London: John Lane, 1911.

Christlieb, Theodore. *Modern Doubt and Christian Belief.* Trans. G.H. Venables and H.V. Weitbrecht. 3rd ed. New York: Charles Scribner's Sons, 1874.

Clark, Katerina and Michael Holquist. *Mikhail Bakhtin.* Cambridge: Cambridge UP, 1984.

Clifford, W.K. *Lectures and Essays.* Ed. Leslie Stephen and Frederick Pollock. 2nd ed. London: Macmillan, 1886.

Clodd, Edward. *Thomas Henry Huxley.* New York: Dodd, Mead, 1902.

Comte, Auguste. *System of Positive Polity.* Trans. Edward Spencer Beesly et al. 1875. Vol. 3. Reprinted New York: Burt Franklin, 1973. 4 vols.

Dale, T.R. '*The Dynasts* and Edward von Hartmann.' *Notes and Queries* 8 (1961): 100–1.

Darnoi, Dennis N. Kenedy. *The Unconscious and Edward Von Hartmann: A Historico-Critical Monograph.* The Hague: Martinus Nijhoff, 1967.

Darwin, Francis, ed. *The Life and Letters of Charles Darwin.* 1889. 2 vols. Reprinted New York: Basic Books, 1959.

Dean, Susan. *Hardy's Poetic Vision in The Dynasts: The Diorama of a Dream.* Princeton, NJ: Princeton UP, 1977.

Dentith, Simon. *Bakhtinian Thought: An Introductory Reader.* London: Routledge, 1995.

Dessner, Lawrence Jay. 'Space, Time, and Coincidence in Hardy.' *Studies in the Novel* 24 (1992): 154–72.

Dickinson, Thomas H. 'Thomas Hardy's *The Dynasts.*' *North American Review* 195 (1912): 526–42.

Drummond, Henry. *Natural Law in the Spiritual World.* Philadelphia: Henry Altemus, 1883.

Du Prel, Carl. *The Philosophy of Mysticism.* Trans. C.C. Massey. 1889. 2 vols. Reprinted New York: Arno Press, 1976.

Duffin, Henry Charles. *Thomas Hardy: A Study of the Wessex Novels, the Poems and The Dynasts.* 3rd ed. Manchester: Manchester UP, 1937.

Eagleton, Terry. 'Bakhtin, Schopenhauer, Kundera.' *Bakhtin and Cultural Theory.* Ed. Ken Hirschkop and David Shepherd. Manchester: Manchester UP, 1989: 178–88.

– *Walter Benjamin: Or towards a Revolutionary Criticism.* London: Verso, 1981.

Eckstrom, Lisa. 'Moral Perception and the Chronotope: The Case of Henry James.' *Bakhtin in Contexts: Across the Disciplines.* Ed. Amy Mandelker. Evanston: Northwestern UP, 1995: 99–116.

Edwards, Duane D. '*The Mayor of Casterbridge* as Aeschylean Tragedy.' *Studies in the Novel* 4 (1972): 608–18.

Elliott, G.R. 'Spectral Etching in the Poetry of Thomas Hardy.' *PMLA* 43 (1928): 1185–95.

Ellis, Havelock. *The New Spirit*. 4th ed. London: Constable, 1926.

Emerson, Caryl. *The First Hundred Years of Mikhail Bakhtin*. Princeton: Princeton UP, 1997.

– 'Problems with Baxtin's Poetics.' *Slavic and East European Journal* 32 (1988): 503–25.

Epstein, Leonora. 'Sale and Sacrament: The Wife Auction in *The Mayor of Casterbridge*.' *English Language Notes* 24 (1987): 50–6.

Firor, Ruth A. *Folkways in Thomas Hardy*. 1931. New York: Barnes, 1962.

Fiske, John. *Outline of Cosmic Philosophy*. 1875. 2 vols. Reprinted New York: Johnson, 1969.

Fitzgerald, Edward. *The Rubaiyat of Omar Khayyam*. New York: Avon, 1967.

Freeman, Janet H. 'Highways and Cornfields: Space and Time in the Narration of *Jude the Obscure*.' *The Colby Library Quarterly* 27 (1991): 161–73.

Friedman, Barton R. 'Proving Nothing: History and Dramatic Strategy in *The Dynasts*.' *Clio* 13 (1984): 101–22.

Froude, James Anthony. *Thomas Carlyle: A History of the First Forty Years of His Life, 1795–1835*. Vol. 2. London: Longmans, Green, 1882. 2 vols.

– *Thomas Carlyle: A History of His Life in London, 1834–1881*. 4th ed. Vol. 1. London: Longmans, Green, 1885. 2 vols.

Gardiner, Michael, *The Dialogics of Critique: M.M. Bakhtin and the Theory of Ideology*. London: Routledge, 1992.

Garrison, Chester A. *The Vast Venture: Hardy's Epic Drama The Dynasts*. Salzburg: Institute for English Language and Literature, 1973.

Giordano, Frank R., Jr. 'The Degradation of Napoleon in *The Dynasts*.' *The Thomas Hardy Year Book* 4 (1973–4): 54–64.

Gittings, Robert. *Thomas Hardy's Later Years*. Boston: Little, Brown, 1978.

Glazener, Nancy. 'Dialogic Subversion: Bakthin, the Novel and Gertrude Stein.' *Bakhtin and Cultural Theory*. Ed. Ken Hirschkop and David Shepherd. Manchester: Manchester UP, 1989: 109–29.

Goodale, Ralph. 'Schopenhauer and Pessimism in Nineteenth Century English Literature.' *PMLA* 47 (1932): 241–61.

Goode, John. *Thomas Hardy: The Offensive Truth*. Oxford: Blackwell, 1988.

Gregor, Ian. *The Great Web: The Form of Hardy's Major Fiction*. Totawa: Rowman and Littlefield, 1974.

Guenther, Conrad. *Darwinism and the Problems of Life: A Study of Familiar Animal Life*. Trans. Joseph McCabe. 3rd ed. London: Owen, 1906.

Haeckel, Ernst. 'Our Monism.' *The Monist* 2 (1891–92): 481–6.

– *The Riddle of the Universe at the Close of the Nineteenth Century.* New York: Harper, 1900.

Haldane, R.B. *The Pathway to Reality.* 2 vols. New York: E.P. Dutton, 1905.

Halliday, F.E. *Thomas Hardy: His Life and Work.* Bath: Adams and Dart, 1972.

Hardy, Evelyn. *Thomas Hardy: A Critical Biography.* London: The Hogarth Press, 1954.

Hardy, Thomas. *The Collected Letters of Thomas Hardy.* Ed. Richard Little Purdy and Michael Millgate. 5 vols. Oxford at the Clarendon Press, 1978–85.

– *The Dynasts: An Epic-Drama of the War with Napoleon.* Ed. Harold Orel. London: Macmillan, 1978.

– *The Life and Work of Thomas Hardy.* Ed. Michael Millgate. London: Macmillan, 1984.

– *The Literary Notebooks of Thomas Hardy.* Ed. Lennart A. Björk. 2 vols. New York: New York UP, 1985.

– *The Mayor of Casterbridge.* Ed. Martin Seymour-Smith. London: Penguin, 1985.

– *The Personal Notebooks of Thomas Hardy.* Ed. Richard H. Taylor. New York: Columbia UP, 1979.

– *Tess of the d'Urbervilles.* Ed. P.N. Furbank. London: Macmillan, 1974.

– *Thomas Hardy's Personal Writings.* Ed. Harold Orel. Lawrence: U of Kansas P, 1966.

Harrison, Frederic. 'Apologia Pro Fide Nostra.' *The Fortnightly Review* 44 (1888): 665–83.

– 'A Few Words about the Nineteenth Century.' *Fortnightly Review* 37 (1882): 411–26.

Hartmann, Eduard von. *Philosophy of the Unconscious.* Trans. William C. Coupland. London: Kegan Paul, Trench, Trubner, 1931.

Hawkins, Desmond. *Hardy: Novelist and Poet.* London: Macmillan, 1981.

Hayles, N. Katherine. *The Cosmic Web: Scientific Field Models and Literary Strategies in the Twentieth Century.* Ithaca: Cornell UP, 1984.

Henrickson, Bruce. 'The Construction of the Narrator in *The Nigger of the "Narcissus"*.' *PMLA* 103 (1988): 783–95.

Hirst, F.W. *Early Life and Letters of John Morley.* Vol. 1. London, 1927. 2 vols.

Hitchcock, Peter. *Dialogics of the Oppressed.* Minneapolis: U of Minnesota P, 1993.

Höffding, Harald. *The Philosophy of Religion.* Trans. B.E. Meyer. London: Macmillan, 1906.

– *The Problems of Philosophy.* Trans. Galen M. Fisher. New York: Macmillan, 1905.

Holquist, Michael. Introduction and Glossary. *The Dialogic Imagination: Four Essays*. By Mikhail Bakhtin. Ed. Michael Holquist, trans. Caryl Emerson and Michael Holquist. Austin: U of Texas P, 1981.

Hopkins, Annette B. '*The Dynasts* and the Course of History.' *The South Atlantic Quarterly* 44 (1945): 432–44.

Horsman, E.A. 'The Language of *The Dynasts*.' *Durham University Journal* 41 (1948): 11–16.

Howe, Irving. *Thomas Hardy*. 1966. Reprinted New York: Collier, 1973.

Huxley, Thomas Henry. *Hume, with Helps to the Study of Berkeley*. New York: D. Appleton, 1898.

– 'S nc nd Morals.' *Fortnightly Review* 40 (1886): 788–802.

– 'Scie...ric and Pseudo-Scientific Realism.' *The Nineteenth Century* 21 (1887): 191–205.

Hynes, Samuel. 'Mr. Hardy's Monster: *The Dynasts*.' *Sewanee Review* 102 (1994): 213–32.

– *The Pattern of Hardy's Poetry*. Chapel Hill: U of Carolina P, 1961.

James, William. *Essays in Radical Empiricism and a Pluralistic Universe*. New York: Longmans, Green, 1947.

– *Pragmatism and Four Essays from the Meaning of Truth*. New York: Meridian Books, 1955.

– Preface. *The Problems of Philosophy*. By Harald Höffding. Trans. Galen M. Fisher. New York: Macmillan, 1905: v–xvi.

Jones, Henry. 'The Philosophy of Religion.' *Speaker* 14 (1906): 477–8.

Kaye, Michael. 'The Possibility of Man's Freedom.' *Philosophy* 2 (1927): 516–31.

King, Kathryn R. and William W. Morgan. 'Hardy and the Boer War: The Public Poet in Spite of Himself.' *Victorian Poetry* 17 (1979): 66–83.

Kramer, Dale. *Thomas Hardy: The Forms of Tragedy*. Detroit: Wayne State UP, 1975.

LaCapra, Dominick. *Rethinking Intellectual History: Texts, Contexts, Language*. Ithaca: Cornell UP, 1983.

– *Soundings in Critical Theory*. Ithaca: Cornell UP, 1989.

Laird, John. 'Hardy's *The Dynasts*.' *Philosophical Incursions into English Literature*. London: Cambridge UP, 1946: 187–204.

'Lange's History of Materialism – Vol. II.' *Spectator* 54 (9 July 1881): 900.

Lepington, Blanche. 'Amiel's Journal.' *Contemporary Review* 47 (1885): 334–52.

Lewes, George Henry. 'The Course of Modern Thought.' *Fortnightly Review* 21 (1877): 317–27.

– *The Life of Goethe*. 3rd ed. London: Smith, Elder, 1875.

'The Limits of Mystery.' *The Academy and Literature* 62 (3 May 1902): 451–2.

Lock, Charles. *Criticism in Focus: Thomas Hardy.* New York: St Martin's Press, 1992.

Lodge, David. *After Bakhtin: Essays on Fiction and Criticism.* London: Routledge, 1990.

Lothe, Jakob. 'Variants on Genre: *The Return of the Native, The Mayor of Casterbridge, The Hand of Ethelberta.' The Cambridge Companion to Thomas Hardy.* Ed. Dale Kramer. Cambridge: Cambridge UP, 1999: 112–29.

Lucacs, Georg. *The Historical Novel.* Trans. Hannah and Stanley Mitchell. Harmondsworth: Penguin, 1969.

Maeterlinck, Maurice. *The Treasure of the Humble.* Trans. Alfred Sutro. Toronto: Musson, 1911.

Mallock, W.H. 'The Late Professor Clifford's Essays.' *Edinburgh* Review 151 (1880): 243–63.

Mann, R.J. 'Darwin on the Movement of Plants.' *Edinburgh Review* 153 (1881): 254–62.

Markham, Felix. *Napoleon.* New York: Mentor, 1963.

Masterman, C.F.G. 'A Statesman's Philosophy.' *Daily News* (4 March 1903): 8.

Maudsley, Henry. *Natural Causes and Supernatural Seemings.* 3rd ed. London: Kegan Paul, Trench, Trubner, 1897.

Maynard, Katherine Kearney. *Thomas Hardy's Tragic Poetry: The Lyrics and The Dynasts.* Iowa City: U of Iowa P, 1991.

McTaggart, John M.E. Review of *Concepts of Philosophy,* by A.T. Ormond. *Mind* 16 (1907): 431–6.

– *Some Dogmas of Religion.* 1906. Reprinted New York: Kraus, 1969.

Mellone, S.H. Review of *Agnosticism,* by Robert Flint. *Mind* 13 (1904): 106–10.

Miller, J. Hillis. *The Linguistic Moment: From Wordsworth to Stevens.* Princeton: Princeton UP, 1985.

Milton, John. *Paradise Lost.* Ed. Merritt Y. Hughes. Indianapolis: The Odyssey Press, 1962.

Mistichelli, Bill. 'Darwinism as Tragedy in *The Mayor of Casterbridge.' CEA Critic* 48 (1985): 69–74.

Morgan, C. Lloyd. '"The Riddle of the Universe": Five Open Letters.' *Contemporary Review* 85 (1907): 776–99.

– 'Three Aspects of Monism.' *The Monist* 4 (1894): 321–32.

Morison, James Cotter. *The Service of Man: An Essay towards the Religion of the Future.* London: Watts, 1903.

Morley, John. 'Three Books of the Eighteenth Century.' *Fortnightly Review* 28 (1877): 259–84.

Morrell, Roy. *Thomas Hardy: The Will and the Way.* Kuala Lampur: U of Malaya P, 1965.

Morson, Gary Saul. 'Parody, History, and Metaparody.' *Rethinking Bakhtin*. Ed.
   Gary Saul Morson and Caryl Emerson. Evanston: Northwestern UP, 1989:
   63–86.
– 'Prose Bakhtin: *Landmarks*, Anti-Intelligentsialism and the Russian Counter-
   tradition.' *Bakhtin in Contexts: Across the Disciplines*. Ed. Amy Mandelker.
   Evanston: Northwestern UP, 1995: 33–78.
Morson, Gary Saul and Caryl Emerson. *Mikhail Bakhtin: Creation of a Prosaics*.
   Stanford: Stanford UP, 1990.
– eds. *Rethinking Bakhtin: Extensions and Challenges*. Evanston: Northwestern
   UP, 1989.
Moses, Michael Valdez. 'Agon in the Marketplace: *The Mayor of Casterbridge* as
   Bourgeois Tragedy.' *South Atlantic Quarterly* 87 (1988): 219–51.
Mozley, J.B. *University and Other Sermons*. 3rd ed. London: Rivingtons, 1877.
'Mr. Footman on Modern Unbelief.' *The Spectator* (21 April 1883): 514–16.
'Mr. Galton's Inquiries into Human Faculty, and Its Development.' *The Specta-
   tor* (11 Aug. 1883): 1029–30.
'Mr. Hardy's *Dynasts*.' *Edinburgh Review* 207 (1908): 421–39.
'Mr. Justice Fry on Materialism.' *The Spectator* (20 May 1882): 655–6.
Myers, Frederic W.H. 'The Disenchantment of France.' *The Nineteenth Century*
   23 (1888): 661–81.
Napier, Sir William F.P. *History of the War in the Peninsula and in the South of
   France from A.D. 1807 to A.D. 1814*. Vol 1. New York: Redfield, 1856.
   5 vols.
Neill, Edward. *Trial by Ordeal: Thomas Hardy and the Critics*. Columbia: Camden
   House, 1999.
'The "New Theology".' *Daily Mail* 12 (12 Jan. 1907): 7.
Noyes, Alfred. 'The Poetry of Thomas Hardy.' *North American* Review 194
   (1911): 96–105.
Orel, Harold. 'Hardy, War, and the Years of *Pax Britannica*.' *Thomas Hardy and
   the Modern World*. Ed. F.B. Pinion. Dorchester: The Thomas Hardy Society,
   1974: 90–105.
– Introduction. *The Dynasts*. By Thomas Hardy. London: Macmillan, 1978:
   vii–xxvii.
– *Thomas Hardy's Epic-Drama: A Study of The Dynasts*. Lawrence: University of
   Kansas Publications, 1963.
– 'What *The Dynasts* Meant to Hardy.' *Victorian Poetry* 17 (1979): 109–23.
Ormond, A.T. *Concepts of Philosophy*. New York: Macmillan, 1906.
Page, Norman. Introduction. *The Mayor of Casterbridge*. By Thomas Hardy. Ed.
   Norman Page. Peterborough: Broadview, 1997.
– *Thomas Hardy*. London: Routledge and Kegan Paul, 1977.

Paterson, John. 'The Mayor of Casterbridge as Tragedy.' Victorian Studies 3 (1959): 151–72.

Pechey, Graham. 'On the Borders of Bakhtin: Dialogisation, Decolonisation.' Bakhtin and Cultural Theory. Ed. Ken Hirschkop and David Shepherd. Manchester: Manchester UP, 1989: 39–67.

'Pessimism.' The Encyclopaedia Britannica. 9th ed. 18 (1885): 684–91.

Pinion, F.B. A Commentary on the Poems of Thomas Hardy. London: Macmillan, 1976.

– Thomas Hardy: Art and Thought. London: Macmillan, 1977.

'Pluralism and Theism.' Times Literary Supplement (18 Jan. 1912): 21.

'Pragmatism.' The Spectator 99 (6 July 1907): 9–11.

Prentiss, Norman D. 'Compilation and Design in The Mayor of Casterbridge.' Thomas Hardy Journal 11 (1995): 60–74.

'Professor Campbell Fraser's Autobiography.' Times Literary Supplement (3 June 1904): 171.

Ransom, John Crowe. 'Thomas Hardy's Poems, and the Religious Difficulties of a Naturalist.' The Kenyon Review 22 (1960): 169–93.

Rashdall, Hastings. Review of The Pathway to Reality: Stage the First, by R.B. Haldane. Mind 12 (1903): 527–35.

– Review of The Pathway to Reality: Stage the Second, by R.B. Haldane. Mind 13 (1904): 410–16.

Ribot, Theophile. The Psychology of the Emotions. London: Walter Scott, 1897.

Ritchie, David. Philosophical Studies. Ed. Robert Latta. London: Macmillan, 1905.

Romanes, George J. 'The World as an Eject.' Contemporary Review 50 (1886): 44–59.

Rose, John Holland. The Life of Napoleon I. Vol. 2. London: George Bell and Sons, 1904. 2 vols.

Ross, E.A. 'Turning towards Nirvana.' Arena 4 (1891): 736–43.

Rutland, William R. Thomas Hardy: A Study of His Writings and Their Background. 1938. Reprinted New York: Russell and Russell, 1962.

Saleeby, C.W. 'The Apostle of Evolution.' The Academy and Literature 65 (1903): 675.

Saunders, T. Bailey. Preface to 'Religion: A Dialogue.' Complete Essays of Schopenhauer. Trans. T. Bailey Saunders. New York: Wiley, 1942: iii–vii.

Schopenhauer, Arthur. Complete Essays of Schopenhauer. Trans. T. Bailey Saunders. New York: Wiley, 1942.

– The World as Will and Idea. Trans. R.B. Haldane and J. Kemp. 6th ed. 3 vols. London: Kegan Paul, Trench, Trubner, 1907.

Schweik, Robert. 'The Influence of Religion, Science, and Philosophy on

Hardy's Writings.' *Thomas Hardy*. Ed. Dale Kramer. Cambridge: Cambridge UP, 1999.

'Self and Space.' Review of *The Metaphysics of Nature*, by Carveth Read. *Saturday Review* 100 (21 Oct. 1905): 527–8.

Seymour-Smith, Martin. *Hardy*. London: Bloomsbury, 1994.

Shaw, W. David. 'The Agnostic Imagination in Victorian Poetry.' *Criticism* 22 (1980): 116–39.

Shelley, Percy Bysshe. *Shelley: Poetical Works*. Ed. Thomas Hutchinson. London: Oxford UP, 1967.

Sherman, George W. 'The Influence of London on *The Dynasts*.' *PMLA* 63 (1948): 1017–28.

Smith, Goldwin. 'The Immortality of the Soul.' *The North American Review* 178 (1904): 717–29.

Smith, Norman. Review of *Why the Mind Has a Body*, by C.A. Strong. *Mind* 13 (1904): 277–81.

'Some Recent Verse.' *Literature* 8 (October 1898): 318–19.

Sopote, M. 'Pragmatism and Religion.' *The Spectator* 102 (23 Jan. 1909): 129.

Southerington, F.R. *Hardy's Vision of Man*. New York: Barnes and Noble, 1971.

Southworth, James Granville. *The Poetry of Thomas Hardy*. New York: Columbia UP, 1947.

Spencer, Herbert. *An Autobiography*. 2 vols. London: Williams and Worgate, 1904.

– *First Principles*. 3rd ed. London: Williams and Worgate, 1875.

– 'Last Words about Agnosticism and the Religion of Humanity.' *The Nineteenth Century* 93 (1884): 826–39.

– *The Principles of Biology*. 2 vols. London: Williams and Worgate, 1864–7.

'The Spiritual Movement in the Nineteenth Century.' *The Spectator* (5 Jan. 1901): 9–10.

Stam, Robert. *Subversive Pleasures: Bakhtin, Cultural Criticism, and Film*. Baltimore: The Johns Hopkins UP, 1989.

Starzyk, Lawrence J. 'Hardy's *Mayor*: The Antitraditional Basis of Tragedy.' *Studies in the Novel* 4 (1972): 592–607.

Stedmond, J.M. 'Hardy's *Dynasts* and the "Mythical Method".' *English* 12 (1958): 1–4.

Stephen, Leslie. *An Agnostic's Apology*. 2nd ed. New York: G.P. Putnam's Sons, 1903.

– *Essays on Freethinking and Plainspeaking*. London: Longmans, Green, 1873.

– *Social Rights and Duties: Addresses to Ethical Societies*. Vol. 2. London: Swan Sonnenschein, 1896. 2 vols.

– *Studies of a Biographer*. Vol. 3. London: Duckworth, 1902. 3 vols.

Stevenson, Lionel. *Darwin among the Poets*. Chicago: U of Chicago P, 1932.

Stewart, J.I.M. *Thomas Hardy: A Critical Biography*. London: Longmans, 1971.

Strong, C.A. *Why the Mind Has a Body*. New York: Macmillan, 1903.

Symonds, John Addington. *Essays Speculative and Suggestive*. 3rd ed. London: John Murray, 1907.

Symons, Arthur. *Arthur Symons: Selected Letters, 1880–1935*. Ed. Karl Beckson and John M. Munro. London: Macmillan, 1989.

Taylor, A.E. Review of *Naturalism and Agnosticism*. *Mind* 9 (1900): 244–58.

Tennyson, Hallam. *Alfred, Lord Tennyson: A Memoir*. Vol. 1. London: Macmillan, 1898. 2 vols.

Thomas, Brook. *The New Historicism: And Other Old-Fashioned Topics*. Princeton: Princeton UP, 1991.

Tolstoy, Leo. *War and Peace*. Trans. Rosemary Edmonds. Vol. 1. Harmondsworth: Penguin, 1957. 2 vols.

Trezise, Simon. 'Places in Time: Discovering the Chronotope in *Tess of the D'Urbervilles*.' *Critical Survey* 5 (1993): 136–42.

Tulloch, John. 'Morality Without Metaphysic.' *Edinburgh Review* 144 (1876): 470–500.

Turner, Frank M. *Between Science and Religion: The Reaction to Scientific Naturalism in Late Victorian England*. New Haven: Yale UP, 1974.

'Unreality and Mr. Haldane.' *Saturday Review* 97 (23 April 1904): 524.

Urwin, G.G. *Notes on English Literature: The Mayor of Casterbridge*. Oxford: Basil Blackwell, 1964.

Wain, John. Introduction. *The Dynasts: An Epic-Drama of the War with Napoleon*. By Thomas Hardy. New York: St Martin's Press, 1965: v–xix.

Walker, W.L. *Christian Theism and a Spiritual Monism*. 2nd ed. Edinburgh: Clark, 1907.

Wang, Shou-ren. *The Theatre of the Mind: A Study of Unacted Drama in Nineteenth-Century England*. Basingstoke: Macmillan, 1990.

'Wanted – A Satisfactory Monism.' Review of *Christian Theism and Spiritual Monism*, by W.L. Walker. *Saturday Review* 103 (11 May 1907): 592.

Ward, James. *Naturalism and Agnosticism*. 2 vols. 3rd ed. London: Adam and Charles Black, 1906.

Weber, Carl J. *Hardy of Wessex: His Life and Literary Career*. 2nd ed. New York: Columbia UP, 1965.

Webster, Harvey Curtis. *On a Darkling Plain: The Art and Thought of Thomas Hardy*. Chicago: U of Chicago P, 1947.

'The Wessex Drama.' *Edinburgh Review* 215 (1912): 93–112.

White, Hayden. *The Content of the Form: Narrative Discourse and Historical Representation*. Baltimore: The Johns Hopkins UP, 1987.

- *Figural Realism: Studies in the Mimesis Effect.* Baltimore: The Johns Hopkins UP, 1999.
- *Metahistory: The Historical Imagination in Nineteenth-Century Europe.* Baltimore: The Johns Hopkins UP, 1973.

White, R.J. *Thomas Hardy and History.* London: Macmillan, 1974.

Wilson, Andrew. 'Concerning Protoplasm.' *Gentleman's Magazine* 247 (1879): 417–35.

Wilson, Keith. '"Flower of Man's Intelligence": World and Overworld in *The Dynasts.' Victorian Poetry* 17 (1979): 124–33.

Woolf, Virginia. *A Writer's Diary.* Ed. Leonard Woolf. London: The Hogarth Press, 1959.

Wordsworth, William. *Wordsworth: Poetical Works.* Ed. Thomas Hutchinson. Revised by Ernest De Selincourt. London: Oxford UP, 1967.

Worsley, A. *Concepts of Monism.* London: T. Fisher Unwin, 1907.

Wotton, George. *Thomas Hardy: Towards a Materialist Criticism.* Guildford: Gill and Macmillan, 1985.

Wright, Terence. 'Space, Time, and Parodox: The Sense of History in Hardy's Last Novels.' *Essays and Studies* 44 (1991): 41–52.

Wright, Walter F. *The Shaping of The Dynasts: A Study in Thomas Hardy.* Lincoln: U of Nebraska P, 1967.

Index

Absolute, the, 32, 38, 40, 44–6, 50, 61, 63, 74–5, 79; and God, 80. *See also* the Unknowable

Adler, Felix, 24, 51

aerial perspectives, 143, 183–7

agnosticism, 5, 21, 45, 68, 84; its dilemma, 51; its effect on naturalism, 22; as philosophy of science, 29; pure, 43; and religion, 53; its sceptical voice, 30–1; species of, 43–4; its tone of neutrality, 17

Alexander, Emperor, 149, 188; as hero-worshipper, 165–6

Allen, Grant, 32

Archer, William, 79

Armitage, E., 28–9, 70

automatism, 59

Bailey, J.O., 77, 82, 225n

Bain, Alexander, 59, 60

Bakhtin, Mikhail, xix, 67, 156, 188, 193; on battles and food, 135; on carnival, 121, 124, 136, 197, 218; on catastrophe, xvi, 121–2, 206; on the chronotope, 196, 203, 204, 216, 233n; on the crowd, 169, 171; *The Dialogic Imagination*, 218; on folk humour, 100, 200–1, 223n; on the grotesque, 81, 219; on language, 95, 139; his language of violence, 217–18; on madness, 189; on the menippea, 183–4, 196–7, 221; on microdialogue, 44, 218; his neo-Kantianism, xix; on the novel, xix, 3–4, 87; on novelization, 168; *Problems of Dostoevsky's Poetics*, 19, 216; *Rabelais and His World*, xvi, 19, 216; on reduced laughter, xiii, 19; on science, 29; on serio-comical genres, xii; on silence, 139; on the superaddressee, 219; and violence, 121, 218–19

Balfour, A.J., 23

battles: Albuera, 136, 203; Austerlitz, 127–8, 203; Borodino, 134, 141; and butcher shop, 134; and carnival, 122–4, 127, 141–3, 206, 210; and dialogue, 138–9; and folkloric chronotope, 210–11; and gambling, 202; and grotesque realism, 122, 132–6, 143; Jena, 130, 203; and language, 137–42; Leipzig, 202–6;